Where to Call When You Don't Know Where to Call

W9-ATA-113

Banking Questions

Federal Trade Commission (202) 326-2000
Information and advice on how to proceed with a specific complaint

Veribanc (800) 442-2657 or (617) 245-8370
To check on the financial health of your bank

Traveler's Aid

American Resort Development Association (ARDA) (202) 371-6700
Trade association for the timeshare industry

American Society of Travel Agents (ASTA) (703) 739-2782

Elderhostel (617) 426-7788
Learning vacations for those 55 and over

Go Camping America hotline (800) 47-SUNNY
Information on RV campgrounds

House swap directory organizations:

   Intervac U.S. (800) 756-HOME

   Vacation Exchange Club (800) 638-3841

Recreation Vehicle Industry Association (703) 620-6003
Offers list of RV clubs, other material

Recreation Vehicle Rental Association (800) 336-0355
For information on renting an RV

Investment Info

American Institute of Certified Public Accountants (800) 862-4272 or (201) 938-3000
Information on a variety of money-related topics

Institute of Certified Financial Planners (800) 282-7526 or (303) 751-7600

International Association of Registered Financial Planners (800) 749-7947 or (915) 544-7947

National Association of Investors Corporation (810) 583-6242
Guidance in starting an investment club

National Association of Personal Financial Advisors (NAPFA) (800)366-2732 or (708) 537-7722
Information from and about fee-only financial planners

Healthcare Information

Group Health Association of America hotline (202) 778-3286
Call for list of HMOs in your area

Health Care Financing Administration (410) 786-3000
Part of U.S. Department of Health & Human Services, offers information about Medicare, Medigap, and Medicaid, among other health-related issues

Joint Commission on Accreditation of Health Care Organizations (708) 916-5800
Offers information on accrediting of nation's hospitals, home health care agencies, and mental health care facilities

Medicare hotline (800) 638-6833
Operated by Health Care Financing Administration of the U.S. Department of Health & Human Services

National Alliance for Caregiving (301) 718-8444
Resource center for caregivers

National Association of Claims Assistance Professionals (708) 963-3500
Members assist consumers with health claims paperwork

National Association of Professional Geriatric Care Managers (602) 881-8008

National Council for the Right to Die: Choice in Dying (800) 989-WILL or (212) 366-5540
Information on living wills, healthcare power of attorney, physician-assisted death

National Hospice Organization (800) 658-8898

Visiting Nurse Association of America (800) 426-2547

United Seniors Health Cooperative (202) 393-6222
Not-for-profit organization helping older consumers in a variety of areas

Support Groups

Children of Aging Parents (CAPS) (215) 945-6900

National Self-Help Clearing House (212) 354-8525
Can put you in touch with specific support groups in your area

alpha books

Retirement Benefits

National Organization of Social Security Claimants' Representatives (800) 431-2804 or (201) 444-1415
A referral service directing callers to attorneys who handle Social Security cases

Pension and Welfare Benefits Administration, Department of Labor (202) 219-8840
For an explanation of your rights under federal law

Pension Benefit Guaranty Corporation (PBGC) (202) 326-4040
Answers questions and offers advice on pensions

Pension Rights Center (202) 296-3778
A legal referral service for pension-related problems

Social Security Administration (800) 772-1213
Has l,300 offices across the nation, but this might be the fastest route to an answer to your question or to order printed material

Elder Affairs

American Association of Homes and Services for the Aging (202) 783-2242
Information on continuing care retirement communities (CCRCs) and nursing homes

American Association of Retired Persons (AARP) (800) 424-3410 or (202) 434-2277
Huge consumer advocacy group offering printed material on virtually any topic of interest to retirees and those planning for retirement

Continuing Care Accreditation Commission. (202) 783-7286 Part of American Association of Homes and Services for the Aging.
Information about CCRCs, including accreditation

Eldercare Locator (800) 677-1116
Collaborative effort of several government agencies; can direct you to local or regional offices that can help you in a variety of senior-related areas

National Shared Housing Resource Center (410) 235-4454

Tax Help

Internal Revenue Service (IRS) Tele-tax line (800) 829-4477 (in some California counties (800) 829-4032)
For automated refund and recorded tax information; or call directory assistance for a local number

IRS free publications (800) 829-3676
Also offers audio tapes and films

IRS tax help lines (800) 829-l040 (for the hearing impaired (800) 829-4059)
To ask questions of a real person; if no response, call directory assistance for a local number

Legal Issues

American Arbitration Association (212) 484-4000
When you think arbitration might resolve your grievance

American Bar Association (312) 988-5000

Equal Employment Opportunity Commission (EEOC) (202) 663-4264
For assistance with age discrimination claims; might also have a local office in your area

HALT, Inc. (202) 437-9600
An organization of Americans for Legal Reform, offers information and assistance on a variety of topics

Legal Counsel for the Elderly (202) 434-2120
Provides information on a broad range of legal and healthcare issues, does some *pro bono* work

National Academy of Elder Law Attorneys (602) 881-4005
Focuses on issues applying to seniors

U.S. Tax Court (202) 606-8754
Hears cases involving disputes between taxpayers and IRS

Insurance Assistance

Insurance Information Institute (800) 942-4242 or (212) 669-9200
Information arm of the industry, geared toward consumer queries

Insurance quote companies: for lowest rates, call

INSurance INFormation (800) 472-5800

Insurance Quote Services (800) 972-1104

SelectQuote (800) 343-1985

TermQuote (800) 444-8376

National Viatical Association (800) 741-9465
Information about insurance for the terminally ill

The COMPLETE

IDIOT'S

GUIDE TO

a Great
Retirement

by Carolyn Janik and Ruth Rejnis

alpha
books

A Division of Macmillan General Reference
A Simon & Schuster Macmillan Company
1633 Broadway, New York, NY 10019-6785

International Standard Book Number: 1-56761-601-1
Library of Congress Catalog Card Number: 94-073518

97 96 95   9 8 7 6 5 4 3 2 1

Interpretation of the printing code: the rightmost number of the first series of numbers is the year of the book's printing; the rightmost number of the second series of numbers is the number of the book's printing. For example, a printing code of 95-1 shows that the first printing occurred in 1995.

Printed in the United States of America

Publisher
Theresa H. Murtha

Associate Publisher
Lisa A. Bucki

Manuscript Editor
Fran Blauw

Production Manager
Kelly Dobbs

Designer
Kim Scott

Illustrations
Judd Winick

Indexer
Bront Davis

Production Team Supervisor
Laurie Casey

Production Team
*Heather Butler, Angela Calvert, Dan Caparo,
Kim Cofer, Jennifer Eberhardt, Kevin Foltz, Joe Millay,
Erika Millen, Erich J. Richter, Robert Wolf*

Contents at a Glance

Contents

Part 5: Law and Medicine—What You Absolutely Have to Know   219

20 About Lawyers   221

Foreword

At some time during mid-life, most of us start looking forward to those years that promise the relaxing reward for a life's labors: retirement. Many of us count on the fact that we can spend our retirement years in perfectly contented, comfortable bliss. Each of us has a unique vision of what that bliss may be—gardening for endless hours; traveling the United States or the world; or even a busy life as a student, volunteer, or part-time consultant.

Often, however, a person who has just settled in for all that bliss has a curious reaction: The reality isn't as perfect as the vision had been. And the natural response to that feeling is to say, "Hey! I want to turn the clock back!"

As with most worthwhile things in life, a *rewarding* retirement doesn't just happen. You have to think about what you want from retirement, decide what you need to do to achieve the retirement of your dreams, and execute your plan (usually over a number of years) faithfully. If you don't start planning for retirement 15 or 20 years before the date, or if you haven't given retirement much thought and don't know where to start, you could miss out on having "golden years" that are even better than your younger years were.

That's where *The Complete Idiot's Guide to a Great Retirement* comes in. This book provides no-nonsense guidance and hands-on steps to help you plan for retirement—whether you're in your thirties, forties, fifties, or just on the brink of completing your career. In this book, authors Carolyn Janik and Ruth Rejnis give you the facts and resources you need to make smart decisions. Most important, they help you identify the right questions to ask yourself; without the right questions, you can't possibly arrive at the right answers.

Recently, many publications and television programs have addressed the challenges of saving enough money for retirement and the question of whether Social Security will be there when *you* retire. If your key concerns center around the financial aspects of planning for retirement, you'll find what you need here. But this book isn't just about money, because you need to think about many life choices before you start counting your pennies.

With both gentle humor and a firm grip on reality, authors Janik and Rejnis encourage you to begin at the beginning in pondering the years to come and help you ask yourself tough questions like those that follow to develop your personal retirement plan:

➤ What do I know about retirement, and what do I need to learn?

➤ Will the resources I'm counting on—like Social Security and a pension—be there for me when I need them?

➤ Do I want to continue living where I live now, or do I want to move into a condo, a special retirement community, or to another country?

➤ What will I do with myself when I have all that time on my hands? Will I be bored? Should I get a part-time job or start a business? Will volunteering be satisfying? Should I retire at all?

➤ How much money will I really need to live where I want to live and do what I want to do? What kinds of investments will get me there? How long will it take to save that kind of money?

➤ Can I protect myself against large taxes or scams targeted toward older people?

➤ How will I manage my estate? How can I write a will or set up a trust?

➤ What's the best way to form a partnership with my lawyer and my physician as I depend on them a bit more?

➤ How will my relationships with others change when I retire? Will I bug my kids? Will I loose touch with friends who still work? Can I find people who share my interests to spend time with?

➤ How will I feel about myself after I retire?

Armed with the information in *The Complete Idiot's Guide to a Great Retirement,* you'll be able to look at each of these questions and arrive at the answers you need to personalize your retirement plan. The authors provide sound advice to help you to steer clear of danger spots and to arrive at a strategy for building the type of retirement you want.

As you read, remember that you're not alone in worrying about where you want to be and how to get there. Also keep in mind that millions of people thrive in retired life every day. With this book, develop your own retirement vision and plan to realize it.

James P. Firman
President and CEO
The National Council on the Aging

Before Dr. Firman brought his 20 years of experience to the NCOA, he was president and CEO of the United Seniors Health Cooperative, a not-for-profit consumer organization. Dr. Firman is widely recognized as an expert and consumer advocate on many issues affecting older persons—including home care, long-term care, and health insurance—and has testified before many congressional committees.

The National Council on the Aging is a private, not-for-profit organization that has worked since 1950 to improve the lives of older Americans and their families. NCOA serves as a national resource for information, training, technical assistance, publications on aging, and more.

Introduction

You might start hearing the background chorus in your late thirties, drearily chanting, "Save... Plan... Retirement's coming. Investments. You don't have enough investments."

By your forties, the voices are louder. In your fifties, the crescendo has you fidgeting as you seriously begin to consider your retirement years. They look pretty bleak, which is why you hadn't thought about them earlier. By your sixties, you are scurrying to catch up, now totally frantic.

Whew—some picture, huh?

Yes, we all know we *should* be planning for retirement, starting just about the time in our late twenties when we finish the spending splurge we embarked on (and wasn't *that* fun!) with our first job or two. But how many of us think more than occasionally about post-65 days in our extreme youth, and even, unfortunately, beyond? There are college loans to repay, mortgages, second mortgages, kids to educate, and a mountain of other expenses that can be categorized as "fun."

So the years go by, with a few dollars put away here and there, and some occasional thinking about retirement, but no *plan*.

An interesting thing about retirement. You've heard the old saw—"I'm retiring, but not from life." It's true, especially with our generation—*our* meaning anyone reading this book. We're all "younger" retirees these days than previous generations were. We choose to do more or less exactly what we have been doing in pre-retirement years, which can be white-water rafting, working, marrying, enrolling in college, and a few dozen other activities. What exactly are we retiring from? Not much besides that nine-to-five job.

Unfortunately, you (and the rest of us) will need the wherewithal to keep up with your pre-retirement lifestyle, or to fulfill your special retirement dreams. Here is where planning becomes so important, so that you do not enter those 20 or 30 more years of your life with shoulda-coulda-oughta regrets about the preparation you did not do.

This book is here to help you get it together. There is no need to panic at the thought of retiring, or to put your hands over your ears so that you do not hear that chorus (or over your eyes so that you do not see all those retirement-planning articles in the print media).

Reading these pages, absorbing their suggestions, and acting on at least some of them will take away the retirement nightmares and replace them with the calm that comes from knowing what is likely to lie ahead, and how you plan to handle those challenges and changes.

You want to be eager, confident, and with a financial picture and lifestyle strategy that, if it doesn't have you broadly grinning, at least brings a bit of a smile to your face.

Now that's retirement!

How This Book Is Organized

To make the reading—and the decision-making—easier for you, we have divided these pages into the areas of your life you will need to consider before retiring, and then we take a look at the time just before R-Day to be sure you're ready.

We should point out that just because we have covered such a wide variety of topics in pre-retirement planning does not mean you can expect all those situations to crop up in your life one day. Not at all. It's nice to know the information is there, though.

We also would like you to note that our suggestions, while we try to personalize them as much as we can, cannot, of course, be custom-tailored for each of you. You have your own unique lifestyle, needs, and wants for retirement. If that isn't complicated enough, this area is always changing—if not from the government, then from the private sector.

We hope that you will take this book as a road map, and then go off and learn more and talk to specialists to put your own stamp on your particular journey. When it comes down to it, of course, you are captain of this particular ship, and you can sail into any waters you choose—navigational decisions we hope will be informed, well-thought-out ones, based on input from knowledgeable sources.

Here is what we've done to help you. This book is divided into six parts, from early thoughts about retirement to The Big Day and beyond:

Part 1, "Reality Pinches," asks you to consider your thoughts about retirement, no matter what your age. Do you really know what is involved here—from your pension to Social Security to figuring out just what you want from those years?

Part 2, "Scoping Out Your Dreams," puts you to work again, this time thinking about how much exactly you will need to fulfill your retirement plan to live... where? We'll help you consider places, as well as specific housing styles.

Part 3, "Pennies from Heaven and Other Sources of Money," gets down and dirty. How are you going to pay for your retirement dreams? We talk about stocks, bonds, real estate, other income sources (such as that pension), work beyond age 65, and good old Social Security.

Part 4, "Covering Your Assets," guides you through protecting what is yours from scary outside forces such as the Internal Revenue Service and scam artists—guarding those assets and squeezing as much profit from them as you can.

Part 5, "Law and Medicine—What You Absolutely Need to Know," considers those two major aspects of life, which grow even more important as you move to and through retirement. We help you with topics from estate planning to healthcare.

Part 6, "Retirement Countdown," moves to the last few years before retirement and helps you with last-minute checkups to be sure you are prepared—financially and emotionally—for what we hope will be truly enjoyable years.

Extras

We've added some brief bonuses, too—icons scattered generously throughout these pages to call your attention to an important tip, to give you a laugh, or to fill you in on background information about a particular point of interest. They are easily recognizable throughout the book:

It's Been Said
These are quotations to enlighten you, brighten your day, or offer a thought-provoking line or two.

Thin Ice
Warnings, cautions, and precarious situations ahead! We'll tell you what to avoid, when to be careful, and when to get help.

Power Word
Using the right word at the right time can make a difference in every business and social situation. Acting, when you don't understand a particular word, can be a disaster. Don't overlook these definitions.

Gray Matter Alert
These points to ponder might give you a new perspective on solving a problem, add something of value to an established process, or suggest ways to save money and improve results.

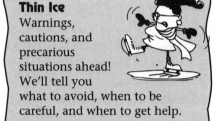

Extra! Extra!
Recorded facts, current issues or opinions, and sources of additional information, these bits of useful material help you understand where things are coming from, why we're where we are, where we might be going, and where to get help.

That's it. Read! Profit! Enjoy!

Acknowledgments

Special thanks to our literary agent, Carole Abel, who made the match between us and this super series.

We also extend a sincere thank you to the many people who contributed their time, effort, and expertise to this project, especially Fran Blauw, William DeLeeuw, Rita Estrella, Elaine and Bob Fendell, Joyce and Bob Fitzpatrick, Joe Janik, Anne M. and John Johnson, Ashok Krishnaswami, Theresa Murtha, Vicky Page, CaroleAnne Pepe, Sophie Stasulewicz, and Joe Tockarshewsky.

Thanks from the Publisher to the Technical Reviewers

The Complete Idiot's Guide to a Great Retirement was reviewed by two experts who not only checked the technical accuracy of what you'll learn here, but also provided insights and suggestions to help you better plan for your retirement. Special thanks are extended to the following two people:

Judith Martindale, CFP, is a certified financial planner (fee only) and registered investment advisor for her financial planning practice in San Luis Obispo, California. She is also a registered principal and branch manager with Tital Value Equities Group, Inc., a registered broker/dealer, and a member of SIPC. She has been quoted by AARP's Maturity news service, *Kiplinger's Personal Finance*, the *Los Angeles Times*, and the *San Francisco Chronicle*, among other publications. She coauthored two personal finance books: *Creating Your Own Future: A Woman's Guide to Retirement Planning*, and *52 Simple Ways to Manage Your Money*.

Lisa B. Stewart, as Manager of the Retirement & Life Planning Programs at the National Council on the Aging, works with human resources and benefits specialists of more than 100 companies and businesses belonging to NCOA's National Institute on Financial Issues and Services for Elders, a membership unit consisting of professionals and leaders in financial and gerontological disciplines. She holds degrees in psychology and gerontology, and worked in a long-term care retirement facility before coming to Washington, D.C. While pursuing her graduate degree in gerontology, Ms. Stewart served on a committee that developed a training program for volunteers providing temporary relief to families caring for adults with Alzheimer's disease. Prior to NCOA, Ms. Stewart worked for an association that develops and sets standards for college and university gerontology curriculum.

Part 1
Reality Pinches

Retirement... *When you're 30 or 40, or even 50, you think it's something old people talk about. But it sneaks up on you. Will you be ready? Or will you be one of the startled?*

If you're ready, retirement can be a 25-year vacation. If you're not, it can make you wish again and again that you'd paid more attention when your parents were giving you advice all those years.

Most experts say most of us are not ready. But it's not too late—in fact, it's never too late to make yourself financially more comfortable. First you need to get an understanding of the concepts behind retirement saving and planning. Then all you have to do is do it!

We're here to help. In Part 1, we'll pinch a place or two to make sure you're with us: "Do you know what it's like to be retired?" or "Do you know how little Social Security will pay?" Or, "Is your pension really safe?" and "Will there, in fact, be a pension?"

After the pinches, we'll give you a hug or two and help you start planning.

Chapter 1

What Do You Really Know About Retirement?

In This Chapter

➤ What makes retirement different

➤ The sources of retirement income

➤ Defining your fears and fantasies

➤ Drawing your future individual retirement profile

What's the image that comes up in your mind when you hear the word *retirement*? Maybe you picture a couple with sterling silver hair. They're flashing smiles on wrinkle-free faces that plastic surgeons would be happy to feature in their trade magazines. And of course, they're busily choosing the right woods on one of Hilton Head's best golf courses. You can just see the Ralph Lauren labels on their Bermuda shorts, and their Jaguar (golf cart) is parked nearby.

Or maybe you get goosebumps when you hear the word. You picture a Formica and Scotchguard living room in a securely anchored mobile home. The only light in the room comes from *Days of Our Lives* flashing from scene to scene on the television screen. You can just make out a human form clipping coupons in the Lazyboy.

Well, you managed to dream up two stereotypical images at opposite ends of the retirement reality chart. In between is the huge, bell-shaped bulge where most of us will fit. What's it really like to *live* the life? What will *your* picture be? Most of the details depend on the choices you make *before* retirement—sometimes, long before.

Some Things Change

Ask any therapist, psychologist, or social worker. He or she will tell you that just about everyone goes through a major period of adjustment upon entering retirement. Why? It's pretty obvious. Two of life's biggest controlling elements change suddenly: time and money.

Time Flies (Or It Doesn't)

The clock radio doesn't go on, the alarm clock doesn't ring. Oh joy! It's Sunday morning every day of the week!

No start times, no deadlines, no meetings, no schedules. You can walk, read, garden, shop, travel, build things, study watercolor, or listen to the grass grow.

And you can get into big trouble (emotional trouble, that is). Many people find themselves disoriented in retirement. From early childhood, for most of us, life has been lived in the rhythm of a seven-day week. We've had days for work or school and days off. Within that overall rhythm, each day also had times when commitments had to be met and times that were unstructured.

Then we retire. Suddenly men and women don't have to be anywhere at any given time. They forget what day it is and they put things off because no one is waiting for the results of their work.

You say you can't imagine a day, a week, a month without markings. Right! And that means you can see the potential problem. If the demands of your job and/or the obligations of maintaining a home and raising a family have structured your life, you will need to think about how time will affect you when there is no structure.

Certainly you've heard people talking about retired friends. "Oh, he's keeping busy," they say with a smile, but there's always that just slightly condescending tone in their voices. Nevertheless, keeping busy is truly a core ingredient for a happy retirement. Time management is just as necessary for success in retirement as it was for survival in the workaday world. There is a difference, however: now you're working for yourself.

Money Shrinks (Or It Doesn't)

It's not so much that the checks stop coming—there are, after all, other possibilities beyond payroll checks. We get pension checks, Social Security checks, dividend checks, rent checks, checks from the stockbroker, checks at the closing, and lots of others (most of which we'll cover in this book). It's that the numbers on the regular-interval checks are often smaller than we were used to and often are fixed for life.

One of the biggest changes in retirement is the loss of potential for making more money for the same amount of time at work. During retirement, there may or may not be small cost-of-living adjustments in your monthly income, but there will be no raises, no new contracts, no new maximums for the job. The possibility of promotion is gone. There will be no annual bonus for work well done.

> **Gray Matter Alert**
> Your job not only structures your time, it also helps to create your social identity. But are you developing a non-working identity that will hold up happily in retirement? As a start, make a list of five things that might identify you when being introduced at a party. Do not include anything to do with your work.

If you are entitled to a pension, the company will tell you how much that pension will give you for the rest of your life. The government will tell you how much Social Security you've earned. What you'll have beyond the fixed figures will be the result of your financial planning before retirement and your creative efforts after retirement.

> **Extra! Extra!**
> Time and money retirement questions will affect more and more people *every single year* in the United States until the middle of the 21st century. Not only are medical breakthroughs increasing life expectancy, but the baby boom, the biggest population bubble in history, is also marching toward those glorious, unstructured days in the sun. The U.S. Census Bureau predicts that when the 76 million people born between 1946 and 1964 reach the traditional retirement age of 65, the percentage of elder Americans will change from just less than 13 percent at the turn of the millennium to 20.7 percent in 2040. By 2050, there will be a slight decrease to 20.4 percent as the baby bust generation influences the statistics.

Some Things Stay the Same

One of the biggest mistakes about-to-retire people make is thinking that everything will be different. The stress of competition and evaluation on the job may be gone, the time demands of working and commuting may be gone, and money may arrive each month without any effort on your part, but *you* will not be an "entirely new person."

If you were never home when you were a working person, do you think you'll be a homebody after retirement? Not likely. You'll still be off fishing or playing golf on weekends, and you'll still be out at community meetings or lectures or movies on week nights. On the other hand, if you usually enjoyed quiet evenings on the couch in front of the television after working all day, do you think retirement will drive you into the local environmental protection group? Or the gourmet dine-around club?

Although the time structure of your day and the sources of your money will change, your personality will not. So relax and be yourself. Remember, however, that continuing to be yourself will mean that your lifestyle patterns will not be much different from what they have always been. Which means that you'll probably need 70 to 80 percent of your pre-retirement income to live comfortably. That's the generally agreed-upon number the financial wizards of the country have come up with. You may be different, but this standard will give you a good working figure for retirement planning.

Important points in charting your retirement course.

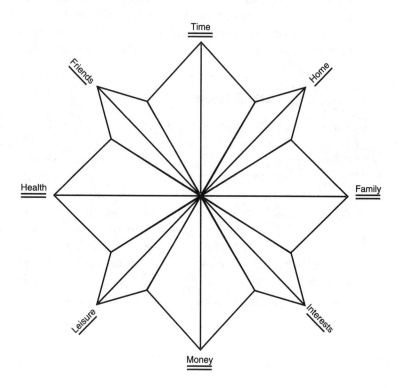

Don't Get Too Comfortable on That Three-Legged Stool

Since the first Social Security checks were issued in 1940, many financial advisors have described the American retirement income system as a three-legged stool. One leg is Social Security and other government programs, including Medicare. Another leg is employer or labor-union pensions. And the third leg is personal savings, including investments and real estate.

For more than 50 years, the majority of Americans sailed along happily thinking someone (Uncle Sam, Ma Bell, "the Union," to name a few) would certainly take care of them when they got old. People buoyantly spent more and more of their income each decade. In the '40s and '50s, the average American was saving almost 11 percent of his or her income each year. In the '90s, estimates set the average savings figure at about 4 percent, which is one of the lowest saving rates in the industrialized world. (Both European and Japanese rates are approximately 12 percent.)

As a result, financial experts say that most Americans don't have enough savings to carry them through their retirement years comfortably. Many will have to work long beyond age 65 to maintain the same lifestyle.

So one leg of the three-legged stool is too short. But that's OK. You still have the other two and you can keep a wobbly balance, right? There's more.

Because of tax laws and employment patterns, which we'll talk about in Chapter 3, many pension programs are no longer available to many Americans. And those who do have pensions waiting for them at age 65 may be very disappointed with their purchasing power. According to the U.S. Bureau of Labor Statistics, 96 percent of pension recipients will not get automatic increases to cover the effects of inflation. If inflation continues even at a moderate 4 percent-per-year rate, the average pension recipient will have less to spend as he or she gets older.

And finally, Social Security will be broke by the year 2030 if it continues to function as it does now. Which means, of course, that it will be "restructured." But we'll talk more about that in the next chapter.

For now, let's just say that a stool with three unsteady legs isn't a very good place to sit out one's golden years. But maybe you want a little more comfort and security, anyway. Taking control of your retirement planning could earn you a nice overstuffed easy chair. So read on.

Extra! Extra!

Why is Social Security going broke when more and more of us are paying in more money each year? Because no one ever thought so many of us would live so long. When the fund was established in 1935, life expectancy was 60 for men and 63 for women. Today we've passed 72 for men and 79 for women but the retirement age has remained set at 65. (It will be raised in the new millennium, however.)

Pop Quiz

OK—in 1,000 words, tell us what retirement will be like for you.

Just kidding. But seriously, it is extremely important that you take some time to identify what you want and what you want to avoid. So we'd like you to work through the four little quizzes that follow. Write down your answers on your own paper, so you'll have as much room as you need. When you're finished with all the quizzes, read over your answers and think about the profile that emerges.

Necessity Quiz

Name five things you can't do without and will continue to spend money on as long as you can. Include the name of the item, how frequently you purchase it, and approximately how much you would have to spend per week to continue purchasing that item at your usual frequency.

Streamlining Quiz

Name five things you won't spend money on during your retirement. (This is *much* more difficult. Hint: Think about expenditures associated with your employment or with the maintenance of a large home.) List each item and the approximate amount you would save each year by not purchasing it.

Dream Quiz

List your five fondest dreams. If money were no object and you had all the time in the world, how would you live? On a scale of 1 to 10 (with 10 the highest) evaluate your inclination to work to achieve at least some part of these dreams. List each dream and its rating on the 1 to 10 scale.

Nightmare Quiz

List your five worst nightmares. This is difficult, but give it a try. List those possible life events (bankruptcy, divorce, chronic illness) that you most fear. Then write down what you would do (your coping strategy) if each event really happened.

Your FIRP (Future Individual Retirement Profile)

Now that you've compiled the Absolutely Will Spend and the Absolutely Won't Spend lists and have come to recognize your fears and your fantasies, it's time to draw a profile of your probable spending habits in retirement. We'll get into this question in much more detail in Part 2, but for now we want you to get a feeling for the level of expenditures you need to have a comfortable retirement without feeling stressed or deprived.

The Retirement Spending Categories activity on the next page shows nine categories of spending, each to be rated on a scale of 1 to 10 (with 10 as the highest). Assume that the mythical "average middle-class American" will rate a 5 in each category. Then put an X on the line where you see your activity and spending in the category.

➤ **Housing:** Always one of the biggest expenditures in retirement. Do you want the luxury of waterfront? Are you interested in the security of a life care community? Or could you be happy with a comfortable senior citizen's (government supported) rental apartment?

➤ **Food & Dining Out:** Do you buy shrimp or spaghetti? How often do you eat out? What's your preference, Wendy's or Top of the Sixes?

➤ **Clothing:** You won't need office clothes, but you might still need furs and black-tie attire. Or do you see yourself in jeans or shorts and T-shirts?

➤ **Transportation:** Will you need more than one car? How luxurious? Include boats and campers in this category.

➤ **Travel:** Include air travel, cruises, tours, hotels, and time-share units; but don't count the cost of your car, yacht, or RV. How often do you plan to go? Will it be camping or touring the world? Or both?

➤ **Entertainment:** How often will you be out on the town? Consider spectator sporting events, theater, concerts, movies, lectures, and weekend seminars.

➤ **Leisure Activities:** Think about participatory sports and hobbies. Skiing, tennis, gardening, oil painting, stamp collecting, and so on. Don't forget the cost of special clothing and supplies.

➤ **Gifts:** Will you continue to buy gifts for family members? Do you plan to make cash gifts during your retirement?

➤ **Medical & Dental:** Certainly no one can predict future health. But right now, do you have higher than average medical bills or are you one of those people who is never sick?

Drawing your future individual retirement profile. Use an X to mark your spending level for each category.

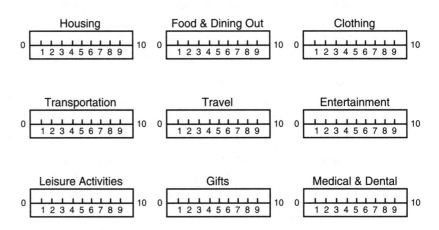

Retirement Spending Categories

Use an X to mark your spending level in each category (10 is highest)

Once you've finished making your marks in these little boxes, you'll certainly know why financial advisors say that you'll need 70 to 80 percent of your current income to get you through retirement comfortably. But you might not be sure what choices are really available for the future and you might not know whether you'll really be able to afford what you want. The rest of this book is about making lifestyle choices, estimating how much money you'll need to facilitate those choices, getting that money, protecting it, and enjoying it.

The Least You Need to Know

➤ Time is usually unstructured in retirement, but time management is still essential to enjoyable days and a positive sense of self.

➤ Fixed income can mean a fixed pension and Social Security benefit. Even more important, however, it also means that there is no opportunity for raises, promotions, and bonuses.

➤ Your personality does not change with retirement, and neither do your spending habits. Or at least not without a lot of effort.

➤ The three main sources of retirement income are Social Security, pensions, and savings (including investments).

➤ In order to predict your future spending patterns, it is essential to know your current spending patterns.

Chapter 2

Counting On Your Old Uncle Sam

In This Chapter

➤ Social Security—as originated

➤ Who's eligible?

➤ Why the money will run out

➤ Why the money won't run out

What are the warm-fuzzy words in a prospective retiree's vocabulary? *Social Security*.

And what are the cold-itchy words in a prospective retiree's vocabulary? You guessed!— *Social Security*.

Will that program be in existence when *you* retire? Will you have to work until you're 75 before benefits kick in? Will you get a smaller check than you now anticipate? Do you have any idea how much you will be entitled to as the system stands now?

Although you want to know the answers to these questions, you might be almost afraid to ask. Everyone seems to be talking about the topic. Who can blame you for wondering, "Just what's going on here?"

Hang in there. We'll tell you.

What Is Social Security, Anyway?

Right now, it's a federal entitlement program and it eats up the largest portion of the national budget (35 percent), followed by defense (24 percent). It's also the program that (according to Congressional studies in 1992) raised the incomes of 9.6 million Americans over age 65 above the poverty level. Without those monthly government checks, the poverty rate for the elderly would have been almost 50 percent instead of the 11.8 percent it was in 1992.

How does it work? Well, it's *not* a savings plan into which you deposit money that you'll get back later with interest. The money that you pay in now is funding the benefits that are being paid out to people now retired. When you begin collecting benefits, those benefits will be paid for by the people who are working and paying Social Security taxes.

Power Word

Social Security is an **entitlement program** because Congress has set eligibility criteria that, when met, automatically qualify workers to receive benefits. Workers pay special payroll taxes into the fund, unlike Medicaid or food stamps, for example, which are financed out of the general revenue and have income requirements for eligibility.

Worse still, you might *not* get back all you put in! One study published in the *Economic Review* (Quarter 1, 1995) showed that a man aged 40 in 1993 is likely to pay in $158,000 more than he takes out. Because women live longer and (alas!) make less, the stats are not quite as bad. The prototype woman aged 40 in 1993 will pay in only $76,000 more than she collects.

On the other hand, the same study projected that a man aged 60 in 1993 will collect $57,000 more than he paid in; a woman aged 60 in 1993 will collect $101,000 more than she paid in.

So should we keep this going? Is it important? Is it essential? The answer is a resounding *Yes!* According to one former Social Security commissioner, few people realize that six out of ten workers in private industry have no pension other than Social Security.

So How Did We Get To Where We Are?

There were wonderful intentions behind the inauguration of the Social Security system back in 1935. It was designed during the administration of Franklin Delano Roosevelt as a sort of, well, frankly, welfare program to provide a financial floor for America's elderly during the Great Depression.

The actuarial team hired by the Committee on Economic Security, the agency that made the studies for the Social Security Act, decided on 65 as the age of eligibility for benefits. They thought 60 was too young, 70 too old.

The first monthly checks sent out were for about $17. To put that in perspective with today's values, the average wage at that time was about $100 *a month*—for those who had work. People had little in savings back then and pensions were not common. That $17 *a month*, not even pocket change today, was a lifeline for many.

To Your Credit

Just about everyone who works fairly regularly in the United States is covered by Social Security. The exceptions are federal civilian employees hired before January 1984, career railroad workers, and a few other working groups.

Before you can be eligible to receive benefits, you need "credit" for a certain amount of work time completed and certain moneys paid into the system. You can earn up to four credits per year, one for each quarter. The amount you must earn to qualify for a credit is adjusted each year for inflation. In 1995, it was $630 in a quarter. Most people need 40 credits (10 full years of working) to qualify for benefits. Some groups, however, have different stipulations for acquiring credits. Among them are the self-employed, domestic workers in private households, farmers, and employees in not-for-profit organizations.

If you earn many, many more than 40 credits, it has no effect on your benefits. The amount of your check goes up only in response to your income during the course of your working career. There is an extra, however. Most people who qualify for Social Security benefits also will qualify for Medicare. Chapters 14 and 23 contain more information on these topics.

Extra! Extra!

Do you know who provides the best phone service to folks calling in to do business or ask questions? The Social Security Administration, according to a 1995 survey by Dalbar, a Boston-based financial news publisher. With its courteous service and knowledge of the subject, the Administration beat out 27 mutual funds and such well-known companies as L.L. Bean, Xerox, and (would you believe) Disney! You can call the Social Security Administration at (800) 772-1213.

How Secure Is This Security?

It's safer than you probably think, which should allow you to exhale that breath you've been holding about now. It might not be in its present state when you retire, but "Washington" expects it to be around. Dare we say permanently?

So what's causing all the commotion? Is this just talk? No, categorically no. Let's look at the problems first, and then we'll talk about what might happen.

> ➤ **The Boom:** All eyes are nervously focused on the expected retirement of 70 million baby boomers beginning in 2012. Considering their demands on the system, experts are predicting that trust funds will be exhausted in 2029.

> ➤ **The Bust:** Besides the baby bust coming directly after the baby boom, birth rates for succeeding years are down in this country. The Social Security Administration shows that birth rates are already below the 2.1 per woman needed for population replacement. They are expected to fall to 1.9. With fewer people supporting more people, there will be a drain on funds. The amount of Social Security benefits to be paid out will begin to exceed the current-year, tax-generated income in 2013. That's when they start dipping into interest income.

> ➤ **Longevity:** We're not just getting older, we're getting really old. When the first $17-a-month checks were issued, recipients were lucky to live a few years beyond 65. Way back in 1900, there were just 3 million Americans, a mere 4 percent of the population, who were 65. By the year 2030, there will be 64 million Americans over 65, which will be 22 percent of the population. People over the age of 85 or older currently make up the fastest growing segment of the population, and Willard Scott's birthday greetings go to an increasing number of 100-year-olds each year. And those Social Security checks keep rolling in.

We're all living longer, and more of us are living 100 years or longer.

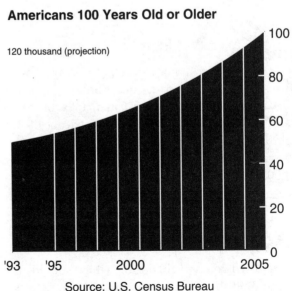

Americans 100 Years Old or Older

120 thousand (projection)

'93   '95   2000   2005

Source: U.S. Census Bureau

➤ **The Trust:** Is made of paper. Currently, the 12.4 tax rate brings in more revenue than is being paid out in monthly benefit checks. The excess is invested in SPDOs (special public-debt obligations) issued by the U.S. Treasury. And what does the Treasury do with the money? It spends it. So the Social Security Trust Fund is really a promise that the government will repay the money with interest. Now when the Social Security Administration starts to call for that money in 2013, what do you think that will do to taxes?

➤ **The Tax Rate:** Most people are not delighted to be paying Social Security taxes on an annually increased maximum amount of wages ($61,200 in 1995). The current 12.4 percent tax rate is either split between worker and employer or paid entirely by the worker if he or she is self-employed. Another 2.9 percent of a worker's entire salary (split or not as before) is earmarked for Social Security's Hospital Insurance (HI). A 1991 advisory council predicted that to finance Social Security benefits in 2020, the tax would have to be increased to 25 percent. Another 1991 panel predicted 31.57 percent. No one believes that Americans will sit still for that.

So what are we going to do? You guessed it: rework the system.

Will Baby Boomers Ever See Big Bucks and Big Benefits?

Social Security was never meant to be a comfort cushion. The idea was to provide all elderly people with enough income to buy the basic necessities of life. The government is unlikely to default on that promise. The big bucks and big benefits for most baby boomers, however, will be the receiving of those monthly payments over many, many years.

The program must be revised. But the revisions will probably be less painful than you anticipate. The first of these revisions is already in place.

As you can see from the numbers in the Social Security Benefit Dates table, the minimum age for full benefits has been raised in a step process. If you were born after 1960, you will have to be 67 before you are eligible. In the future, the minimum age probably will be raised even higher.

When you can expect Social Security benefits to begin.

Social Security Benefit Dates

Retirees, Spouses, and Divorced Spouses

Full Benefit at Age	Date of Birth*
65	Jan. 1, 1938 or before
65 + 2 months	1938
65 + 4 months	1939
65 + 6 months	1940
65 + 8 months	1941
65 + 10 months	1942
66	1943–Jan. 1, 1955
66 + 2 months	1955
66 + 4 months	1956
66 + 6 months	1957
66 + 8 months	1958
66 + 10 months	1959
67	1960 or after

Widow(er)s and Divorced Widow(er)s

Full Benefit at Age	Date of Birth*
65	Jan. 1, 1940 or before
65 + 2 months	1940
65 + 4 months	1941
65 + 6 months	1942
65 + 8 months	1943
65 + 10 months	1944
66	1945–Jan. 1, 1957
66 + 2 months	1957
66 + 4 months	1958
66 + 6 months	1959
66 + 8 months	1960
66 + 10 months	1961
67	1962 or after

*Month and date are January 2 unless otherwise shown

Source: Social Security Administration

How much will you get? On January 1, 1995, the average monthly benefit for a single retired worker was $698. For a worker and spouse, the average benefit was $1,178. Benefits have been raised over the years in response to cost-of-living adjustments (COLAs). COLAs may be smaller in the future, however, because they are set by Congress each year. In fact, your check might not change much for years at a time.

In today's plan, your benefits increase 4 percent per year for every year you delay retirement up to age 70. In the future, you may be encouraged even more strongly to keep on working without claiming benefits.

As the Social Security system is reworked, more affluent people may receive smaller benefits. And the benefits themselves may be taxed for higher income retirees.

And, yes, Social Security taxes may increase.

> **Gray Matter Alert**
> If you plan to start collecting Social Security after 1996, you may never see a check. But don't worry. You'll get your money. Awaiting Congressional approval is a bill to switch to electronic funds transfer as a means of distributing benefits. The move is expected to save billions of dollars, but it won't be fully implemented until the end of the century.

Back to Rugged Individualism

Perhaps by some magic at the turn of the century, everyone will start thinking of 65 as older middle age rather than the beginning of old age. And we'll all work a little harder and longer and try to be positive about the cuts in Social Security. Remember, there was no Social Security at the turn of the last century. People *saved* for their old age! Is that a not-so-new idea whose time has come again? Read on!

> **It's Been Said**
> *The one with the primary responsibility to the individual's future is that individual.*
> —Dorcas Hardy, Director, Social Security System (as reported on March 5, 1987 in the *Christian Science Monitor*)

The Least You Need to Know

➤ To qualify for benefits, you must earn a certain minimum amount in 40 quarters (10 years) of working.

➤ Social Security benefits are not likely to disappear.

➤ There will, however, be changes in the system. Some have already begun.

➤ There will be increased incentives to work longer and save more.

Chapter 3

Pension Checks and Personal Savings

In This Chapter

➤ What's in a pension plan

➤ Inflation and your buying power

➤ What you have coming and why

➤ Is *your* pension really safe?

➤ Seven ways to save

You say you want more than the roof over your head and bread on the table. You want walls and Palladian windows, or at least good storms and screens. And you'd like some French wine and cheese with that bread, thanks, or at least a good Californian. So you'll take Social Security for all you can get, add your pensions, and supplement with your savings.

How rosy is this picture? Well, it needs a reality pinch. So let's do an overview of the American pension system and a quick survey of opportunities for saving and investing. This will give you a feel for the money source arena. In Part 3, we'll tell you how to participate in *and win* at the games that are played there.

Company Pensions Defined

When all is said and done, the American pension system divides into two categories: *defined benefit programs* (DBs) and *defined contribution programs* (DCs). Defined benefit programs are the old tried and true: The company tells you what you deserve and then sends you monthly checks for the rest of your life, after retirement. These programs cost the employee nothing but are expensive indeed for the employer. Which explains why so many companies are now canceling out of DBs in favor of the newer and less expensive defined contribution programs. With DCs, the employer promises to make certain contributions to your retirement plan savings but does not guarantee any level of retirement income. Sometimes the amount the employer will be contributing is dependent on how much *you* are also contributing.

Extra! Extra!

Honors for the first corporate pension plan in the United States go to **American Express**. In the 120 years since they established their fund in 1875, most of our larger corporations, labor unions, not-for-profit companies, and government agencies initiated plans (and funds) of their own. Today, pension funds are one of the most powerful class of investors. Their assets include billions of dollars in stocks, bonds, and real-estate investments.

The Benefits of Defined Benefits

How will you get that monthly pension check when your employer took absolutely nothing out of your paycheck over the years? According to federal law, a company with a defined benefit program must annually pay into and set aside in a trust fund the money necessary to support your promised pension benefits. Trust fund moneys are invested (wisely, everyone hopes) so that they will grow far faster than inflation. When you retire, you begin to draw monthly payments from the fund.

Who and How Much

Because of the expense of creating and administering these funds, defined benefit programs usually are available only in companies with 250 employees or more. And in most cases, you need to be employed by the company for at least five years to participate in the pension plan.

How much will you get from your DB plan? Each firm has its own rules for calculating pension payments. Usually, your check is based on a factor of years of service combined with salary—sometimes the average salary over your entire term of employment or sometimes the average of the last several years. (The average of the last several years is usually better!) Some pension plans offer a flat benefit that is not based on your dollar earnings but is affected by the number of years you worked for the company. Your employer is required to make available to you an annual statement of your benefits. You can learn more about this subject in Chapter 13, "Stretching Your Pension Dollar."

> **Thin Ice**
> Let's say that after three years, you leave the company for greener pastures. In the next 15 months, you discover the grass is not so green and return. In some companies, this *break in service* wipes away your first three years of credit toward your pension benefits, forcing you to start again at year one. *Negotiate for bridged time!*

Staying Power

Although defined benefit programs offer the comfort and security of a guaranteed income for life, they are not the perfect solution to living-the-good-life concerns. Why not? Because most plans specify the exact amount you will receive every month as long as you live. Fortunately, we live longer and longer; unfortunately, the purchasing power of the dollar does not remain fixed.

The Social Security Administration's "best estimate" for moderate inflation in the foreseeable future is 4 percent per year. Accepting that rate and assuming that you'll live to 80 at least, take a guess at your purchasing power 15 years after retirement.

Give up? You'll be able to buy only 54 percent of what you bought when your pension started.

If you're one of the lucky few, your DB pension plan allows for cost-of-living increases. According to the U.S. Bureau of Labor Statistics, only 4 percent of the retired Americans currently receiving pensions are that lucky. Their luck is not limitless, however, because most cost-of-living adjustments are at the employer's discretion. And because giving out money is involved here, you'll find that most employers are very discreet indeed. Generally, increases do not even approach the rise in the Consumer Price Index.

> **Power Word**
> COLA is not a soft drink. The initials stand for Cost Of Living Adjustment. Check to see if your pension plan provides for automatic or periodic COLAs. Or any COLAs at all.

Inflation will cut back your spending power over time.

Purchasing Power of Your Pension Dollar Fifteen Years After Your Retirement Date

If the rate of inflation is 3%

You will have <u>61%</u> of your purchasing power

If the rate of inflation is 4%

You will have <u>54%</u> of your purchasing power

If the rate of inflation is 5%

You will have <u>46%</u> of your purchasing power

Another disadvantage of defined benefit programs affects people who change jobs frequently. Accrued DB pension credits cannot be transferred from one employer to another. This fact can mean a significant reduction in total pension for some individuals. (We'll get into the details a little farther along in this chapter.)

The Contribution of Defined Contributions

There are many types of defined contribution plans. The common thread, however, is that each DC employer promises only a certain level of contribution to your retirement savings and makes absolutely no promises about how much money you'll have when you actually do retire. You can end up with more than you would have gotten on a defined benefit plan, or you can end up with less. Much of the responsibility is yours and, in some cases, you can even participate in the management of your invested money.

Most employers like DCs because they cost less. Many employees like them because accumulated pension funds can be transferred when moving from one employer to another. Other employees, however, dislike them because of the uncertainty of benefits and the need to participate in savings and management. But we're getting ahead of ourselves again. Before we get into changing jobs and other pros and cons, let's take a look at some of the various types of defined contribution plans you might encounter.

401(k)s and 403(b)s

These plans are virtually identical. Both allow employees to contribute pre-tax dollars to retirement savings programs, within limits set by the federal government. While the money remains in these accounts, it is not subject to income tax. The 401(k)s are for people who work in corporations, while the 403(b)s are for people who work for not-for-profit organizations.

Many companies add to their employee's retirement savings by contributing a stated amount in matching funds. A dollar-for-dollar match is extremely generous. More common is 50 cents from the company for each employee dollar. The money then is invested in stocks, bonds, money market funds, or other investments. It continues to grow tax-free until withdrawals after age 59 1/2. Chapter 13 gives you more information about this excellent investment.

ESOPs (Employee Stock Ownership Plans)

If your company has an ESOP, both you and your employer can contribute specified amounts of money, which are then used to buy stock in the company. Choosing this plan as your primary retirement fund, however, is an immense show of faith in your employer. Think about it: There is no diversification of your retirement holdings—all your eggs are in one basket. And remember: Even the best companies can go downhill, sometimes for reasons beyond their control. Choosing an ESOP as a supplementary program, however, can be quite worthwhile.

Profit-Sharing Plans

When profit-sharing plans determine retirement savings, most employees work a little harder. Or at least that's what many companies like to believe and want the public to believe.

Profit-sharing plans are a safe road for the employer. They require that the company make an annual retirement fund contribution equal to a certain percentage of your salary. The catch is that the percentage can change each year because it all depends on the company's profits. It could be 20 percent in a good year or 0 percent in a bad year.

Money-Purchase Plans

These DCs are similar to profit-sharing plans, except that the employer must contribute a *fixed* percentage of your salary to your retirement fund each year. The dollar amount of the contribution might change if your salary goes up or down, but company profits for any given year will not affect the percentage rate.

SEP Plans (Simplified Employee Pension)

Often called SEP-IRAs, these are defined contribution plans for small businesses with 25 or fewer employees. With much reduced federal red tape, they allow the employer to set up an IRA for each employee. There is usually some matching of employee contributions at an agreed-upon level.

Moving Your DC Plan

If you have a defined contribution plan and you change your employer, you have 60 days to roll over the lump sum distribution of your retirement funds into your new employer's DC retirement plan. You can also roll over the funds into your IRA if you prefer, or if you remain unemployed.

Gray Matter Alert
Withdrawal of funds from an IRA before age 59 1/2 can be very expensive. Your money will be subject to federal, state, and local income taxes *and* a 10 percent early withdrawal penalty from Uncle Sam. Roll over!

It is extremely important—no, *absolutely essential*—that the funds are transferred directly from one employer's account to the other's or directly into your IRA. Electronic funds transfer is the safest means to accomplish this. Do not accept a check for the lump sum. Because of a 1993 law, if you're not yet 59 1/2 and you take hold of a distribution check, even to carry it from the office to the bank, the company will withhold 20 percent for income taxes and Uncle Sam will slap a penalty on top of that. More in Chapter 13.

One, Two, Three... How Many Pensions Will You Get?

There was a time, when our parents and grandparents were young and even before, when companies took care of their employees and employees were fiercely loyal to their companies. You went to work for, let's say, "the telephone company" at age 20 and got a gold watch and a pension 45 years later. As every baby boomer will tell you, it's a lot different in today's employment marketplace!

Statistics now show that by age 65 American men have held an average of 10.7 jobs, and American women 12.2 jobs. Just over a third of men have stayed with one employer for more than 20 years and only 15 percent of women have stayed with one employer for this amount of time . Although the swinging-tree-to-tree days of the '80s are over, there is still a tumultuous job market out there with a variety of job-changing pressures.

Why is this important? Because people who work for companies with defined benefit plans are sometimes hurt financially if they change jobs frequently. A study by the Employee Benefit Research Institute in Washington found that, all other factors being equal, the person who had four different employers at 10-year intervals over a lifetime career would get almost $20,000 less pension *per year* than the person who had just one employer.

Take a careful look at the Changing Jobs Can Change Your Pension graph. You'll see that job changes in the early years of employment don't make too much pension difference. But job changes after age 45 can be devastating.

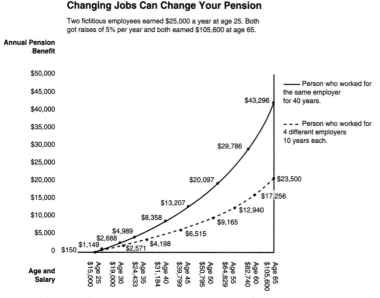

Changing Jobs Can Change Your Pension

Two fictitious employees earned $25,000 a year at age 25. Both got raises of 5% per year and both earned $105,600 at age 65.

This graph shows an example of how multiple jobs can affect your pension benefits.

Source: Employee Benefit Research Institute

The marginal change in benefit as a percentage of pay is the annual change in the present value of a deferred annuity for an employee in a final pay plan that pays an annual annuitized benefit of years of service times 1 percent of final pay. The present value of the deferred annuity is based on the annuity purchase price of 8.60 and a discount rate of 8 percent. Wages for both employees are assumed to increase 5 percent annually.

What's more, if you change jobs very frequently or have several interruptions in your career (as many women do because of child rearing), you might lose pension eligibility with some of your employers. Most employers require at least five years with the

Power Word

Vested has nothing to do with clothing. In pension language, it means having met the plan requirements for the legal right to receive pension benefits based on your years of service. Your benefits start when you attain retirement age, usually 65.

company before you are vested in the pension plan. So if you're thinking of a job change and getting close to the five-year mark, try to hang in there!

If you change jobs often but always work for companies with defined contribution plans, it's possible that you could go into retirement with only one source of pension income, because DCs can be accumulated into one plan and moved when you move. More likely, however, you'll get some DB checks, one or more DC checks, and perhaps a draw from your Individual Retirement Account (IRA). More about the IRA later.

Is Your Pension Really Safe?

Although pension funds must be held in a managed trust account, the money you think you are entitled to may not be there yet. And you can thank a deficit-conscious Congress for creating this scary scenario.

What happened? Well, money contributed to pension funds is not subject to taxation. So in 1987, legislation was passed in the Omnibus Budget Reconciliation Act that prohibited companies from taking into account projected pay raises and employee years of service when putting money into defined benefit pension plans for future retirees. It was thought that this act would prevent companies from building untaxable pension surpluses and thus increase federal tax revenues.

Great theory, but the law has also resulted in many pension plans becoming or about to become underfunded. During the coming decades, as the baby boomers earn higher and higher incomes, rack up more years in the company, and approach retirement, employers will have to make larger and larger annual pension fund contributions. Many experts fear that many companies will cancel their defined benefit programs when faced with the increased dollar demands.

Can they do that? Yes, they can. A company does not have to file bankruptcy or even be in financial trouble to justify termination of its pension plan. In fact, more than 30,000 American companies have dropped their defined benefit pension plans since 1980. Most have substituted some form of defined contribution plan.

"Whoa!" you cry. "What happens to the pension I was promised?"

It's probably still safe, although your benefits may be frozen at the markers (date and years of service) at which the plan was terminated. Your safety net is in place because of another, earlier, act of Congress. In 1974, the Employee Retirement Income Security Act (ERISA) was passed. It now governs pension plans.

ERISA also established the Pension Benefit Guaranty Corporation (PBGC), which acts for pensions much the same as the FDIC acts for savings. If a company wants to terminate its pension plan, PBGC requires it to prove that it has enough funds to pay all the scheduled benefits for currently retired and vested employees. If PBGC is satisfied, the company usually buys an annuity from an insurance company to pay pensions. That means you'll get your pension checks from XYZ Insurance Company rather than the company you worked for all those years.

If a company declares bankruptcy and has an underfunded pension plan, PBGC takes on the responsibility for paying your pension. You might not get everything you were promised, however. There are maximums for annual payments to individuals ($30,886 in 1995) and the agency does not cover health plans or other retirement extras. Also, this insured coverage only extends to private-company pension systems (which includes individuals in union-sponsored plans). It does not cover the plans of not-for-profit groups, government employees (federal, state, or local), and professional associations such as doctors or lawyers.

It also doesn't have quite the stature of the FDIC. The PBGC is funded by insurance-like contributions from the companies whose pension plans it guarantees. In addition, it has the authority to borrow up to $100 million from the U.S. Treasury. But that leaves open to question what would happen if many companies shut down at the same time. The $100 million wouldn't last more than a few months. Would our government then come to the aid of its elderly? Let's hope that question never needs to be answered.

So *will* you be getting a monthly pension check? Probably. The Smart Money people are still counting on both Social Security and pensions, but they're also putting away plenty of personal savings and investments both for safety's sake and to add the downy feathering that most people want in their retirement nests.

Which brings us quite handily to savings. Let's take a quick introductory tour of personal savings and investment opportunities. Later, in Part 3, we'll go into more detail.

Thin Ice
When a private-company pension plan is about to be terminated, the plan must send you a *Notice of Intent to Terminate* letter. Don't panic. The Pension Benefit Guaranty Corporation (PBGC) is on your side and you'll soon get a *Notice of Plan Benefits* letter. You can write to them at PBGC; 2020 K St., N.W.; Washington, DC 20006 or call (202) 326-4040.

It's Been Said
Wine maketh merry: but money answereth all things.
—Ecclesiastics 10:19

Seven Ways To Save

So **Merrily! Merrily!** went out in the blaze of glory that was the '80s. You now know that you can no longer coast along buying now and paying later, expecting that there will, of course, be more money later. And it looks as though none of us can spend, spend, spend, expecting that we will be taken care of when we can no longer work.

Oh, there's a cushion. But if you want real comfort, you've got to provide it yourself. Providing starts with saving, and there are a lot of ways to save.

What follows is a menu. We'll describe the dishes in detail in Part 3.

In the Bank

It used to be that there were savings accounts that paid you interest—the rate capped by law. Rates float free now, but the savings account still exists. Banks also offer certificates of deposit (CDs) at rates fixed for certain periods of time and money market accounts. Chapter 9, "Cash Equivalents—Your Piggy Bank," gives you more details and information.

Insurance

Insurance companies offer a menu that includes both protection and investment opportunities. Term life insurance might be an option for a young family, whereas an annuity might be perfect for someone approaching retirement. If you're wondering, "What's the difference?," you're not alone. You'll find answers in Chapter 17, "Protection for Your Possessions."

Bonds

There are many, many kinds of bonds. All of them take your money and promise to return it with a fixed amount of interest at a specified time. But when you've seen one bond, you haven't seen them all. There are levels of investment safety, and they don't all match the security of Series EE. Read Chapter 11, "Bonds—Your Money Earning Money," before you buy a bond.

Stocks

When you buy stocks, you buy ownership shares in corporations. Many people have achieved their financial goals by trading on the stock market. Some people have also lost money. Read Chapter 10, "Stocks—Your Ownership Interests."

Mutual Funds

There are stock mutual funds, bond mutual funds, and diversified mutual funds. If you feel uncertain of your own investment decision-making or you would prefer professional management of your investment money, this may be the way for you. *Mutual funds* are pools of money invested by a fund manager to achieve a specific goal. They offer the added security of allocating your assets to a wider range of investments, which could include stocks, bonds, real estate, and even futures. You can read about mutual funds in Chapters 8 through 12.

Real Estate

Yes, your home is an investment. But many people also make money investing in multi-family houses, rental condominiums, houses that need renovation, and vacation properties. You can also explore Real Estate Investment Trusts (REITs), Real Estate Limited Partnerships (RELPs), joint ventures in land development, and mortgages. You learn more about real estate in Chapter 12, "Real Estate—Your Hands-On Money Maker," and Chapter 16, "Home! The Biggest Asset for Most People."

Gold and Collectibles

Gold is probably the oldest investment vehicle and still has value the world over. It is not always the best possible investment, however. Collectibles such as art, rugs, stamps, cars, and so on are riskier investments because they have limited markets and high commissions and mark-ups for resale. But some savvy collectors have made fortunes. You learn more about cash equivalents in Chapter 9.

The Least You Need to Know

➤ Company pensions can be one of two flavors: defined benefit plans or defined contribution plans.

➤ Defined benefit plans promise you a certain monthly pension. You have no control over those benefits and must become vested to qualify for them.

➤ Defined contribution plans make no certain promises about your pension dollars. You might, however, have some control over the management of your retirement fund money.

➤ If you change employers and are given a lump sum distribution of your retirement savings, you *must* have the money moved directly from one retirement account to another within 60 days. If you accept the money, even touch the check, you will pay taxes and fines.

31

➤ Changing jobs frequently, especially after age 45, can negatively affect the pensions you will receive.

➤ Pension plans can be terminated. You will, however, receive what is owed you. The Pension Benefit Guaranty Corporation provides this insurance.

➤ Savings beyond the pension plan are essential for a secure and comfortable retirement.

Chapter 4

How To Get What You Want and Avoid What You Don't

In This Chapter

➤ Points on the retirement lifestyle spectrum

➤ What percentage of your pre-retirement income will you need?

➤ Risk tolerance and your route to financial security

➤ Five essential elements in every investment decision

➤ Where to get more planning aids

How to get what you want and avoid what you don't. What are we saying! Never mind *get* what you want. Sometimes it's hard to *know* what you want!

Which is exactly the point. In this chapter, we'll help you define your needs, set your goals, and evaluate your resources for reaching them. And if that sounds like work to you, it is! But don't stop reading. A little extra work is often well rewarded. Especially when you're working with money.

Why Bother?

Imagine this scene, if you will. There you are near the end of a day, 3,000 miles from home, running a meeting that's bogged down in power struggles and worrying that you'll miss the red-eye and have to spend another night in this overbooked town. On break, you call home only to discover that your oldest has brought chicken pox home from school (which means the younger two will probably get it too), the water heater sprang a leak and the plumber who fixed it left a bill for $587.43, and your financial advisor called to suggest you change to a growth-oriented mutual fund, which is, of course, more risky but will probably provide more money for an active retirement. *What?*

Yes, it's hard—very hard—to think about retirement when you're still trying to earn enough money to survive, and maybe get ahead a bit. And besides, how can anyone know what life will be like 10, 20, or 30 years from now?

There's no way to get rid of the crystal-ball factor when planning for the future. You think you have a perfect view, then something shakes the crystal ball and when the mist clears, it's a whole new picture.

It's Been Said
Our life is frittered away by detail... Simplify, simplify.
—Henry David Thoreau, 1817-1862

"So why even try?" you say. "Why not just do the best you can and go forward?"

You can't mean that or you wouldn't be reading this book. But we'll answer anyway. Because if you don't outline your retirement goals and work toward achieving them, you'll have to take whatever you get when you get there. And you may not like it. So set out now to define what you want and get it.

Determine Your Goals

If a picture is worth a thousand words, maybe a good story is worth 50 statistics. Read about Susan and Suzanne.

Susan earned a Ph.D. in psychology, opened her own Park Avenue office in New York City, and worked in two metropolitan hospitals as a domestic violence consultant until

It's Been Said
...be busy, and you will be safe.
—Ovid
43 BC-17 AD

she was 60. When she retired, she chose a log cabin in the hills of North Carolina. She and her husband raise geese and grow most of their own vegetables. In the community, she's just Mrs. Jones.

In her suburban community, Suzanne was just Ms. Smith, a high school teacher for 30 years. Eligible for an early pension, she took it. And she took off. Three-week international vacations several times a year, motor trips, long weekends, and most dinners out (and we're not talking Wendy's). She started and expanded a mail-order educational supply and software business, wrote a book on parent/teacher communication, and became a speaker at educational conferences. And she considers herself retired.

How do you see yourself? We can't exactly blame you if you don't align with either Susan or Suzanne. They are unusual people because they drastically changed their lifestyles. As we've already said, most of us really want to keep on living pretty much the same as we've been doing. Which is why experts predict that you'll need a retirement income of about 70 to 80 percent of your pre-retirement figure.

The "about" and the 10-point spread of that prediction, however, leave a lot of space for adjustment. In fact, some people go 10 percentage points in the down direction. So it's important at this point that you set *your* retirement income goal. The number you come up with will depend on some specific lifestyle choices, which we'll help you to define in Part 2. It will also depend on your current financial status and saving patterns, which can still be changed if the goal you want is different from the current predictions. Let's look at some of the variables.

Nearer to 80 percent. Your retirement income needs may be high if:

➤ You want to acquire and do some of the things you've been waiting for. In other words, live better!

➤ You will have to make a mortgage payment or pay rent during your retirement.

➤ You haven't been saving much of anything over the years or you made some investments and lost money.

Nearer to 60 percent. Your retirement income needs may be low if:

➤ You want a quieter and simpler life.

➤ You will own a home free and clear of debt by the time you retire.

➤ You have been saving between 10 and 20 percent of your annual income or you will get a substantial inheritance by the time of retirement.

About 70 percent. Your retirement income needs will be about average if:

➤ You plan to live in the same lifestyle that has been determined by your pre-retirement spending patterns.

➤ You will make some monthly housing payments, whether to pay off the balance on your mortgage or to support a vacation or seasonal home.

➤ You diligently saved between 5 and 10 percent of your gross income during your working years.

So what's your goal? A simple life or a busy life? Do you plan to continue earning some significant income during retirement or would you prefer that your savings and investments free you up to have as many lazy days as you please?

Unfortunately, you can't just pick one, snap your fingers, and make it so. Despite the best of plans, life happens and it sometimes gets in the way. But you can move in a direction that leads to what you want. Let's see what the main roads look like.

Mapping Your Route

There are almost as many ways to reach a financial goal as there are people to pursue it. In Part 3, we're going to discuss the nuts and bolts of many of these ways. By that time, you'll probably have added several ideas of your own too. Right now, however, you need to consider some of the basic concepts of financial planning.

High Speed or Safe?

More than anything else, investment choices come down to risk. The first question you should always ask is, "How much risk feels comfortable?" Within each savings and investment vehicle, from real estate to stocks, from bonds to mutual funds, you'll find various levels of risk. The trick is to develop a portfolio that suits your goals and needs but doesn't raise your anxiety level beyond normal tolerance. T. Rowe Price Investment Services, Inc. suggests the profiles in the Balancing Time and Risk in Portfolio Planning graph. But the time/risk profile could be applied to almost any investment vehicle.

OOOOH...

Power Word
Portfolio has nothing to do with artists when you're talking about money! It's your *combined* holdings of a variety of stocks, bonds, real estate, commodities, or other assets. The benefit of a portfolio is that you reduce your investment risk by diversifying your dollars into several different types of investments.

In this graph, safety (dark gray) is lower risk, income (white) is moderate risk, and growth (light gray) is higher risk. T. Rowe Price and most other investment advisors suggest more conservative choices as one gets closer to retirement and more risk-taking if one has many working years before the anticipated retirement date. But if you examine the graph carefully, you'll see that there are different portfolio blends suggested for different risk tolerance within each age bracket.

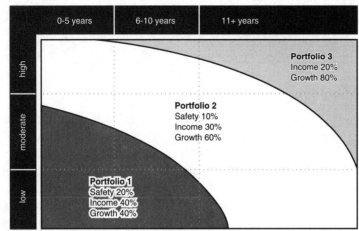

Balancing Time and Risk in Portfolio Planning

Investor's Time to Retirement

| 0-5 years | 6-10 years | 11+ years |

Investor's Risk Tolerance — high / moderate / low

Portfolio 3
Income 20%
Growth 80%

Portfolio 2
Safety 10%
Income 30%
Growth 60%

Portfolio 1
Safety 20%
Income 40%
Growth 40%

Source: T. Rowe Price Investment Services, Inc.

The amount of risk you can handle and the amount of time you have until you retire affect the kinds of investments you should make.

Knowing the Road

Besides your risk tolerance, your knowledge of and familiarity with an investment vehicle is also very important to your strategy. Generally, the more you know in a field, the more likely you are to succeed. Let's take real estate investment as an example. If you are familiar with the common uses of CC&Rs in condominium law but you don't know a 10-penny nail from a finishing nail, you would probably do better by choosing condominium rental apartments rather than fixer-uppers as your investment vehicle. In the financial marketplace, you might be familiar with *puts* and *calls* but not with *zero coupon*. In that case, you might want to stay with the stock market while you're doing some research on bonds.

The Long Haul

Another factor in investment choice is life expectancy. Because more and more Americans are living as much as 30 years after retirement, many who are approaching the gold-watch date are choosing investments that are likely to produce income for many years to come as well as keep pace with inflation. This consideration correlates with the tendency to go for high risk/high return investments in youth and "reliable" investments as retirement approaches.

Extra! Extra!

We met a man at a real estate investment conference in Florida who admitted to being 87 years old. Asked why he was so interested in buying and managing rental property, he replied, "I'm stocking up for my old age."

Roadside Assistance

If you feel insecure in your knowledge of an investment vehicle, you also can decide to get help rather than just looking elsewhere. There is a great deal of free information available. (We mention some of it at the end of this chapter.) And you can start out by investing in companies that professionally manage investments in that area. That's why mutual funds are so popular. With some care and research, you can find a company with funds whose goals and investment patterns match your own. You learn more about this process in Part 3.

Gray Matter Alert
Anyone can hang out a shingle that reads **Financial Planner.** The designation *Registered Investment Adviser* (RIA) requires only the filing of a form and paying of a fee to the Securities and Exchange Commission (SEC). The designation *Certified Financial Planner* (CFP) requires education and an exam. Look carefully before you leap!

On the other hand, some people hire a financial planner to assist in developing and implementing their savings and investment plan. A good planner can be, quite literally, worth his or her weight in gold. An incompetent one (and they exist in abundance) will not only charge you for services but also lose money for you. You learn more about professional financial advice in Chapter 8, "Ground Zero—Where Do You Stand?"

The Five Major Factors

Whether or not you use professional advice, you should be aware of and evaluate five basic elements in every investment you consider: security, income, profit potential, liquidity, and tax impact. As you do your evaluation, remember that these five factors are always in a balancing act. It would be as rare as hens' teeth to find all five at the same level in the same investment.

Security

Of course we're talking about safety. Ask yourself, "How safe is my money? Can I lose some of it or all of it under certain circumstances? Are there any guarantees?" Money in savings accounts insured by the FDIC is considered safe. But after interest and inflation are taken into account, you probably won't be any richer five years down the road than you were when you deposited the money. Commodities and junk bonds are not considered secure investments, but there is the potential for great profit and great loss.

Income

Everyone knows that income is money. When discussing investments, however, income is specifically the money you'll get on a monthly, quarterly, or annual basis from your investment. Whether it comes in under the alias *rent*, or *dividends*, or *interest*, it's still income. When you begin collecting Social Security benefits , however, income from investments in any given year does not count toward the maximum allowed earned income before benefits are reduced between ages 62 and 69.

An income-producing investment such as a multi-family house or a blue-chip stock may have very little potential for profit but be valuable because it is secure and dependable. The same can be said for some bonds, notes, and mortgages. Some income-producing investments, however, also have growth potential. And some are not especially secure. Whether this is a good investment for you depends entirely on your needs and goals.

> **Thin Ice**
> The standard warning is *don't put it all in one stock*, but putting it all into the stock *market* can be almost as dangerous. Build your retirement nest egg with a diversity of investments. Stocks can be balanced with real estate, bonds, mortgages, gold, and collectibles. Down in one market often means up in another.

Profit Potential

The possibility that your invested dollar will increase, maybe double or triple, is commonly referred to as *growth*. Growth vehicles are usually the most risky. In real estate, however, and in some kinds of collecting, profit potential may not correlate with risk at all. Generally, this is an area where knowledge counts, big time.

Liquidity

Not at all related to the laws of the non-solid state in physics, *liquidity* in investments means the ability to convert an asset to cash. An investment is liquid if it can be sold at any given time without financial loss because of time pressure. An investment is *illiquid* if the seller must wait for a buyer or lower the price significantly in order to attract a buyer. Real estate usually is considered an illiquid investment; stocks are liquid investments.

Tax Impact

There are few money-makers that taxation doesn't affect in one way or another. The problem is that "the way" is not consistent across the board. Some bonds are indeed tax free, many investments are tax deferred, and some financial decisions carry tax penalties. It's important to know the taxation policies associated with your vehicle of choice. If reading tax law puts you to sleep, you might want to talk with a tax accountant or tax advisor before diving into anything.

Asset Protection

Working hard, saving, and investing wisely doesn't necessarily mean you'll get what you want in retirement. *Everyone* wants to be rich, or at least secure, and not everyone respects the rights, goals, hard work, and dreams of other people. It's a shadowy world we live in, rarely black and white, right and wrong. There are individuals, companies, and forces everywhere that will take your money. Sometimes the taking is illegal, but as often as not, it's perfectly legal.

The most legal of the phantoms waiting in the shadows for your money is, of course, the IRS. They play a tough game with more rules than any one person could possibly remember. Often, if you know those rules, you can use them to your benefit. But "I didn't know" is *not* an acceptable excuse for mistakes. There are stiff penalties for incorrect reporting, calculation errors, or moving money without adhering to the rules. We'll try to alert you to danger points whenever we can, but it's essential to remember that IRS rules are subject to change. We strongly recommend that you consult with a competent tax advisor regularly.

Smaller than the IRS but still potentially tough and costly are the taxing authorities of state and local governments. You need to be aware of state income taxes and inheritance taxes and the potential for senior citizens' breaks on local tax bills. If you spend extended periods of time in a foreign country, you'll also need to be aware of foreign residency tax rules. Again, we'll try to alert you to important points as we go, but it's essential that you get professional advice for your particular questions and situations. There's more information about taxes in Chapter 18, "The Tax Man Cometh."

So much for the open hands of the government—how about companies and individuals? Anyone who has ever filed an age discrimination suit can tell you how cold and uncaring a company can be, especially when money is involved. Money is also the demon in most divorce cases and estate battles.

The fact is, you can't live without it—not well, anyway! So your challenge in planning for a great retirement is not only how to save and invest the money you need, but also how to keep as much of it as you can. Which brings us to lawyers.

Extra! Extra!

According to the American Bar Association, 88 percent of American lawyers work in metropolitan areas and tend to specialize. Lawyers in rural areas and small cities tend to be general practitioners. Studies show that Americans hire lawyers most frequently about financial/consumer matters, work-related matters, personal injury, real estate, estate planning, and marital issues.

Most people will need the services of a lawyer at several points in their lives. Why? Well, when it comes to protecting our assets, most of us stand alone in this life. Lawyers can help you tap the support available in the legal system to protect your assets from and against every kind of challenge. We'll spend some time in Part 5 telling you how to find and work with a good lawyer.

So What Do You Know?

Ok, can you acknowledge that the dream of someone taking good financial care of you as you grow older is just a dream? Social Security might keep you from being hungry and cold, but that's about it. Defined benefit pensions are being phased out, and you'll have to manage your own savings in defined contribution plans. Just about all of you will have to save to make retirement comfortable. And some of you will have to work.

The Sources of Retirement Income pie graph shows the Social Security Administration's estimate of sources of retirement income for retirees now over 65 who made more than $29,000 in 1992. *More than half the income is derived from investment/savings and work!*

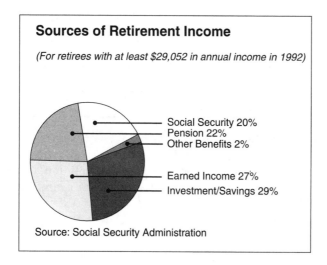

Sources of Retirement Income

(For retirees with at least $29,052 in annual income in 1992)

Social Security 20%
Pension 22%
Other Benefits 2%

Earned Income 27%
Investment/Savings 29%

Source: Social Security Administration

Here's Uncle Sam's estimate of where most people get their retirement income.

Think about the fact that you must save and invest, and that you might have to continue working at least part time after you retire from your primary career. What do you know, what are you interested in, what can you do that will help you to save money, invest it profitably, and perhaps earn more money during your retirement? To help you sort ideas, fill out the following lists. You might be surprised where the information leads you. And you might want to do the lists over again after you finish reading this book!

Here are some of the categories you might consider as you work through these exercises: stocks, real estate, insurance, mortgages, mutual funds, bonds, gold, collectibles, hobbies, work skills, and community service.

➤ Potential investment vehicles in which you have some knowledge or experience. Try to evaluate your level of expertise or experience.

_____

_____

_____

_____

➤ Investment vehicles in which you have some interest. Note why you are interested!

_____

_____

_____

_____

➤ Hobbies or work skills that might be used for extra income in retirement. Tell how.

_____

_____

_____

_____

A Source List of Some Planning Aids

Retirement planning is a hot topic right now. A great deal of information is available, some of it free for the asking. The trick is to get it, read it, and put it to good use. The following is just a sample to get you started.

From Your Government

There are Social Security Administration offices in many cities. Stop in, or you can write to them at Department of Health and Human Services, Social Security Administration, 300 N. Greene St., Baltimore, MD 21235. If you prefer to call, they have a toll-free number that is answered on any business day, from 7:00 a.m. to 7:00 p.m. Call (800) 772-1213. Among the booklets available are *Understanding Social Security* (#05-10024) and *Retirement* (#05-10035).

Upon request, the Social Security Administration will do a personal earnings and benefit estimate for you. The service will show your Social Security earnings history and estimate how much you have paid in Social Security taxes. It also estimates your future benefits. Ask for form SSA-7004-SM OP-7. As of January 1995, everyone over the age of 60 automatically will receive a benefit estimate.

From a Consumer Advocate Group

The American Association of Retired Persons is one of the largest trade associations in the nation. It publishes *Modern Maturity* magazine and offers numerous booklets and pamphlets on retirement planning. Contact them at AARP; 601 E Street N.W.; Washington, DC 20049. Call them at (202) 434-2277 or (800) 424-3410.

From an Investment Broker

Many investment companies offer free retirement-planning kits. Most are excellent, but be aware that these companies do want to sell you their products. The following is just a sample of what's available:

Aetna Insurance Co.
151 Farmington Ave.
Hartford, CT 06156
(203) 273-0123
(800) 238-6260
Free booklet: *Retirement Made Easy*

Fidelity Investments
P.O. Box 629724
Dallas, TX 75262-9724
(800) 544-4774
Free booklet: *A Common Sense Guide to Planning for Retirement*
Software: *Fidelity Retirement Planning Thinkware*, available at $45

T. Rowe Price
P.O. Box 89000
Baltimore, MD 21289-0250
(800) 638-5660
(800) 225-5132
Free collection of booklets: *Retirement Planning Kit*

Vanguard Group of Mutual Funds
Vanguard Financial Center
P.O. Box 2600
Valley Forge, PA 19482
(800) 662-7447
Software: *Vanguard Retirement Planner,* available at $15

The Least You Need to Know

➤ You will need between 60 and 80 percent of your pre-retirement income to be comfortable in retirement. The percentage that applies to you is determined by your lifestyle in retirement and your financial status when you enter retirement.

➤ In choosing the investment vehicles for your retirement savings, it is essential to consider your level of risk tolerance.

➤ Every investment should be evaluated from four different perspectives: security, income, profit potential, and liquidity.

➤ To protect your assets, get what you want, and avoid what you don't, you should use the professional skills of tax and financial advisors and a good lawyer.

Part 2
Scoping Out Your Dreams

Decisions, decisions, decisions. Now comes some of the fun part of retirement planning—seeing what you want, and then calculating what it is likely to cost. When the moment comes for you to retire, there will be a symbolic cutting of the cord that for so many years linked your home and your workplace. Snip—it's gone. Not only do you not have to show up for work every day, but you also do not need to live reasonably close to that job.

Now what? Perhaps, over the years, you have given some thought to those newly cleared hours and the many choices they will offer you in every area of your life. Or maybe, prior to reading this book, you have not. As you read on, try to do some serious "work" toward determining, and then shooting for, the lifestyle you truly want in retirement. After all, if not now... when?

THAT'LL BE $18.25 FOR THE NEXT 20 MINUTES...

Chapter 5

Free Time Isn't Always Free

> **In This Chapter**
>
> ➤ Estimating the cost of your favorite activities—full time
>
> ➤ Considering the possible cost of your dream projects
>
> ➤ Making serious travel plans
>
> ➤ Taking a closer look at yourself in retirement

OK, you're all geared up now. You're going to do some heavy duty financial planning and you're going to have plenty of money for retirement—right?

Well, *almost* right. There's just one little question still hanging around out there. Think about this: *How are you going to know how much money is "plenty?"*

As we said in Part 1, one of the big changes of retirement is that your time becomes your own. You're probably going to fill most of it doing the everyday things (chores and all) that already are familiar to you. But 40 hours a week is a lot of extra time, and you're likely to find yourself also doing at least some of the things you've always dreamed of doing. The trick is to estimate how much all that *doing* will cost.

It's Been Said

*"I just **love** having fun!"*
—Selma T. Archer, age 79 (more or less), while jumping in the surf on a south Florida beach

Your Tried-and-True Favorites

Because you're going to want activities that are enjoyable—yes, fun in some form or another—throughout your retirement, you can assume that you'll continue to do most of the things you choose to do in your free time now. But you might be surprised at what you now are actually *choosing* to do. And you might be surprised at how much it costs.

To get an idea of how you are spending your current free time, fill in the Pre-Rretirement Hobbies and Interests survey that follows. Now, don't just say, "OK, OK, later." This is important. It's really the best way to predict the pattern of your days in retirement. Or at least the hoped-for pattern. Don't forget to imagine yourself in each season. Activities usually differ in response to the weather.

Use this worksheet to see how you're presently spending your free time.

Pre-Retirement Hobbies and Interests Survey

Activity (Think about everything you do that's not work.)	How many hours in a typical week? M Tu W Th F Sa Su	Cost per hour	per day	How many weeks in each year?	Total expenditure each year

Once you've filled out the worksheet, you'll have a grip on your free-time choices and your current spending patterns for those choices. Then try to visualize yourself with enough money and no demands on your time. Ask yourself, "How would I choose to spend my time?" Would you play golf three days a week? Five? Seven? How many days a year would you spend skiing? If you're a theater buff, would you spend your time seeing plays or would you get involved in a community theater group?

After you come up with an estimate of how many hours or days per week you would like to spend pursuing your current hobbies and interests, multiply that number times the cost of one hour or day on the worksheet. Now you have a cost per week estimate.

Then consider the seasons again. If you move to another climate, will the amount of activity per season change? Will you be out boating in March? If you change to a different housing style (from a single family house to a condominium, for example), will changes in your responsibilities allow you a longer season in some activities? In short, will you play more golf and do less gardening?

Now estimate the number of weeks in each season that you will engage in your favorite activities. When you come up with that total, multiply it times the cost per week, and you will have an estimate for how much per year you will spend on each of your current hobbies and interests. Subtract what you currently are spending, and you'll have the amount of additional money needed.

The Dreams You've Dreamed

Now this part is harder. Almost everyone knows some retired person who talked for years about all the fishing, woodworking, oil painting, or writing he or she was going to do as soon as the time was available. Then the person retired, fished, woodworked, painted, or wrote a bit and soon found a part-time job or got involved in volunteer work. So much for fantasy hobbies.

"But I'm different," you say. You're absolutely positive you're going to track your genealogy through North Dakota, Arkansas, Brooklyn, Glasgow, and eastern Germany (or maybe the area you want actually became Poland). All right. How much do you think that will tax your retirement budget?

Thin Ice

Some newly retired people spend thousands of dollars on hobby supplies and equipment and then use what they bought very seldom, if at all. It's better to go forward one step at a time. Start with beginner-level equipment, take on a small project, or sign up for a course at night school before you commit to major cash outlays for a dream hobby. Best of all, if you have the time: Try to start that hobby *before* you retire, so you'll know if it's an interest you want to pursue later, and you will also have a good idea of costs.

Whether you have 30 years or 3 years before your retirement, right now is an excellent time to think (realistically) about the new things you will want in your new lifestyle. Have you dreamed about restarting the piano lessons you quit when you turned 11? Or perhaps you'd like to follow the example of Malcolm Forbes and take up hot-air ballooning. Both are possible, both cost money, and both could be real. It depends on what a person wants and how much money is available. So let's do a dream analysis. Cost analysis, that is—no need for help from Dr. Freud.

The Retirement Dream-Activity survey that follows will help you separate the *must haves* from the *maybe I'd like tos*. In the Experience column or on a separate sheet of paper, write down how much time you already have spent in this field and what you know about it. The cost of equipment is more a one-time expenditure (or at least an infrequent expenditure), whereas the cost of lessons and supplies might well be computed weekly.

Right now, for purposes of estimating your retirement financial needs, you can ignore the Maybe I'd Like To... column.

"So why did you make me write it out?" you ask. Because it's important to list and acknowledge the *maybes* as possibilities—just possibilities. Until you think it through, it's very difficult to differentiate a dream *must have* from a dream *maybe*.

In the future, you may indeed pursue those *maybe* interests, but in all likelihood you'll do so only if you have *extra* money. You shouldn't try to save enough money for everything! You want to focus on and plan for the activities you want most.

Retirement Dream Activity Survey

Now plan what you'd like to do.

What you dream of doing (do NOT include travel)	Experience	Approximate cost of equipment	Approximate cost of supplies and lessons - per week	Weeks per year	Check One	
					Must have	Maybe I'd like to...

Add up the cost of equipment. That figure probably will loom as a major expenditure sometime within a year or so after you retire. Then add up the weekly estimate of supplies and lesson costs, and multiply this by the number of weeks per year you think you'll pursue that particular hobby or interest. The figure you get will be another addition to your basic cost-of-living needs after you retire.

Be sure that you consider that dollar amount as a part of your requirement—don't expect it to come from petty cash or extra disposable income. If the activity was important enough to enter it into the Must Have category, it probably is essential to your health and happiness in retirement. Remember that your interests—not your job—will define and create you, the person, after retirement.

Gray Matter Alert

For couples only! If you'll be going into retirement together, you should copy these worksheets and each do one, separately. Allow for both your *musts*. When you share activities, however, the cost per couple usually is less than twice the cost for one person.

Extra! Extra!

According to an American Association of Retired Persons (AARP) study, travel ranks as one of the top leisure activities for both men and women over age 50. American seniors spend close to $500 *million* a year on vacations, the report found. Two-thirds of them prefer to make their own travel arrangements rather than go on a package tour.

Jaunts and Far-Away Places

Retired people travel for pleasure more than working people. But not all of them fly the Concorde or sail the QE 2. Most fly or sail tourist class and many choose to drive—some in motorhomes. Sometimes trips are long and multi-faceted. Sometimes just an overnight holiday satisfies the urge to get away.

Even those footloose and fancy-free people who can amuse you for hours with travel stories may be spending much less on their pastime than you think. They know better than to sign up for frilly, escorted tours and big-name hotels. Often, you'll find them at an Elderhostel, on a university vacation, with a senior group tour, on a home exchange plan, using a timeshare, or seeking out international bed and breakfasts. Elderhostel, home exchanges, and timeshares are explained in detail in Chapter 28, "Travel Time."

What's your style? Or do you like to browse the vacation buffet? You might indeed choose a luxury cruise for one trip, but then a wilderness camping experience for another.

That's great! Variety is still the spice of life, right? But we've got to ask you to put away your "I'll go wherever and whenever the spirit moves me" attitude for just a bit, and consider how much travel and what types you hope to experience in your retirement. The answers you come up with will help you to determine how much extra cash you'll need for travel. Use the following surveys to compare how you travel now to how you'd like to travel when you retire.

Your Current Travel Patterns Survey
List the vacation travel you have done in the past 5 years.

Place	Transportation (plane, ship, car)	Accommodation (hotel, apartment, camp)	Approximate cost of vacation

Make an honest assessment of how often you travel now.

Your Retirement Dream Travel Survey

Type of vacation	How many each year?	How much time?	Approximate cost
Resort			
Foreign travel			
Cruise			
Guided tour			
Touring by car or motor home			
Camping			
Bed 'n breakfast/short trips			

*Use this worksheet to see how often you'd like to travel during retirement **and** to estimate that cost.*

We'd like you to look back at the trips (vacations, not business-related trips) you've taken in the past five years.

"Why so long?" you ask. Because you may see a pattern emerge. If you do, it probably indicates a travel preference and you'll probably continue it into retirement. So take that amount of travel and consider it "normal activity." This activity is counted when we say you'll need 70 percent of your current income to live comfortably in your retirement. What we need here is an estimate for the amount and cost of the *additional* travel you hope to do.

We know these are rough estimates at best. But think this through. Do you see yourself taking four long trips a year? One long and many short? Extended trips of several months? All-day jaunts or long weekends? Try to come up with a pattern you would enjoy and then try to estimate the extra annual cost, beyond what you spend now. You need that figure to help set your retirement savings goal.

Back to Your FIRP

Now go back to the Future Individual Retirement Profile you put together in Chapter 1. How accurate were your initial predictions in the Travel and Leisure categories? These are two aspects of your lifestyle that are especially subject to change in retirement. So revise your predicted spending points if that's appropriate and keep the figures you came up with in this chapter at hand. They're essential in determining how much you'll need to save during your working life.

But hold on. You're not quite ready to do that yet. You still need more work on this scoping out your dreams project. After leisure activities and travel, the only aspect of your life more likely to affect your wallet and your well-being is housing. And housing seems to affect everything, every day, and through all the years. So, of course, we're going to spend the next two chapters talking about just those things. (We need two chapters because housing is both *where* and *what*.)

The Least You Need to Know

➤ You'll probably continue your current leisure activities into retirement, but they will cost you more because you'll have unlimited time to spend on them.

➤ You may or may not pursue the activities you've always dreamed of doing but have not yet done. You will have to decide which are most important or most feasible and how much you are willing to spend on them.

➤ You almost certainly will do more vacation traveling after you retire. If you don't want your travel money to come out of your food budget, however, you must estimate how often you will travel, what type of vacations you will take, and how much you want to spend per year.

Okay, Let's Put the Good Life in Its Place

Before selecting the exact type of dwelling that will be your retirement home, or perhaps the first of several retirement addresses, comes the matter of where that spot will be situated in this global village.

You will find that the world is your oyster, the sky's the limit, and all of the other clichés that apply to this topic. Read about them now, in a nutshell.

City Mouse, Country Mouse—Where Do You Fit In?

In a 1993 article, the *New York Times* noted a rise in the elderly population in New York City. Some of the increase came from folks just living longer, but there was also, the article stated, a small but continuing growth in retirees leaving more serene towns for New York City, where almost 1.3 million people over the age of 60 live. No numbers on the newcomers were available, but the phenomenon could be verified, the article continued, by people who work with the elderly there.

Why would retirees—and some quoted in the article were in their eighties and nineties—move to an urban area characterized as overpriced, crime-ridden, congested, and just plain unlivable? They are city people. They found in New York City a variety of social programs to assist them with their needs and problems, so that they could take advantage, as much as their health and desires allowed, of the many cultural advantages of the Apple.

It's Been Said
This is where the action is ...
—a woman said to be 90 years old, in a newspaper article about the elderly moving to New York City for its services and excitement

If you are nodding your head while reading this, then you understand. You are one of them.

Of course, in many instances, city living can be expensive. Rents are higher than in most small towns or hamlets. Houses in town can carry stratospheric price tags. Food and other day-to-day expenses are high. On the other hand, in a large enough city, a car might not be necessary, with the availability of public transportation. For out-of-town excursions, there is always the car rental agency. That would be one major cost saving.

If the city is your dream and you are on a more or less tight budget, investigate the least costly way you can live there. Houses in neighborhoods undergoing restoration usually are less costly than those completely refurbished. (You will, of course, have to take into account the funds you will need for the fixing up, although the community might have low-cost neighborhood improvement loans to assist you.) You also can buy a two-family house and use the rental income to help defray city-living costs.

A condominium or cooperative apartment could be less costly than a house. Or you might decide on a loft apartment. In many cities, loft living is trendy and still quite inexpensive, and residents are not all young, struggling artist types either. Every loft neighborhood has its share of retirees who decided not to live a stereotypical retirement life.

Finally, you might give some thought to renting an apartment. Chapter 26, "Another Look at Housing," gives you more information about rentals.

Squeak, Squeak

Rural life can be quite affordable, if you're the country-mouse type. Some houses that are far from primitive carry reasonable price tags compared to houses in the city or its surrounding towns, and many fixer uppers are downright steals. The intrepid homeowner might turn a little patch of land out back into a vegetable or fruit garden, saving even more retirement dollars.

You would be wise to try living in the outback for a vacation or two before committing yourself to life there full time. You might find that you miss certain things. Your nearest neighbor could be too far away, the quiet a tad too still. Old houses with inadequate wiring for your high-tech gear, unpaved roads, problems with water—all could trap those who are still seeing rural areas through those rose-colored glasses.

Retirees also should think about the availability of social and healthcare services out in the wild, or even the not-so wild. Where will the doctors, hospitals, and walk-in health clinics be in the spot you are eyeing?

It's Been Said
The country makes me nervous. You've got crickets and it's quiet and there's no place to walk after dinner and there's [sic] screens with dead moths ... you've got the Manson family, possibly ...
—Alvy Singer (Woody Allen) in *Annie Hall*

Hey, What About the Suburban Mouse?

Oh, we almost forgot. Wasn't it a children's story that introduced us to the city mouse and the country mouse? That tale must be at least 50 years old. Since over the last half century there has been a third choice, and a sizable one it is: the suburbs.

This lifestyle is certainly a viable option for retirement. Interestingly, those bedroom communities are not the sole province of young families any more, and are not always '"sterile"—an adjective frequently applied to them by those turning up their noses at that lifestyle.

Here is an interesting statistic. In 1994, the American Association of Retired Persons (AARP) released a study that found that 62 percent of the nation's population over the age of 60 reside in suburbia. These could well be folks who lived in those towns for many years and do not want to move simply because they have retired (see the next section, "Staying Put"). Or, they could be retirees who moved to a particular community to be near their children and grandchildren who are living the suburban life.

Drawbacks? Noise from children could be annoying at times. Housing costs might be a more serious concern. The large suburban house can carry a large mortgage and an equally sizable property tax bill and maintenance costs.

Still, if a suburb is your choice, you might be entitled to a senior citizen tax break on property taxes offered by your town, and you also may be able to convert part of your house to a rental unit or take in a roomer to help swing expenses. Many communities have neighborhood help programs to assist retirees with house painting and other home-related chores at little or no cost to the homeowner. To find help in the community you've chosen, contact that town's senior services agency or office on aging. You can try your regional office of the U.S. Department of Housing & Urban Development (HUD), too.

Or, you could elect to move to a cozy, affordable condominium in the suburb that interests you.

Where are the retirees?

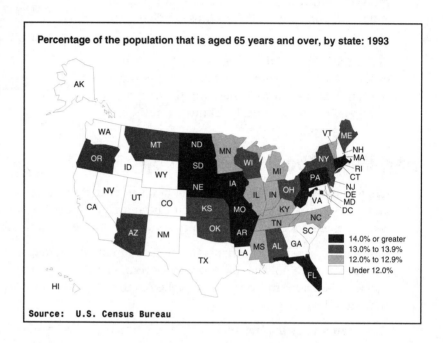

Percentage of the population that is aged 65 years and over, by state: 1993

14.0% or greater
13.0% to 13.9%
12.0% to 12.9%
Under 12.0%

Source: U.S. Census Bureau

Staying Put

"What's all this talk about moving?" you ask. "There's nothing wrong with staying right here on Sycamore Street."

You are not alone in your choice, unmovable one. Although retirees who relocate are the focus of most media feature stories, there are many more people over 65 who would not think of taking off for parts known or unknown.

Again from AARP: A study released in 1993 found that 84 percent of those 55 years old and older want to stay in their present homes and never move. The overwhelming number of retirees seem to prefer the comfort of a home and town they know well, with good neighbors and friends nearby, not to mention children and grandchildren. Whether those polled will want to stay in their homes a few years down the road—or will be able to—remains to be seen.

Extra! Extra!

Virginia Hopkins Phillips of Onancock, Virginia, lived in the same house from her birth in 1891 until a few months before her death in 1993 at the age of 102. Posthumously, she won the Guinness Book of World Records award as "Most Durable Resident."
—*Old Farmers Almanac*

Moving is a major stress point in most lives, even if that move is a long-desired one. Ordinary details of life we take for granted now loom as serious concerns in a new locale—finding new doctors, a dentist, a veterinarian, a lawyer, even a hairdresser. Making friends, many feel, is also more difficult as we grow older.

Relocating is expensive, too. Moving across a few states will cost several thousand dollars. There is the expense of the new home and its closing costs, too, which are likely to run a few thousand dollars.

If you stay where you are now, your home could be paid for or nearly so at retirement time.

Here, too, as with the suburban house, if your place becomes too big for you, you can convert part of it to a separate apartment to rent or take in a roomer.

Hometown Homework

You will get more from your retirement years where you are now if for a while you approach living there the way you would if you were new to town. You'll look around for sightseeing attractions, of course, but also investigate services for retirees.

Look into social programs for seniors. There could be a city or county office on aging that can assist you with medical and tax forms, help you find someone to share your home, and lend a hand with any of your other concerns as you move through retirement. Perhaps your town offers seniors discounts on public transportation, purchases in certain shops, and so on.

Also, check to see whether there are rehabilitation centers, assisted-care facilities, and nursing homes near where you are. Those needs may be years down the road, if you need them at all, but if you want to stay in Hometown, it's nice to know that your community will be able to fill all, or almost all, of your retirement check-listed items.

College Towns—a New Retiree Attraction

Here is a sort of new trend in retirement lifestyles, or at least one that is becoming more prominent: moving to a college town. That may be a true small town, with a college and its few hundred students, or it could be a big city. For example, Morningside Heights, a New York City neighborhood, is a sort of college town for Columbia University.

Gray Matter Alert

If you want to tour college campuses and towns with an eye toward moving to one of them, why not sign up for some Elderhostel learning vacations, which often are conducted on college campuses? You can learn more about Elderhostel in Chapter 28, "Travel Time."

Many people want the stimulation and busyness of an academic environment when they retire. Usually they sign up for courses at that college, which might be offered free to seniors (just for auditing, or listening, not enrolling for credit). They poke around the many bookstores in town, enjoy stopping in coffeehouses, and frequent the theater that shows foreign films.

If you fit this profile to a T, you certainly have plenty of college towns to investigate, if you don't already have a favorite in mind.

Well, You Won't Live in a Dorm ...

Housing opportunities run the gamut in college towns, but, in general, the area around the campus is obviously the priciest. You are paying for the most distinguished homes and the convenience of walking to campus.

If you find single-family houses too costly in the community that interests you, you might try for a two-family dwelling. Renting out the second unit can bring you an extra income, and there is never a shortage of would-be tenants in a college community.

Developers are always quick to spot a trend, and they have in recent years been constructing new-home developments near college campuses. You do not have the college atmosphere in those communities, of course, but you might enjoy the pool, tennis courts, and other amenities you would have to forego with one of the older houses in town.

... But You Might Live on Campus

This could come as news to you. There are now about 20 college campuses around the country that offer housing to retirees right on the grounds of the school.

The campuses vary in the housing they offer seniors—both rental and ownership styles, high- and low-rise buildings, and what various prices will buy you in the way of amenities and services.

If you are interested in learning more, contact your college alumni office. (Interestingly, to take just one example here, around 40 percent of the residents of The Colonnades at the University of Virginia in Charlottesville are graduates of that school. The Colonnades, developed by Marriott Corporation, features 180 apartments and 40 cottages.)

So You Want Better Weather

And you are willing to move to get it? Let's take a look.

First, a few words about terms. *Climate* is a pretty steady thing. A town's or state's climate is determined by its geographic location, distance from the poles and from the equator, proximity to bodies of water, and so on. That is why winters are cold in Minneapolis, milder in New Orleans, and even warmer in Key West, Florida.

Weather makes up a climate and is variable. One day, it is rainy in Minneapolis; two days later, it's snowing; and the day after that storm, the sun is shining.

You probably want to move to a climate that will provide you with more of the daily weather you like, right?

Extra! Extra!

Contact the Chamber of Commerce in the community that interests you and ask for weather data. Also ask for the cost-of-living figures for that town. They might also have statistics for other parts of that state, so you can calculate whether you are moving into a low- or high-cost region. If the Chamber can't help you, ask someone in the reference department of that town's public library.

Mountain People

Do you love crisp winter days and winter sports, especially skiing? Heading for a winter sports community can be an excellent move. On the practical side, the home you buy can be used in the summer time as well. Spring, summer, and fall are marvelous seasons in the mountains. Many ski towns, large and small, have lively social programs designed to attract off-season vacationers.

You also won't feel that you have to escape your dream spot in the summer. It certainly won't get too hot in or around the mountains, will it? If it does, it's likely to be far steamier out on flatter land. So you stand to get a good value from your housing invest-ment, as long as you choose the town and the house or condo wisely, as you would any real estate purchase.

However, there are a couple of points to keep in mind here—considerations that could affect your retirement budget. One is that many skiing communities, and new towns cropping up near them, have been experiencing tremendous growth over the last few years as folks from more troubled spots flee to what they feel is God's Country Filled with Good People. Services such as water, roads, police, and other services may be strained, even if the developer must absorb some of those costs. That growth spurt also might bring a need for new schools—a tax bill you will have to foot without having any use for those facilities.

By all means, vacation in your intended community for several years before buying, and talk to residents about zoning, taxes, growth, and other local issues—especially hot ones. See how you like life there in the off months, and when you're vacationing in the "high" season, think about how you will cope with living there day to day with the vacationing hordes. You might feel different as a resident than you do as a visitor.

Another consideration is health. Developing even non-life-threatening health problems some day might keep you from enjoying those cold winters. Retirement services could be skimpy because the town is geared toward a younger population. A changing health picture could mean you will want to leave your winter haven—an unexpected, expensive move.

Sunny Side Up

Then there are those who thrive in the sunshine, and feel a chill when the temperature drops below 60 degrees. Recognize anyone here?

Moving to warmth and sunshine is many a retiree's dream. For thousands that means Florida, which has been called, as the joke goes, *God's waiting room*. If you plan to move to the Sunshine State 15 minutes after being handed your gold watch, you probably have vacationed there many times over the years. You know the communities that interest you.

That familiarity will help make your move as smooth as possible. Housing is cheaper in quite a few parts of Florida than it is in many other parts of the country, helping stretch your retirement dollar.

But this is about climate and weather. So here is a question: Have you taken any of those many vacations to Florida in August? Uh-huh. And what about you folks heading for the desert when you retire? Have you visited in August? Mmmmmm.

Both groups need to spend a vacation week or two in a dream spot in the off season which, if it is warm in winter, is likely to be broiling in summer. They tell you in desert areas like Arizona or Palm Springs, California, "Oh, but it's a dry heat so it really doesn't seem that bad." Not bad? Most people find that 120 degrees is HOT no matter which way you analyze it.

Retirees who have moved to Florida and desert areas move back out again for a number of reasons. Sometimes they miss their home town, friends, and children. Sometimes they miss the change of seasons. But often, they leave because they cannot stand all that sunshine day after day, and they especially cannot take the summer heat (or the bugs, another complaint, or the fact that some desert areas are so brown, with so little green, that they do not seem real).

Gray Matter Alert

If you move to a hot climate and are going from one air-conditioned building to another much of the year, join the local branch of the Sierra Club, or volunteer at a nature preserve. Or, think of some other way get to know the ocean or desert, the birds, trees, and other living things special to your region. It will help you settle in and get you outdoors once in a while!

The solution for many people appalled by heat in their new retirement community—heat that lasts half a year or longer—is to rent or buy a small place miles away to which they can escape for a few of the more intolerable months. That costs money, of course—money that can be totally unexpected in retirement calculations. It's simpler just to try it before you buy it—all of it.

A word here about hurricanes. They are a reality along the coasts of Florida, Georgia, the Carolinas, Louisiana, and Texas. There are no statistics, of course, on whether someone has not retired to those regions because of the possibility of a big storm. However, it would seem that folks who really want to live in those parts of the country will, telling themselves the chance of their being hit directly is remote (it is). They also will say that really big storms hit infrequently, (they do), and they'll take the advice of local authorities when storms seem to be brewing, and also will take advantage of hurricane-preparedness programs in their communities.

Tornadoes hit those states, too, of course, and they certainly cause paths of destruction in the Midwest as well. If your retirement haven will be in California, you will have to take the threat, and sometimes more than merely the threat, of earthquakes along with your sunshine.

Extra! Extra!

There are now 3.2 million 60-plus residents in Florida, representing 24 percent of that state's population, according to 1995 statistics from the Florida Department of Elder Affairs. That same 24 percent, the department notes, will be the proportion of retirees to the overall population nationwide in 20 years.

New Escapes

Small but growing retirement destinations are parts of the Carolinas, Georgia, Tennessee, Mississippi, Arkansas, and Alabama. They offer milder winters than those in the northeast or north central states and somewhat cooler summers, especially in mountain areas. Some communities are actively courting the retirement clientele. Many of those who move there have chosen their new homes precisely because of the climate. A bonus, they have found, is that they are closer to family and friends in their hometowns than they would have been in warmer-weather states, making return visits easier.

If you want to poke around those areas, the state's tourism department, located in the state capital, can provide literature on those areas and even direct you to specific towns that might interest you.

The Best of Both Worlds

Finally on the weather front, you might want to stay where you are now, and rent or buy a place to get away for a few months in the winter or summer, avoiding at least some of the weather you dislike where you are now. If that is your choice, figure the cost of that accommodation into your retirement figures, and don't forget auxiliary expenses such as air fare to your destination, car rental, and so on. If you want to learn how to *s-t-r-e-t-c-h* out that visit to many months, read the next chapter, "And the Roof Over Your Head."

Considering Safety

Naturally, you will want your retirement spot to be safe. Truth be told, though, crime affects everyone these days, even in the teeniest hamlet. Some places are more secure than others, of course, and you can create some degree of safety wherever you go by using your smarts and staying aware at all times of your movements and surroundings.

Retirees are particularly concerned about crime because they often seem to be sitting ducks for criminals. They move more slowly than youngsters, their reflexes are slower, and perhaps they are a shade more trusting of their neighbors.

Yet you *can* move to Chicago, New York, Los Angeles, or Miami and live the rest of your days without ever seeing a crime, let alone being the victim of one. A lot depends on the community and home you choose, your own habits and attitudes, and, let's face it, luck.

You might contact the police department of the town that interests you, and ask for the crime statistics for the previous years (if you can get your hands on a few years of data, you can trace the growth or decrease of certain crimes). How many police officers are there in town? If it's a large metropolitan area, are there police substations or mobile units? Are crimes mostly against property? Is the town so off the beaten path, seeing little through traffic, that crime is low? Are car thefts a major problem? Are the most common cars stolen the same model and year as your auto? That might make you think about having a garage with the home you buy, if you haven't already made that a must. Take advantage of any help a police department can offer. It's solid information, and free.

Talk to your real estate agent in that community, too. Ask if it's true that corner houses are far more likely to be broken into. Is a certain neighborhood particularly open to burglaries because it's only a block to the interstate, offering criminals a fast getaway? Note which homes have bars on the windows. Why? Has that location experienced a number of break-ins?

Do Fence Me In

Here is a fairly recent development on the security scene that you can find in every state, and with numerous housing styles. It's the gated community. Some are built new with guardhouses or electronic devices to restrict entrance, while others have been converted to that state after fear of crime among residents.

Ask at any gated subdivision that you are considering whether there is a guard on duty 24 hours a day, or just for one shift. Check several times in your househunting to be sure the guard is on duty when he or she is supposed to be there. Are you willing and able to pay your percentage of the fee for personnel, equipment, and upkeep of the gatehouse building? Can you live with the lack of spontaneity in having to have visitors announced?

An electronic card or a numeric code system to allow you access can be less costly than a fulltime guard, but it's important to inspect the gate. Some of them are simply railroad-crossing type gates that anyone can slip under, and not iron grilles.

Thin Ice
Are you really safe in gated communities? One critic noted, "The first time the pizza delivery man comes through, everyone knows the code." But it's the *perception* of security that's important, security experts say.

Will you pay for your security? Of course. One New York planner noted the 50 gated communities he studied on the subject of safety were fetching prices as much as 50 percent more than identical homes in ungated subdivisions just a few blocks away. Nationwide, there are some 30,000 residential communities closed off to public access in some form.

On Foreign Soil

Living out of the country might be your choice for the 65-plus years, and that is not a totally uncommon decision. As you can see from the U.S. Population Abroad chart, Americans are residing in a number of foreign countries—and we aren't talking about service personnel, either.

As this State Department data illustrates, many Americans choose to live in other countries for a variety of reasons, including, among others, proximity to family and reasonable cost of living.

U.S. Population Abroad, by Country

(In thousands. As of October 15, 1992. Data taken from the annual noncombatant personnel evacuation requirements report, which is used solely to estimate the number of potential U.S. citizen evacuees from a given country in a crisis.)

Area	Resident U.S. citizens *	Area	Resident U.S. citizens *
Argentina	13	Italy	104
Australia	62	Jerusalem	43
Canada	296	Mexico	539
Costa Rica	23	Netherlands	19
Dominican Republic	97	Panama	36
Egypt	17	Portugal	26
France	59	Saudi Arabia	40
Germany	354	South Korea	30
Greece	32	Spain	79
Hong Kong	24	Switzerland	27
Ireland	46	United Kingdom	255
Israel	112	Venezuela	24

* Totals represent broad estimates and may include some non-U.S. citizens, as well as dual nationals.

Source: U.S. Dept. of State, unpublished data, 1993

You might want to live in the country where you still have relatives and roots. Canada has a number of American residents. Mexico has attracted attention for its reasonable, even inexpensive, lifestyle that is drawing retirees, among others. Perhaps you have vacationed in a particular spot often over the years and now want a permanent home there. Or it could be a second home you're considering buying in another country.

As you can imagine, Americans considering a home abroad need to exercise caution and do lots of research. There are many rules and regulations for living and buying property in each country, making it impossible to set down here exactly what the demands are where you might be heading. But, generally speaking, here are the major points to look for:

➤ Be sure the country that interests you is welcoming to foreigners, especially Americans. Just because you were born there does not mean you will be welcomed back.

➤ Will you be able to rough it there, if need be? We *are* used to our comforts here.

➤ What is the country's political situation? At peace? Tense? What if, overnight, it becomes unfriendly to foreigners living there? What will happen to your property, not to mention your life?

➤ Look into whether outsiders can buy property and how that purchase is handled. In some parts of the Caribbean, for example, it can be difficult for Americans to own real estate. If your choice is one of the more fashionable London neighborhoods, you probably will have to buy your home with a long-term lease. Land in choice Belgravia and other West End sections of that city are owned by the Duke of Westminster and his family. You rent from him, although the rental, in this case, is considered a form of ownership.

➤ The cost of living in your foreign country might be higher than it is here. Inflation may be rampant. You might not profit from your investment, or indeed even get your money back because of currency fluctuations.

➤ Consider the cost of traveling back and forth to visit family and friends here.

➤ In the vacation-home vein, will you become tired of visiting the same spot every year? Who will keep an eye on it when you're back in America?

➤ When you do move abroad, be sure to register with the U.S. embassy or consulate nearest you. One of the services that office can provide is letting you know about serious political changes in that country, such as an evacuation.

➤ Be sure that you have a valid will (there is more about this subject in Chapter 21, "A Will, Perhaps a Trust, and Other Legal Paperwork"). If you die abroad without one, a consulate officer becomes the executor of your estate and must track down your next of kin. If relatives cannot be found quickly, you could be buried in a potter's field in that country. Incidentally, the U.S. State Department notes about 6,000 Americans die abroad each year.

➤ Finally, contact your local IRS office for a copy of their booklet #54, *Tax Guide for U. S. Citizens Living Abroad*, to learn about your rights and responsibilities to Uncle Sam while in a foreign land.

Extra! Extra!

A good way to examine life in another country is by living there as the residents do, not from a hotel room. Try trading your home for someone's in the country that interests you. See Chapter 28 for more about home swaps.

The Specifics of Buying

Generally, you will have to shop for your home in that country, dealing with sales agents there. Real estate commissions are likely to be higher than the usual 6 percent we pay here. Closing costs can run 15 percent of the sale price, compared to 3 to 6 percent here. Foreign countries also often include a *transfer tax* or *stamp tax* or whatever other name that levy goes by there, which is usually a few hundred dollars.

You will have to apply for a mortgage in the country of your choice (although you can stop in at a branch of an American bank there to see what it has to offer). Lenders, you will find, will finance a smaller percent of the sale price than Americans do—say, 50 percent. You are apt to find the seller financing a loan for the buyer virtually unknown.

Does it all sound pretty expensive? It can be, although prices of homes in some countries can be quite reasonable indeed. The key here is spending plenty of time in your expected new home country and learning as much as you can from real estate agents, bankers, lawyers, and other homeowners.

Check with the American Chamber of Commerce where you are looking for some answers to your many questions. Generally, foreign embassies, consulates, and tourism offices in America are not helpful with real estate purchases, although they can provide you with a raft of information about other aspects of life in various countries.

The Least You Need to Know

➤ Do you want to live in the sun? Do you wish you could move back into town? You have many options in this mobile society, affording you the opportunity to find your dream spot somewhere among those many choices.

➤ Sometimes a move won't work out, or sometimes it needs a little fine-tuning to smooth out the uneven edges. In either case, you might end up spending more retirement money than you had planned. After reading this and the next chapter, though, you will know what problems could arise.

➤ If you have read this chapter and still think home is best—both your present community and your house or apartment there—hey, that's all right, too. Staying put is a very popular option.

And the Roof Over Your Head

You now are going to decide, if you haven't already known for years, what type of home you want for retirement. But there is a point to be made here that was not likely to be included in retirement books written 15 or 20 years ago.

The term *retirement home* traditionally has described where you will live after you retire—usually, the only place you will have in those years. However, today's retirees—younger and in better health than those of earlier years—are likely to have several addresses after turning 65.

You might plan for... well, 90 is not an unthinkable age these days. So in the 25 years between 65 and 90, your tastes might change, your needs might turn around, and other aspects of your life might have you buying and selling two or more "retirement" homes.

Let's start with the first one.

Residential Communities with Restrictions

For those of you who have spent most of your adult life in an apartment or a house in the city or suburbs, but not in a subdivision that has an owners association, the type of community you will come upon as a househunter for a retirement place might astonish

It's Been Said
The good neighbor looks beyond the external accidents and discerns those inner qualities that make all men human and, therefore, brothers.
—Martin Luther King, Jr.

you. They can be single-family developments, patio homes, townhomes, or condos. They also can be recreation vehicle parks.

The tie that binds here—the list of what you can and cannot do in those enclaves—is what could make you fightin' mad. "It's my house," you will probably say, "I'll do whatever I like." (No, you won't.)

On the other hand, many of you will find those restrictions comforting. You do not want to stand by while your next-door neighbor delightedly erects a jumbo satellite dish on his front lawn. You might not want the noise of children nearby. You might not want to see unmowed lawns. Your mantra, like that of most folks who live in communities with restrictions, is *property value*.

As you read the next several paragraphs, you will decide which group you fall into, and that will be one more retirement choice you will have made.

"Adults Only"—All Others Just Visit

These developments can come in all housing styles, price ranges, and parts of the country. Some have elaborate recreational facilities, others aren't fancy at all. What they have in common is that they are child-free.

The purpose of the "over 55" community (or the "over 62" or whatever age is determined by the developer) is to make certain that, generally speaking, at least one owner in at least 80 percent of the homes there is at or above that minimum age. Other restrictions might be no children under 18 as permanent residents, or no children of any age.

Of course children will be allowed to visit any time you wish on a daily basis, and they are likely to be allowed to spend two or three weeks with you, if you like, a few times a year.

If you aren't sure yet whether this is the community for you, it is important to know that residents are very serious about enforcing those covenants. If you are single and 57, and marry someone with young children, you probably will be asked to leave. If, as a retired couple, you wind up having your 14-year-old grandson move in with you permanently, you are no doubt going to have to move. Anyone violating the rules is often subjected to verbal attacks by other residents. One retired couple who took in their two grandchildren for four months while the youngsters' father was away in the 1991 Persian Gulf conflict had to field dozens of vicious, anonymous phone calls from residents of their 300-unit plus subdivision. That was not an unusual reaction. What can a community really do? To take the issue to its furthest point, the association can get a court order to force you to sell your home if you ignore that restriction.

According to a 1988 amendment to the U.S. Fair Housing Act, if it follows certain legal guidelines, a development can be a legitimate empty nest community without being accused of discriminating against children.

Homeowner Associations

Homeowner associations also have become popular over the last half dozen years or so. These are—usually, but not always—single-family home developments bound together by their own covenants of dos and don'ts. But here the community has residents of any age. What should concern you prior to buying is the *owners association covenants*, which must be adhered to and can cover any number of issues about life in that community—the color you can paint your house, the roofing materials you must use for repairs, what can or cannot go on your front lawn (that satellite dish, for example), whether you can use your driveway to work on cars for pay (probably not), and on and on. The owners association also charges monthly or annual dues, which all owners must pay. (They are not usually inordinately high, and are used for maintaining the common areas, perhaps building up a legal defense fund if one is ever needed, publishing a newsletter, and so on.)

If an owners association exists where you are looking, you probably must join. It is a condition of buying your home.

It should be noted here that these communities do see that the community remains attractive and that property values are maintained. They foster a great sense of neighborliness, too. Many provide newsletters and social programs for residents. Just be sure you read those covenants carefully before signing a sales contract.

Gray Matter Alert
If you are househunting in any subdivision with a name prominently shown at the entrance to the community, be sure to ask about covenants. Some real estate agents forget to present them to would-be buyers, and it doesn't occur to some sellers either. Still, you will be held to that community's restrictions once you move in, even if you say you did not know the rules.

So You Still Want to Build Your Dream House

If you had a particular house in mind for some time, and are determined to treat yourself to just what you want at retirement... good idea.

Having a home built exactly to your specifications and every desire can be an exciting, creative, rewarding experience. It can be an expensive and frustrating journey into the unknown, too. What's good about this unique form of homebuying at retirement is that you will have the time to devote to the project, to talk to the builder or architect, to hang around the job site, and to make sure all is going well. For many, trying to balance work with the many demands of builders, subcontractors, and the rest contributed to exclamations of "Never again!"

No doubt you have acquired a small library of books, magazine articles, plans, and scraps of paper with tips from friends—all with advice on having a home built. So here we will consider only points that might not have occurred to you, especially *vis-à-vis* a retirement home.

You know, of course, that building always takes more time (which you will have) than expected, and more money than what you have budgeted. The latter could be a problem for you—perhaps not if you are building prior to retiring, when you still have a salary coming in, but going over and above the projected cost with a retirement income could wreck your carefully planned calculations. No matter when you are building, add a few thousand dollars to your price projections, even to what might have been quoted to you by the builder. The cost of building materials might go up (does it ever go *down*?) and you might, at the last minute, opt for more costly extras, or other features or furnishings in your new home that were not scribbled into the original plans.

You might want to consider incorporating features into your new home now that could be invaluable some day. Such features might include doorways that are at least 36 inches wide in the event that you need to accommodate a wheelchair, built-in grab bars in the baths, and bathrooms large enough to allow for turning a wheelchair around. You might also want a stairway wide enough to accommodate a chair lift. Retrofitting can be expensive, and whether you are laid up for a short time some day or for the long term, you don't want to wish in hindsight that you had made those installations.

Also on this subject, if you are constructing a two-story house, you might want to plan the rooms so that you can live on the first floor if you want or have to, and can close off the second floor (or maybe convert it to a rental unit some day).

Having the home you always wanted will no doubt be immensely satisfying, but be sure that that house is not so strikingly individualistic that resale becomes a problem. You may have seen houses like that occasionally, usually designed by architects for their own use. Take care that your home is not so offbeat, so much of a statement of "you" that you will have to stay there the rest of your life, whether you want to or not, because nobody seems to want to buy it. That means, usually, no dome home, or one built into the ground, or even, in some locales, a one-bedroom house... You get the picture.

You might be able to get away with offbeat in a resort community where buyers could be interested in only a second home, but you might prefer not to gamble even there.

You do not want to spend your first few retirement weeks or months squabbling with the builder about problems with the house. Read the builder's warranty carefully to be certain you understand what protection you are being offered. If you have any questions about coverage, be sure to clarify what's what before finalizing your purchase.

> **OOOOH...**
>
> **Power Words**
> **Townhomes** are usually an architectural style—two-story attached buildings operating under the condo form of ownership. **Patio homes** are separately owned, like single-family houses. Although the units are attached, residents own the ground in front of and behind their individual homes. Both communities usually have an owners association.

A warranty is only as good as the warrantor. A 10-year warranty the builder is offering from an independent third-party warranty company is best. If the builder does not repair defects, then the warranty company will. You are likely to find that only the best builders will qualify for those policies, but then you are looking for someone whose work is good, aren't you?

Finally, it is wise not to buy land for your retirement home too many years away from your targeted building date. Too many things can change in your life over the years—even where you decide to retire. Land can be a chancy purchase at best—certainly it is not a real estate investment—and a good deal can change around any acre you purchase. The pristine wilderness acre you bought in 1985 could be just around the corner from a mini mall and multiplex theater in 2004, the year you plan to begin building your country home. You will never, of course, purchase land you have not seen or land with no roads, no water, no sewage, or no electricity. After all, this is a dream house you are expecting, not your worst nightmare.

Condos and Co-ops

Both condos and co-op housing styles are solid, and have been increasingly popular over the last 30 years. For many retirees, they offer the value of ownership with the convenience of low maintenance and more manageable living quarters. Keep in mind, however, that condos and co-ops mean communal living. While a burden will be taken off your mind in some respects, you will have some responsibilities here, too.

A Condo Is Like a House, But...

When buying a condominium, you receive a deed and you own your apartment outright, the way you would with a single-family house. You secure a mortgage from any lender you choose, and you can sell your apartment to anyone you like.

You also own an undivided percentage of the community's common areas. Those are the walkways, greenery, clubhouse, tennis courts, parking lots, and so on. When you buy into a condo community, you are handed various documents—a prospectus, rules and regulations, and so on, spelling out your responsibilities, which include contributing your share to maintain those common areas and other expenses attached to running the community. Read them carefully and have a lawyer look them over, too. This is a more complicated purchase than a single-family house—you will need legal counsel.

Here are some points to give special attention to as you shop for condos:

➤ Keep in mind that soundproofing, or the lack of it, is the most common gripe of condo owners.

➤ One of the documents you and your attorney will want to give close attention to is the community's financial statement, covering the last three years if possible. Does it have a reserve fund for emergencies—repairs or replacements, attorney fees, or whatever else could crop up unexpectedly?

➤ There are, of course, many older complexes, some of them having a certain cachet in town, and some even with a waiting list of would-be buyers. But the older community may now be badly in need of major repairs and replacements. If there is no reserve fund for those expenses, guess who could be hit with a costly assessment for them just when he or she is moving in? Keep that in mind as you look at communities approaching, or far beyond, the 10-year-old mark.

➤ You will be paying a monthly fee to cover maintenance of the common areas and other communal expenses. Check to see when that amount of money was last increased. If you will be on a fixed income, you might have a problem paying an ever-rising maintenance charge.

➤ Ask how many renters there are in the community in which you are interested. Most lenders frown on too high a percentage of renters to owners—that's a range of 30 to 50 percent renters, depending on the lender—and could decline your mortgage application.

➤ Make it a point to talk to residents. They are the ones who can tell you what life is *really* like in that community.

➤ Finally, beware of overbuilding where you are looking. Too many condo complexes within a few miles of one another could mean you will have trouble selling your unit when you want and at the price you are asking.

Condo and Co-op Sales **Seasonally Adjusted Annual Rates**			
	1992	1993	1994
United States	366,000	401,000	437,000
Northeast	78,000	86,000	96,000
Midwest	67,000	73,000	75,000
South	115,000	131,000	145,000
West	106,000	111,000	120,000

Source: National Association of Realtors

The number of condos and co-ops continues to rise. Too many in the same immediate area can lead to a drop in value if there is not a strong buyer's market for them.

The Cooperative Apartment

There are far fewer co-ops than condos nationwide, but you could have several cooperative choices where you are, and you might have wondered about them as a possible home during your retirement.

A *co-op*, first of all, is not a real estate purchase. Here you buy shares in a corporation that owns the building. The number of shares you own is proportionate to the size and location (within the building) of the unit you buy. Those shares entitle you to a proprietary lease on that unit. Co-op owners pay a monthly maintenance fee, which represents their proportionate share of the complex's expenses for the underlying mortgage, plus the same expenses a condo owner would pay—maintenance, staff salaries, and so on.

Also, because you can finance an apartment with a co-op loan, you might have that monthly expense as well. This is not a mortgage. It is simply a loan a lender calls a co-op loan because that's its purpose. It takes into account the special conditions of co-op buying (it is not real estate, you are tied to the co-op cooperation, and so on). Yes, you do have to be approved for admittance to the building by the co-op's board of directors, so of course when you sell, you must have that prospective buyer okayed by the board.

Is a co-op a sound purchase? Yes, of course. Co-ops are very popular in metropolitan areas like New York City, Miami, and Washington, D.C., where a number of rental highrises have been converted to cooperative status over the years. As with buying a condo, just be sure the location is good and the building is physically and financially sound. And, just as you will with a condo, here you will be handed reams of printed material you will want to go over with a lawyer: a prospectus, financial statement, and so on. You can call a house inspector, too, just as you would with a single-family home purchase. Here, the inspector will be looking at the unit that interests you, plus the building's master electrical, plumbing, and heating systems.

When it comes to selling, which is better? The single-family house is in more demand and usually sells faster than the condo or the co-op. Which is better between the condo and co-op? Well, the condo is real estate, which makes the sale easier and often faster than the co-op, which requires board approval of the buyer. That is not to say that a co-op apartment cannot be a wise buy. If the co-op is chosen properly (for good neighborhood, appearance, good condition of the building, and financial stability of the corporation), it can be an excellent housing choice.

Golf Course Complexes Are Not Just for Golfers

Not everyone wants to move to a community along a golf course to play several rounds a week, although this is how retirees often are perceived.

Would you believe there are folks who do not play the game at all, but who want to live in a golf community? Believe it. According to the National Golf Foundation, a Florida-based organization that tracks golfing trends, 60 to 70 percent of those who buy a house in a golf-course community do not play the game.

What's the attraction here? Golfers and non-players both like all the green space, and typically those communities are beautifully landscaped. If you live right on the fairway, you don't have a road in the back of your house and you don't have a neighbor's yard backing up to your yard. Then there is the "prestige" of living in a country-club community, with the activities that go along with that membership.

On the opposite side of the ledger? Well, residents who live along fairways can expect to see golfers tramping into their yards occasionally, hot on the trail of a lost golf ball.

Prices in these communities run the gamut, depending on where in the country they are and the lavishness of the development. You could pay as little as $80,000 for a home that does not front on the golf course. Or you could spend more than $500,000 for a top-of-the-line dwelling.

Tips for Buyers

You will have plenty of questions to ask as you hunt for a house in a golf community. Here are some you might not think of:

➤ Will the price of your home include country-club membership, or is that additional? Some clubs sell memberships for as little as $750 a year, while in others, entry fees can run $25,000 or more, and then a few hundred dollars in monthly dues.

➤ Is the golf course a public, semi-private, or private one? Living on a public course will, of course, lower your membership fee, but it also allows people who are not residents to use the course.

➤ Speaking of people who are not residents, will your guests be allowed to play on that course? How many of them at one time? What is the fee?

➤ If you are passionate about the game, check out the country club's golf professional. He or she should pay attention to all members, no matter what the level of their skill.

➤ For serious golfers, the quality of the course will be of interest. Who designed it? Who maintains it? What type of grass is on the greens? Are you allowed to use a cart in all areas, or only in specified sections of the course? Is the clubhouse posh or minimalist? Those extras will affect membership dues.

Gray Matter Alert
Do you have a dog or cat or two? When buying into any residential subdivision, into a condo or co-op, or even moving in for a stay in a recreation vehicle campground, be sure to check whether that community accepts pets. You don't want to move in, only to find out they do not (another good reason for a careful reading of covenants). How many animals are permitted? Is there a size or weight restriction? Must a dog be leashed (almost certainly)?

➤ Be sure you can live with the covenants that go along with buying into a golf community, which are pretty much like those found in any development with an owners association.

Look ahead. Do there seem to be too many golfing communities where you are house hunting? Overbuilding already may have occurred, according to some specialists in the field. Some developers have experienced financial problems over the last half dozen years. You want to be sure your community is solid and that resale prospects for your home are good. You can check out the developer of the community you're considering with your state or local Department of Consumer Affairs.

On the Road, RV Style

There's a lot to be said for retiring in a recreation vehicle (RV), as thousands of seniors crisscrossing the country in them will tell you.

Owning an RV means that you can follow the sun throughout the year if you choose. You can visit friends, children, and grandchildren around the country. An RVer pays no expensive hotel or restaurant bills. There is a casual lifestyle here, too, allowing those who can no longer rough it to feel they are in some way camping out. In fact, parks accommodating RVs are called campgrounds.

For many retirees, parking a recreation vehicle in a campground also means meeting up with old friends. This is a lifestyle often chosen for the camaraderie that exists among motor home owners. Through camping clubs, retirees can meet at conventions, organized tours, rallies, or, of course, right on the campgrounds. Many campgrounds offer recreational activities such as potluck suppers, bingo nights, and dances.

The appeal to retirees shows in the statistics. Nearly half the nation's nine million RVs are owned by Americans who are 55 and older, according to the Recreation Vehicle Industry Association.

A Closer Look

If you plan to adopt this lifestyle for at least part of the year after retirement , you naturally will spend some or many vacations in an RV (Chapter 28, "Travel Time," gives you more information on RVs).

When it comes to buying, you certainly have a variety of designs and features from which to choose, for full- or part-time traveling. There are mini-motor homes, bi-levels, fold-down camping trailers, and on and on. Still, generally speaking, what we are talking about here is a home on wheels. All the necessities for living can be contained within that vehicle, or you can be hooked up to what you need (water, sewage, electricity) at a campground.

You can pay anywhere from five figures for a used, simple RV to more than $250,000 for a top-of-the-line new one with all the bells and whistles. They are purchased like cars are and, similar to cars, they depreciate in value, although not at the same speed.

RVers can park their homes on wheels in any of the nation's 16,000 campgrounds. Rentals run about $20 for just the RV space, and $30 to $50 per night if you want hook-ups to services included. Long-term rental rates will be cheaper—a growing number of northern retirees choose to park their RVs in a southern campground for the entire winter. Some pauses for thought about this lifestyle? Well, you probably will be doing a lot of driving, especially if you do not want to spend too much time at one campground or in one state. You might want to haul your automobile behind you, so that you can use it when you arrive at your destination for short trips—to stores, for example. That can be a lot of wheels to handle until you get used to the maneuvering. Also, gasoline can be expensive (you'll probably get eight miles a gallon or worse), and prices are likely to get much higher in the future.

Be sure you can afford the costs of maintaining, registering, and insuring the vehicle, too, which can add up to a tidy figure. You also will need to be certain that you can park your RV at home with no problem from an owners association (most will not allow them to be parked in a driveway for more than a few days) or from local ordinances if you are planning on parking your RV in the street. If you cannot park your RV at your home or in the street, and you cannot make arrangements with a family member or friend to keep it for you, you will have to pay to hold it in a storage facility.

That's it. If you'd like to know more about this lifestyle, and about the folks who swear by the open road, you can write for a free copy of the annual *Woodall's Discover RVing*, at P.O. Box 5000, Lake Forest, IL 60045. Or, call (800) 362-7989.

Taking to the Water

Pooh—you're not interested in the traditional house with four walls. Your neighborhood, you are determined, will be the sea—or at least on the sea tied to the land along the coast. Your address will be a marina.

Maybe you already have a boat and are looking forward to living full time on it when you hit that magic retirement age. Or perhaps you will trade in the boat you have now for a larger model that will become your retirement home. On the other hand, maybe you're the type whose only boat is floating in the bathtub. But you have vacationed on boats many times over the years, and you know that when you retire you want to sail off into the sunset—literally.

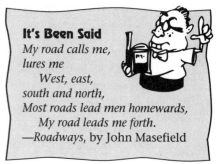

It's Been Said

*My road calls me,
lures me
    West, east,
south and north,
Most roads lead men homewards,
    My road leads me forth.*
—*Roadways*, by John Masefield

If you expect to spend 24 hours a day on your boat most days of the year, perhaps at the local marina where many of your good friends already live, you might consider a houseboat or pontoon, which offers space and is more stable than some other craft. You can liken them to living in a small camper.

If you want to hit the high seas from time to time, the choice is yours. You might prefer a sailboat, if you intend to cruise around the world, for their economy and seaworthiness. Or, you could go with a power boat for traveling the thousands of miles of inland waterways in this country.

As a rule of thumb, you probably will want a craft at least 30 to 40 feet long by 10 to 12 feet wide if you are going to live aboard comfortably.

Extra! Extra!

Boating is good exercise. The motion beneath you, even when the boat is docked, keeps you moving, whether you are aware of it or not. Your arms especially are rarely totally still.

Slip rental charges cut a wide swathe. You can pay anywhere from $50 to $1,000 a month. The higher end, of course, is for a very fancy marina, usually in a resort locale in high season.

If you want to learn more about this lifestyle, you can send for a free copy of *Living Aboard*, a newspaper for and about its 2,500 subscribers who, obviously, live on a boat. Write the paper at 141 North Roadway, New Orleans, LA 70124. It costs $12 for a one-year subscription, which comprises six issues.

Paying for Your Pleasure

You can pay cash for your boat, and a lot of sailors do. This is not a hobby or lifestyle taken up by those who have to watch every penny. If you have a craft larger than 30 feet, you can obtain what is called a *ship's mortgage*, which is more or less comparable to a house mortgage, although, of course, your ship is not real estate.

Boats, new or used, can cost anywhere from $10,000 to more than $1 million. A likely figure for a 30- or 40-foot craft is around $80,000, although that can vary substantially depending on the part of the country, manufacturer, condition of the boat, extras, and so on.

You can apply at almost any bank (and some credit unions) for a loan, which most lenders will be happy to provide. Boaters, as mentioned, can well afford to carry payments. There are very few *chargeoffs* (people who do not pay on their loans) for this type of borrowing, bankers say.

The down-payment requirement is likely to be 10 to 20 percent. Some banks, if you are a good customer, will waive that, but you might want to put something down anyway. There could be negative amortization with your craft somewhere along the line, which means that it may depreciate in value faster than you can pay it off.

Most boats, like cars, do depreciate but, like RVs, at a slower rate than automobiles. There are always exceptions, of course. Some boats hold their value to the time of resale, bringing the seller almost or exactly what was paid for the craft.

Back to your "mortgage." The length of these loans is likely to be a minimum of 12 years and a maximum of 20. Your best bet might be to ask for 15 years, to avoid the possibility of that negative amortization with the longer term.

Interest rates usually are lower than with an auto loan (for an A-rated buyer), and not a whole lot higher than for real estate. You also might want to look into a home equity loan on your present residence to finance the boat, which would mean using it as a second home.

Your Principal Residence—It's More Than a Voting Address

There are snowbirds who will spend much of the year in their northern homes, and then head toward the sun for three or four months in the winter. Others will live in their homes—wherever they happen to be in this country—through the winter, but then leave the state for their summer place in April and stay through September. Retirees can do that. Often family members will say "I want to call Faye and Kevin. Where are they these days?"

All that movement can be enough to make one's head spin. But wait a minute. If you plan that lifestyle after retirement, you must make a major decision: If you will be living in two states, where will your permanent residence be? Yes, it will be the spot from which you will vote, but a primary address means more.

There are tax implications involved in your choice. You will want to know how the two states in which you will be residing treat retirement income, like Social Security and pensions. What about estate taxes? Does each of the states have a personal income tax? What about property tax relief for seniors? Are there trade-offs you will have to weigh? Florida has no state income tax, for example, but it does tax the value of such intangible assets as stocks and bonds.

There are a good dozen taxes and fees that might apply to you in the two states in which you will live some of the time. To make an informed decision about which state should be your primary residence, call each state's Department of Finance, and ask about all taxing possibilities. Perhaps those offices also offer printed material that can help you with your decision.

You also will want to ask that finance department what constitutes taxable residency within its borders, and how you can apply for a primary residency status.

You can request a copy of the free *State Tax Laws Guide*, published by AARP's mutual funds, run by Scudder. The guide features a breakdown of each state's tax structure, including provisions for senior taxpayers. Call (800) 322-2282, extension 8238. *Relocation Tax Guide*, a booklet to help you pinpoint the dozen or so tax areas you will want to know about when comparing states, is published by AARP. Call (800) 424-3410.

The Least You Need to Know

➤ If you are interested in communities with owners associations, be sure you understand what you can and cannot do in those developments. Carefully read the covenants and any other documents they give you before you decide to buy.

➤ If you don't like the geographic area or home you have chosen for retirement, be prepared to move. Sometimes it takes a little fine-tuning before you get a move just right.

➤ Budget for a retirement home, of course, but be prepared for upsets: rising condo maintenance fees, property taxes, and other housing expenses.

Part 3
Pennies from Heaven and Other Sources of Money

Money! Maybe it doesn't buy happiness, but it sure can do a lot to help you forget whatever it is you're unhappy about. So we all want it. Yet no one has discovered the secret of spinning straw into gold, and no one seems to have that hen with the hard-to-birth eggs.

Personally, we'd both just prefer a nice $10 million winning lottery ticket. Wouldn't you?

Oh well, because neither magical nor paper winnings seem to be the lot for most of us, let's get into Part 3 and gather some information on how to make the money we earn grow at maximum capacity. We'll cover savings, stocks, bonds, real estate, your pension, Social Security benefits, and working after retirement.

Chapter 8

Ground Zero—
Where Do You
Stand?

In This Chapter

➤ Convincing evidence that invested money increases

➤ The factors that influence how much you must save

➤ About that financial planner

➤ Assessing your current financial status

➤ Your risk profile and investment plan

By now, you've thought about the kind of lifestyle you want in your retirement and you've estimated the percentage of your pre-retirement income that you'll need "to live in the manner to which you've become accustomed," as they say. So what's left? Just how to get the money.

"But that's easier *said* than done!" you say.

You're right. But it's very unlikely that you'll be successful unless you *try*. So step in. And then just put one foot after the other.

Not On Trees—But It Grows

Financial advising is anything but a science, and it's darn hard to get two advisors to agree, ever. But there is one thing they all agree on: Start saving early!

The earlier you start saving and investing, the more money you are likely to have at retirement. And that's not just because you saved harder and longer. It's because money grows.

"Not that much," you say, "I can start in my forties and make up for my wild 'n woolly thirties."

Yes, you can, but you will have to contribute more than you might expect. Take Chuck and Charlie, for example. Charlie, the good-time guy, didn't start saving until he was 45, but then he saved faithfully. Every month he contributed $100 to his tax-deferred retirement account. Because this is a fictitious story, we can tell you that his money made a return of 8 percent each year. Of course, all the dividends were reinvested until Charlie reached age 65. At his retirement, he had just less than $60,000.

His cousin, Chuck, was the kind of guy who *would* save as much as he *could*. So he started saving $100 a month in his tax-deferred account at age 35. He also made a return of 8 percent each year, with all dividends reinvested until he was 65. At his retirement, he had just more than $140,000.

That's a difference of more than $80,000. But Chuck only contributed $12,000 more than Charlie. So good-times spending of an extra $100 a month for 10 years cost Charlie almost $70,000!

Extra! Extra!

Imagine that you rubbed a lamp and Genie popped up and made you an offer. You could choose to get $1 million in cash or a magic penny that would double in value every day for a month. Which would you choose? The million? Think again. If you had a 31-day month, the doubling penny would net you $10,737,417 and change. So much for the power of dividends reinvested.

So How Old Are You Now?

OK! OK! You believe us! But now you want to know how much you should save each month to have enough for the lifestyle you want throughout your retirement.

That's one of the hardest questions to answer because the number has so many variables. And believe it or not, some of the *variables* have variables. Let's run through them:

➤ **Your age.** As we said, the earlier you start, the better your chances are for achieving your goal.

➤ **Your expected retirement age.** Not everyone chooses 65. If you want to retire early, you must start your investment plan sooner and plan to increase your savings at a greater rate. If you plan to work into your seventies, you may reach your goal earlier, or you can choose to save less per month.

➤ **Years in retirement.** Which is a euphemism for life expectancy beyond retirement age. Of course, we know you can't possibly predict that, but your friendly IRS has. They've even made a prediction for couples! Look over Table 8.1.

Table 8.1. Expected Number of Years in Retirement

Expected Retirement Age	For Individual	For Couple Same Age
55	29 Years	34 Years
60	24 Years	30 Years
65	20 Years	25 Years
70	16 Years	21 Years
75	13 Years	17 Years

Source: Internal Revenue Service life expectancy tables

➤ **Rate of return on your investments.** This is the slipperiest of all the variables. It depends on the kind of investor you are (aggressive and risk-taking or cautious and conservative, or somewhere between) and it depends on your success rate. Some investments may return 12 percent in a good year, but 6 percent in a not-so-good year. Some years, your entire portfolio may average out to 9 percent, and some years it may average 7 percent. Most financial advisors figure an 8 percent or 9 percent return when estimating the amount of savings needed for retirement, but that's a number that has to be reevaluated often. You learn more about keeping tabs on your rate of return in just a bit.

➤ **Rate of inflation.** This eats your money. Remember the pie graph in Chapter 3, "Pension Checks and Personal Savings," which showed you how your pension's purchasing power would decrease over 15 years? Well, that bad news about the decreasing value of the dollar also affects your saving *for* retirement. Assuming a 4 percent per year inflation rate and a 9 percent annual return on your investments, and assuming that you're 45 years old and will work to age 65, you will need to save $3,587 per year in order to have $200,000 when you retire. *But* if you want today's $200,000 of purchasing power when you retire, you must save $7,858 per year!

Using these same inflation/rate-of-return assumptions, T. Rowe Price Associates has estimated that the following amounts of savings are needed to have $200,000 of today's purchasing power at age 65:

Current Age	Savings
35	$648,680
40	$533,167
45	$438,225
50	$360,189
55	$296,049

➤ **Tax rate.** This is always subject to change by the government and to adjustment according to your increasing or decreasing income. A rate of return of 9 percent on an investment is not 9 percent in your pocket after you factor in the taxes you must pay.

If all these numbers are making your head spin, you can get help. Most financial advisors will run your profile through a computer for you and come up with the numbers required to meet your retirement savings goal. Or, you can do your own figuring with the help of your own computer. There are several software programs available.

Power Word

CPI is the Con-sumer Price Index, also known as the Cost of Living Index. It is deter-mined monthly by the Bureau of Labor Statistics and includes the costs of housing, food, transportation, and electricity. Inflation normally is measured by changes in the CPI.

OOOOH...

T. Rowe Price, the company that did the earlier calcula-tions on the effects of inflation, offers its Retirement Planning Kit for PCs at $15. You can call the company at (800) 541-7861. Or, you might investigate two other programs: *Retire ASAP*, from Calypso Software at (800) 225-8246 or (206) 822-8581; and *Harvest Time*, from Retirement Planning Systems at (800) 397-1456 or (214) 490-3339. All three programs will help you calculate how much you must save with all variables accounted for. And even as we write, most of the larger investment brokerage houses are coming out with new retirement planning programs. Call your favorite broker and ask if one is available.

Is There a Financial Planner in Your Future?

Bet you thought we were going to suggest professional guidance, didn't you? Yes, that's a possibility, and we'll tell you about it in just a second. But first, it's important you realize that the most important financial planner in your future is *you*.

It's difficult to think 30 years ahead to retirement when you're grappling with little league, mortgage payments, ballet lessons, braces, and Huggies. It's even more difficult to think about saving for retirement when you're grappling with college costs! But unless you step away from your day-to-day concerns on a regular basis and try to evaluate where you stand financially, you may look around one day and find yourself on a precipice, or in a very deep ravine.

So we're going to take you through an assessment of your current financial status. It will help you to determine how much you'll need for the future and how much you can afford to save. But it's essential you understand that this assessment is just a point in time. It is absolutely certain to change. And you absolutely *should* do it over and over again. Once a year is good, preferably the third week in April, right after you mail your annual IRS envelope and before you put all those papers back into drawers, files, boxes, or wherever you keep them.

As a part of your annual financial assessment, you should review the rate of return on your portfolio. Naturally, you'll be watching your rate of return for each individual investment much more than annually, sometimes even daily, but a periodic overview is essential. Especially if you have a diversified portfolio (which everyone should have).

About that professional financial planner? They come in all shapes and sizes, with backgrounds and knowledge just as variable. If you are considering hiring one, it's essential that you ask about fees before your first visit. Fee structures may be based on time, commissions, or a combination of the two.

When the fee structure is based on time, you pay by the hours spent working on your behalf, just as you would pay your lawyer. If the financial planner makes recommendations for investment purchases, you execute those purchases through your broker. The financial planner does not get a commission. Many people believe that you get unbiased advice when you consult a planner whose fee is based on time spent.

> **Gray Matter Alert**
> One of the most common reasons for losses in the stock market is overreaction to the daily fluctuations in price. Many neophytes sell near a bottom and buy near a top. OOPS! Statistics show you'll do better if you go in for the long haul.

It's Been Said
If you can count your money, you don't have a billion dollars.
—J. Paul Getty

On the other hand, you'll pay nothing for time spent when you consult a planner whose fees are paid in commissions. These people focus on getting you good investments—or, of course, they lose their clients. Some people complain, however, that their focus is too much on "favorite" investments and not enough on genuine financial planning for the future.

When financial planners work on a combined commission/time-spent basis, you can get the best of both fee structures, or the worst. Hourly fees should be lower, but that's not always the case. Purchase recommendations should be appropriate to your financial situation, but again that's not always the case. So frequently evaluate the quality of the advice you're getting and don't be afraid to change to another financial planner if you are feeling dissatisfied.

Before you choose your first financial planner, make several calls and compare prices. Also ask what services you can expect for those fees. And, finally, ask about credentials— including education, professional experience, and professional designations.

Planners who have passed their CFP exams are represented by The Institute of Certified Financial Planners at 7600 E. Eastman Ave., Suite 301, Denver, CO 80231; (303) 751-7600 or (800) 282-7526. This organization will send you a list of CFPs in your area at your request. Membership qualifications are more stringent for the RFP designation at The International Association of Registered Financial Planners at 307 E. Texas Ave., El Paso, TX 79901; (915) 544-7947 or (800) 749-7947. Every member has had at least four years' experience in planning; holds a college degree in business, economics, or law; has earned a CFP, ChFC, or CPA designation; and has a securities or insurance license. You can write to them also for a list of members.

If you want to use a fee-only planner (one who is paid for time spent and therefore likely to give unbiased advice) you can contact the largest association of fee-only planners: the National Association of Personal Financial Advisors (NAPFA) in Buffalo Grove, IL. Call them at (800) 366-2732 and they'll send you the names of members near you.

Your Current Financial Status

The first step in evaluating your current financial status is to calculate your current net worth. Your *net worth* is simply the total of what you own minus the total of what you owe.

What you own commonly is called an *asset*. Assets generally include your home, personal property, insurance cash value, securities, cash accounts, and retirement savings plans. What you owe usually is called a *liability*. Liabilities include your credit card debt, your mortgage, your balance on the car loan, and even your yet unpaid college loans. In fact, your liability is the total of your outstanding debt.

You can calculate your net worth by filling out the Calculating Your Net Worth worksheet. This will take some time and effort. But do it, please. It's no worse than a mortgage application and, when you finish, you'll have a point of comparison for each of the coming years.

Calculating Your Net Worth

Cash and Equivalents	Assets	Liabilities
Money markets	____	
Savings accounts	____	**Credit Card Outstanding Balances**
Checking accounts	____	_____
CDs	____	_____
Other	____	_____
Investments		_____
Mutual funds	____	
Stocks	____	**Investment and Education Loans**
Bonds	____	_____
Insurance cash value	____	_____
IRA	____	_____
401k or equivalent	____	_____
Keogh	____	
Other	____	
Real Estate		**Mortgages and Home Equity Loans**
Home	____	_____
Vacation home	____	_____
Rented property	____	_____
Other real estate	____	_____
Miscellaneous		**Automobile, Boat, RV, or other Loans**
Automobiles	____	_____
Jewelry	____	_____
Gold	____	_____
Collectibles	____	_____
Other valuables	____	
Total Assets	$ ____	Total Liabilities $ ____

Total Assets minus Total Liabilities equals Net Worth _____

Use this worksheet to take a snapshot of your current financial status.

After you finish estimating your net worth, try to estimate where you are in your lifetime financial plan. To do this, use the Looking at Your Progress Toward Your Goals worksheet to list your goals on one side of the page and your progress toward those goals on the other. Don't worry if the best you can do is ballpark figures or if the ballpark changes from year to year. Life is a process, something like a rose unfolding from a tight bud to a full-blown flower, and change is not only inevitable but essential. Work with change, work *toward* goals, but always be flexible. Don't ever let a number you write down on a given day in one year rule your life for years to come.

Enough wise advice. Let's look at the list.

Use this worksheet to estimate how close you are to reaching your financial goals.

Looking at Your Progress Toward Your Goals		
	What you want	**What you have**
Home	_____	_____
Vacation home	_____	_____
Investment property	_____	_____
College funds	_____	_____
Savings	_____	_____
Stocks, bonds	_____	_____
Other securities	_____	_____
Retirement accounts	_____	_____
Gold and jewelry	_____	_____
Cars	_____	_____
Recreational vehicles	_____	_____
Boats and other toys	_____	_____
Insurance	_____	_____

Is There a Money Manager in Your Future?

Many people who want to invest their money, but don't want the anxiety of choosing and watching individual stocks or other investments, select mutual funds. In fact, mutual funds have become the widest held investment vehicle in the nation.

What are they? Really nothing more than pools of money organized by an investment company and managed by professionals (called *portfolio managers* or *fund managers*). Each fund has certain goals to be used as guidelines for its investing. Goals like "aggressive growth" or "growth and income" or "income and security." When choosing a fund, you should check carefully to be sure its goals match your investment goals.

And you'll have plenty to choose from. There are funds in stocks, bonds, options, commodities, real estate, and money market securities. The total number of funds available to the public changes almost every week. Right now it is hovering at around 6,000.

We'll tell you more about mutual funds in the next several chapters as we discuss the investments they hold. Meanwhile, if you want to get started on your own research, you can call some of the larger funds and investment firms. Your mailbox soon will be crammed full.

Extra! Extra!

Here are some phone numbers for a beginner's foray into the mutual fund marketplace:

Charles Schwab Funds: (800) 526-8600
Dean Whitter Funds: (800) 869-3863
Dreyfus Mutual Funds: (800) 645-6561
Fidelity Group of Funds: (800) 544-8888
Kemper Group of Funds: (800) 621-1148
Merrill Lynch Mutual Funds: (800) 637-3863
Morgan Stanley Funds: (800) 548-7786
Scudder Group of Mutual Funds: (800) 225-2470
T. Rowe Price Mutual Funds Group: (800) 638-5660
Vanguard Group of Mutual Funds: (800) 662-7447

And this is only a small sample from among the largest and most widely known!

The Financial Pyramid

Don't confuse the classic financial pyramid with the scam selling schemes that are called pyramiding. *Pyramiding* is building with money borrowed on paper or sometimes non-existent values. Like a house of cards, the structure is doomed to fall.

The *financial pyramid* is a conceptual diagram of risk structure in investing. The most liquid and secure investment vehicles appear at the bottom, the most risky at the top. How you distribute your money on the pyramid usually determines the amount of risk you are taking with your investments. And, as usual in life, the more risk you take, the more possibility of high and/or fluctuating returns; the more security you seek, the less possibility of high and/or fluctuating returns.

The classic financial pyramid, with some investment vehicle examples.

Highest Risk Greatest Potential for High Returns

Futures, Options, Foreign investments, Junk bonds, Penny stocks, Undeveloped land, Collectibles — Speculation

Common stocks — Short-term growth

Blue chip stocks, Treasury notes and bonds, Corporate and municipal bonds, Ginnie Maes, Annuities, Residential real estate — Income and long-term growth

Cash, Money market accounts, Short-term CDs, treasury bills, Savings accounts — Liquidity, security, and stability

Lowest Risk Lowest Returns

Your Changing Risk Profile

Your inclination to take risks usually depends on three factors: your personality, your sense of financial security, and your age. It's very unlikely that your personality will change over the years, and you already know whether you like risk taking. Your sense of financial security might change, however, in response to how much money you actually have or in response to career prospects or changes in your personal and family life. Your age *will* change.

Most financial advisors suggest a larger proportion of higher risk, higher yield investments for younger people and more secure and liquid investments for older people. Within the overall recommendations, however, investment profiles still vary according to personality and financial security.

Take a look at the graphs covering risk profiles. They were created by Scudder Funds, Inc., one of the nation's largest investment houses. Consider your personality, your financial status, and your age. Then place yourself in a circle.

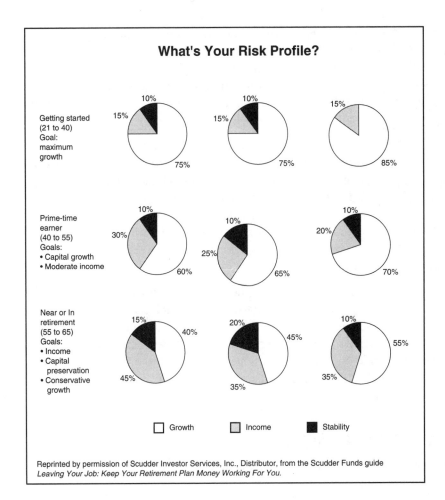

What's Your Risk Profile?

Getting started
(21 to 40)
Goal:
maximum
growth

Prime-time
earner
(40 to 55)
Goals:
• Capital growth
• Moderate income

Near or In
retirement
(55 to 65)
Goals:
• Income
• Capital
  preservation
• Conservative
  growth

☐ Growth　　☐ Income　　■ Stability

Reprinted by permission of Scudder Investor Services, Inc., Distributor, from the Scudder Funds guide
Leaving Your Job: Keep Your Retirement Plan Money Working For You.

*Can you find
your comfort zone
in these portfolio
recommendations?*

Custom Tailoring Your Plan

There's no investment package out there, *anywhere,* that will serve all 35-year-olds, or all 50-year-olds. Or all women, or all married people, either. Every person is unique, and every person should have an investment program suited to his or her goals, financial situation, knowledge, and personality.

This doesn't mean that there aren't mutual funds that are well suited to your needs and objectives. There are. But mutual funds aren't the only way to invest, and for some people they are the wrong way. If you're a hands-on person, for example, rental real estate may be much more interesting, satisfying, and ultimately rewarding. If you're something of an obsessive/compulsive with a thirst for knowledge in selected subjects, rugs or paintings may be an attractive addition to the opportunities in the financial marketplace. If you *like*

Thin Ice

A rush to make up for lost time can be disastrous. If your money has been under your mattress for years, don't grab it all, pull on your bathing suit, and jump into the financial marketplace pool. The people in snappy business suits standing around that pool are sales agents, not lifeguards. Choose your investments carefully. And keep reading—you're not even halfway through this book.

gambling, research, and those moving strips across the bottom of the television screen (the ones with stock exchange identifying initials), you might do your own stock picks. If nothing interests you but interest rates, bonds might be your bread and butter. Or maybe you want it all.

Then again, maybe you'll want different opportunities at different times in your life. That's what makes the process of ongoing financial decisions so challenging and so interesting. Needs change, and so do resources. And that's why it's so very important that you develop at least a nodding acquaintance with as many investment vehicles as you can. The chapters that follow in Part 3 will be your primer.

Your goal is to come up with a diversified portfolio that suits your current needs and also helps you accomplish your future goals. Whether you currently choose not only your mutual funds but also your particular fund managers by name, or you make all your investment decisions as a loner, you always should remember that you are never committed to only one operative method. Diversity and flexibility are success tools in the investment marketplace. Whatever works for you. Just do it!

The Least You Need to Know

➤ Starting early on a saving and investment program is the biggest single advantage to accomplishing retirement security.

➤ When developing an investment plan, you must factor in your age, your expected retirement age, the expected number of years in your retirement, the expected rate of return on your investments, the rate of inflation, and taxes.

➤ It is essential that you see yourself in the role of financial planner.

➤ An annual assessment of your financial status helps to adjust and focus investment strategy toward goal achievement.

➤ It is essential that you choose investments that fit your ability and inclination to take risks.

Cash Equivalents—
Your Piggy Bank

Even in this world of rampant plastic and enterprising electronics, everyone needs cash—at least sometimes. You might take off for a three-week trip to Europe with three credit cards and $200 in cash. Theoretically, the credit cards will get you everything you need, including foreign currency whenever you want it, but you take the cash, just in case.

The investment marketplace is a little like that, too. There are so many vehicles to choose from, so much promise, so much hope, so much opportunity. You're ready to take some risk, you're ready to do the work required. But you want to keep a little cash around.

The Value of Cash at Hand

Ask any investment advisor, and he or she will surely tell you that short-term or liquid-cash assets such as money market accounts and CDs are the least likely vehicles to bring in an acceptable yield on your money. They may point out that the interest you'll earn may just keep pace with inflation, if that. And they're right.

So why keep any money in cash assets when you could send it out there to make 8 percent? Or maybe get into high adventure stuff and double it within the year?

Because everyone needs a sofa. Something comfortable, something that you *know* will be there after work. Something that's warm, non-threatening, and non-demanding, no matter what the weather—outdoors or in. And something that has small change under the cushions.

Cash investments provide liquidity, which means ready access to your money. (Sometimes even at 2:00 a.m. with an ATM machine!) They also act as stabilizing factors in an investment portfolio. There's no up or down. You have what you have and you know you can get it whenever you want it. There's a comforting feeling in that.

It's Been Said
To turn $100 into $110 is work. To turn $100 million into $110 million is inevitable.
—Edgar Bronfman, Chairman, Seagram Co.

So how much should you keep in your "piggy bank?" Some experts suggest six months worth of income. Others, however, believe this is too much, especially for younger people who find it hard to accumulate such a large figure. And if you do keep six months of income in cash, they argue, you should realize that it's not working very hard for you. Depending on your job security, credit rating, and definition of what is an "emergency," you might aim for keeping 10 to 15 percent of your annual income in liquid assets. If you're feeling insecure and anxious, however, go for the six months.

Savings Accounts

Until the end of the 1970s, a *bankbook* was a piece of cardboard folded around a few pages, much like a passport. You came into the bank for a deposit or withdrawal, and you handed your bankbook to the teller. The teller ran your book through a machine that printed the transaction and your new balance. Everyone in town—in fact, everyone in the nation—got the same rate of interest—either 5.5 percent in a savings and loan or 5.25 percent in a bank.

But in the early 1980s, banking was fully deregulated. It became a competitive industry. That industry now offers myriad savings and investment options. *Bankbooks*, or *passbooks*, are rarely seen today, although some banks do still give them out to customers who request them. More common is the statement savings account (often combined with a checking account in the same bank). Each month, bank customers receive an accounting of their activity, their interest, their charges, and their balance.

Interest rates are competitive and reflect both the local and national economies, but they remain generally low—sometimes even hovering around 2 percent. Banks can compound interest daily, weekly, monthly, quarterly, or the newest innovation—*continuously.* The more often interest is compounded, the better for you.

But the big bonus in savings accounts is federal government insurance. The Federal Deposit Insurance Corporation (FDIC) fully insures deposits up to $100,000. If an FDIC bank fails, you get every penny you deposited back plus interest. So if you should happen to have several piles of fresh, newly bundled bills totaling $100,000 in each pile, you will, of course, open several accounts at different banks. Or you can stay in the same bank and open several different accounts—one with your spouse, one with your #1 son, one with your #2 son, one with your daughter, one with all three kids... you get the idea.

If you choose to use a credit union rather than a bank or savings and loan association for your savings account, you may get slightly higher interest rates and sometimes lower fees. Your deposits also will be insured up to $100,000 if you see the NCUA (National Credit Union Administration) sign. Savings and loan bailout legislation in 1989 set up the National Credit Union Share Insurance Fund to be administered by NCUA. You're almost as safe as you are with Uncle Sam.

> **Gray Matter Alert**
> If you'd like to check on the financial health of your bank or any other in the nation, you now can do it by phone. *Veribanc* at (617) 245-8370 or (800) 442-2657 will tell you if your bank rates one, two, three, or no stars (three is best). For a fee, Veribanc will send you a written report on the bank you specify.

You'd Like a Money Market... Fund or Account?

Many people confuse money market funds, which are mutual funds (and not insured by any government agency), with money market deposit accounts (MMDAs), which are bank products (and insured by the FDIC). Let's look at the other differences and the similarities:

> ➤ Both are considered liquid-asset vehicles. You can get your money out when you want to. With MMDAs, however, you usually are limited to three checks or transactions a month. Funds don't limit the number of checks, but they usually do impose a minimum amount for each check—$100 or $500, for example.

➤ Yields on both are competitive. Actually, banks can pay whatever they want in interest, but they usually want to pay as little as the market will bear. Bankers usually adjust their rates on a weekly basis (most often on Wednesdays) in response to what other banks are offering, what mutual funds are offering, the expected direction of short-term interest rates (particularly Treasury bills), and the state of the economy in general. MMDAs do not have management fees. They sometimes do impose service fees, however.

➤ Money market mutual fund managers compete to get the best return on the invested dollar, which is determined by successful reinvesting rather than any designated index. They generally choose those short-term securities that offer good returns with the least risk. Among their common investments are Treasury bills, CDs, commercial paper, and banker's acceptances. Generally, there is a management fee of less than 1 percent (.75 percent is the current industry average), which is deducted automatically from the yield.

➤ MMDAs earn interest on the actual cash that is deposited. In money market mutual funds, the investor owns *shares*. Since 1976, however, asset value has been maintained at $1 per share. No one in this industry intends to "break the buck," since it is advantageous to investors to know that the number of shares they own is equal to the number of dollars they have invested.

➤ All interest earned on MMDAs is taxable. Money market mutual funds come in both taxable and tax-free funds.

➤ The yields on money market mutual funds usually are higher than those on MMDAs.

Power Words
A **rate** is the interest that a bank promises to pay on an investment. A **yield** is the interest that has been paid on an investment. So when you're looking to deposit your money, you ask for the best rate. When you take your money out, you talk about the yield on your investment.

You can open a money market deposit account (MMDA) at most banks. Money market mutual funds are available from mutual fund companies, stockbrokers, and many insurance companies. If you already are investing in securities, you may be able to get into a money market fund through an asset management account at your brokerage firm. In these accounts, interest, dividends, and profits from the sale of stocks can be moved automatically into a money market fund, to be kept there until you decide your next move with the money. Besides being very convenient, these accounts usually pay the highest return of the money market vehicles.

Certificates of Deposit (CDs)

CDs are available from banks, savings and loan associations, and credit unions; they are insured like savings accounts by the FDIC or NCUA. Essentially, when you purchase CDs, you lend the use of your money for a specified period of time and you get paid interest. CDs come in denominations as small as $100 and as large as $1,000 or more. The most common *terms* (time periods for maturity) are three months, six months, one year, and two years, but some CDs run three and five years. No fee is charged to buy a CD.

If you compare CDs to statement savings or MMDAs, you will see that there is a slight disadvantage to a CD because your money is not completely liquid. Which means you can't necessarily get and use it whenever you want it. You have to wait for the CD's term to end. The terms are indeed short, but if you want or need to withdraw your funds before the maturity date of the CD, you will be charged a penalty. In some cases, the penalty actually could cause you to get back less than you put in. On the other hand, CDs usually pay higher yields than the other standard savings instruments and the early withdrawal penalties are tax-deductible.

CDs are especially attractive when rates are unstable, because they allow you to lock in on a relatively high rate for a specified period of time.

"Great," you say, "but what if rates go *up* after I buy my CDs?"

Most experts recommend that you do *not* put all your investment money into one CD at any one point in time. Instead, they recommend a technique called *laddering*, which can be used with any fixed-income security. When you ladder, you spread your money among several CDs that mature at whatever intervals you choose. If rates have gone up during an interval, you'll have some money to reinvest at maturity. If rates have gone down, you'll still be holding some CDs at the higher rate. The following illustration shows an example how $5,000 might be laddered.

You can buy CDs at most financial institutions, but you shouldn't limit yourself to your local banks. CDs are available through the mail or through electronic funds transfer if you want to deal with banks nationwide directly. CDs also are available through many brokerage firms. Those sold through brokerage firms still are insured by the FDIC as long as your investment is $100,000 or less.

> **Thin Ice**
> Watch out if CDs are part of your IRA! (If you don't know about IRAs, read Chapter 13.) If a CD that is held in your IRA matures and your bank mails you a check, you will be hit with federal tax penalties! Banks are not required to notify you of maturity on CDs. So ask about bank policy before you put your money in. Make arrangements for notification or reinvestment to suit *your* goals.

How to ladder $5,000 in CDs with different maturities.

$1,000 in a 3-month CD

$1,000 in a 6-month CD

$1,000 in a 1-year CD

$1,000 in a 1 1/2 year CD

$1,000 in a 2-year CD

Extra! Extra!

So you want to hunt for the best CDs nationwide? You can get a lot of help. Highest yields around the country are published in most financial newspapers such as the *Wall Street Journal* and in many monthly financial magazines such as *Money* and *Kiplinger's Personal Finance* magazine. If you're really into CDs and willing to spend some money to make some, you can subscribe to financial newsletters such as *100 Highest Yields* at P.O. Box 088888, North Palm Beach, FL 33408-8888; (800) 327-7717.

Do You Remember Bond a Month?

Yes, the United States government still sells savings bonds. You can buy them at any bank or sometimes through payroll-deduction programs. They come in denominations of $25, $50, $75, $100, $200, $500, $1,000, $5,000, and $10,000.

So you can buy in big chunks or little chunks. But you cannot buy as much as you want. The rule is that you are not allowed to buy more than $15,000 worth in any given year.

Series EE bonds sell for half of face value and the money you put into them is absolutely safe—you'll get it returned to you plus interest because it's backed by your government.

(Whether you'll get it back with the same buying power is another question, however. That degree of safety depends on the rate of inflation.)

Series EE bonds have no set maturity date and do not pay interest until you redeem them—which you can do at any time from six months after buying them to 30 years later. As of May 1, 1995, redemption in less than five years yields 5.25 percent (the rate is subject to readjustment at intervals), and after that you get 85 percent of the average of five-year Treasury-note yields.

Are they a good investment? Well, you often can do better in other savings instruments that are just about as safe and liquid. The advantage of savings bonds is that you don't pay federal income taxes until you redeem them and you avoid state and local taxes.

Gray Matter Alert

If cashing in Savings Bonds to pay college tuition, couples with an adjusted gross income below $63,450 in 1995 may not have to pay federal income tax on interest earned. The tax break gradually diminishes with more income and disappears at $93,450. See your tax advisor for current numbers and write to Consumer Information Center, Pueblo, CO 81009 for the pamphlet *U.S. Savings Bonds: Now Tax Free for Education*.

If you want to collect interest annually on your U.S. Savings Bonds without cashing them in, you can exchange a minimum of $500 worth of Series EE to Series HH. You then can collect 4 percent per year on the face amount, but you must pay federal income tax on those interest payments in the year you receive them. This interest income is exempt from state and local taxes, however. Series HH bonds mature in 10 years.

T-Bills Make Money

Do you have more than $10,000 that you want to put away profitably, with maximum safety and short-term liquidity? Then Treasury bills may be an appealing investment vehicle.

You can buy T-bills through your brokerage firm or a bank for a small fee, currently about $25, or you can buy directly from the federal government or any Federal Reserve Bank or branch with no fee. T-bills come in denominations from $10,000 to $1 million. The 13-week maturity and 26-week maturity bills are auctioned to the public every Monday, and the 52-week maturity bills are auctioned once a month.

You do not have to attend an auction to buy a T-bill. Most of the bidders are professional government securities traders. Instead, you fill out a form called a *tender*. The tender signifies that you are making a *non-competitive* bid. Along with the tender, you submit a check for at least $10,000 (the minimum for a T-bill). You have then agreed to accept the

OOOOH...

Power Word
The word **discount** in the investment world is not like **SALE** at your favorite store. Sometimes it costs you money—when you get a mortgage, for example—but other times, it's the money you make, as in discount bonds. When talking about any kind of bond, *discount* is the difference between its current market price and its face or redemption value.

yield that is determined by the competitive bidding of those professional dealers. Like almost everything else, that yield is determined by supply and demand.

T-bills are called a *discount* security because they don't pay interest. Instead, you pay less than the face value of the bill when you buy it. At maturity, you get the full face value back. The difference between purchase price and face value is your yield. The confusing part, however, is that you must put up the full face value when you submit your tender. Once the yield is determined at the auction, you receive a check for the discount. Then you receive the face value again at the maturity date.

Is your mind totally boggled? OK, suppose that you want a $10,000 T-bill. You put down your $10,000 with your tender. The Monday auction produces a yield of 5.26 percent. You then receive a check from the government for $500, which is the discount. So you've really put up only $9,500, right? The $500 is your return on your investment because at the end of the bill's term, you receive a check for your invested $10,000, the principal.

Being an individual, non-professional investor is what brings on the confusion here. If you were a pro, you'd simply pay $9,500 at the auction and get $10,000 at maturity.

Still interested? Despite all this paperwork, you'll never get a certificate for your investment. Records are kept in government computers. It's no wonder that most Americans invest in T-bills through mutual funds.

You must pay federal income tax on your yield from a T-bill in the year that the bill matures or is sold. However, T-bills are free of state and local taxes. Yields on T-bills usually are slightly lower than on money market funds. Most analysts point to the absolute security of the investment (backed by the good faith of the U.S. government) as the reason. Some say that money market funds do better because they have some diversity.

The Glitter of Gold

"Gold has been around forever. It's the international currency. You can't lose with gold!" That's what a lot of people say. And they're wrong.

Most financial advisors consider gold a speculative investment. It is most valuable in times of high inflation, and its value tends to move in the opposite direction of paper assets such as stocks and bonds. Most forms of gold investments do not provide income. For example, there is no annual interest paid on the gold bar in your safe deposit box. Most investors who want to make money by holding gold must wait until gold prices go up. Unfortunately, these prices go down almost as often as they go up.

If you choose to collect gold bullion, be aware that you will need a safe place to keep it. Safe deposit boxes in bank vaults are an option, but add in their cost when calculating your profits. If you keep your gold at home, be sure your insurance covers it. And be wary of here-today-gone-tomorrow dealers when you buy or sell!

Other ways to buy gold are certificates, shares in precious metals mining companies, mutual funds that buy precious metals mining stocks, and futures and options (among the most risky investment vehicles). You can read more about trading and futures in the next chapter. At this point, let's just say that gold is *not* an investment that you can keep at the bottom of your sock drawer.

Investments You Can See, Touch, Smell, Etc.

Your Avon representative might tell you that those old bottles are worth a fortune. Maybe. But don't count on financing your retirement with the pirate's head aftershave bottle or the pink glass rose that once held face cream.

Antiques and collectibles, along with such other things as gold coins and bullion and real estate, are known as *hard* assets. You own substance—something you can touch—as opposed to the "paper" ownership that stocks represent and the "paper" promised income of bonds. In times of national disaster or hyperinflation, these investments tend to increase in value. They are *not* liquid assets, however, because finding a buyer willing to pay what you think is market price might take a long time.

Like almost everything else that is sold in the world, the price or worth of collectibles is governed by supply and demand. But just because something is rare doesn't mean that it is valuable. (If there is no demand for hens' teeth, what will they sell for?) On the other hand, something may be in demand, but have a plentiful supply. (Everybody buys toothpaste, but there's more than enough to go around.)

So how do you know if something has worth in the collectibles market? Sooner or later, most owners get a professional appraisal, or two, or three. The two major trade groups in personal property appraisal are the Appraisers Association of America (AAA) and the International Society of Appraisers (ISA). Before you pay anyone anything for his or her professional opinion, ask if they belong to one of these groups and ask what services they will provide and what it will cost.

For more information, contact the Appraisers Association of America at 60 East 42nd Street, New York, NY 10165, (212) 867-9775. You also can contact the International Society of Appraisers at 500 N. Michigan Ave., Suite 1400, Chicago, IL 60611-3796, (312) 661-1700.

Although it is certainly unwise for most people to build their entire retirement plan on collectibles, you probably can add to your wealth with the cultivation of particular interests. This is an area where knowledge of the field is essential to success. Although acquiring and maintaining that knowledge can demand a great deal of time in pre-retirement years, your field of expertise and investment can provide both pleasure and financial return after retirement.

Now, just for fun, think about the many, many things you might collect. Antique furniture, glass paperweights, very old books, baseball cards, antique cars, coins, stamps, Hollywood odds and ends, paintings, pottery, oriental rugs, vintage wines... the list could go on almost forever. Just remember, however, that amassing your collection is not synonymous with amassing your fortune. Don't spend money that should be going into your IRA on antique cars!

The Least You Need to Know

➤ Most financial advisors suggest that investors keep about 10 percent of their investment funds in low-risk and liquid-investment vehicles, which means cash-accessible items.

➤ Although similar, money market deposit accounts and money market funds are not the same beast.

➤ Unless you are very certain that rates won't go higher and you won't need any of the money, do not put all your available funds into one Certificate of Deposit. CDs should be laddered for maximum return and accessibility of funds.

➤ Series EE savings bonds do not pay interest until you redeem them. Federal income tax, therefore, is also not due until redemption. EE bonds and HH bonds are free of state and local taxes.

➤ If you want to invest $10,000 or more in a secure instrument for a term of less than a year, Treasury bills may be right for you.

➤ The value of gold tends to move in the opposite direction of paper assets, such as stocks and bonds.

➤ Collectibles can increase both wealth and pleasure in retirement, but you cannot rely on them as a source of income.

*tak
tak
tak*

Chapter 10

Stocks— Your Ownership Interests

In This Chapter

➤ Risk on Wall Street may be less than you think

➤ Choose a broker—at a price

➤ Get a money manager—stock mutual funds

➤ Words for the wary

➤ Three investment modes: aggressive, income, and turbulent

➤ Sources of advice and information

Believe it or not, there are only three (legal) ways to earn money: work and get paid by an employer, allow someone else to use your money and collect interest, or own a business.

"Oh *come on*!" you say. "What about real estate? What about the stock market?"

We knew you were going to say that. Real estate is a business if you buy, rent, or sell what you own with the intention of making a profit. And so is investment in the stock market. When you own stock, you own a share of a company. In other words, you own a piece of a business.

Buying and selling investment interests in business is what the stock market is all about. And millions of Americans make millions of dollars doing just that every year. Some also lose money.

Risk on Wall Street

If you've never invested in stocks or been around people who do, you may think of Wall Street as another continent somewhere, with subcontinents or countries called *Nasdaq*, *AMEX*, *NYSE*, and other unpronounceables. And if you were asked to visit among these countries, you might feel a bit like a 10-year-old trying to hold on to a pocketful of quarters at a carnival.

But the stock markets are not as risky as you might think. Oh, sure, they have their moments... the crash of '29, the plummet of October 19, 1987, and an assortment of other roller-coaster rides before, between, and after. Yet over the long haul, stocks have provided Americans a better return on their money than any other investment.

Gray Matter Alert
To diversify for your safety net, you would need to own stock in at least 10 companies in a variety of industries. That's virtually impossible when entering the market with a few thousand dollars! *Unless* you let the combined power of many people, much money, and full-time management commitment work for you. You guessed it: mutual funds. More to come.

According to statistics published by Ibbotson Associates, if you average out the ups and downs of the market for the 70 years between 1924 and 1994, you will see that large common stocks have provided an average rate of return of 10.2 percent and small U.S. stocks 12.21 percent. That puts stocks running neck and neck with the national average for real estate, considerably better than bonds, and far, far better than savings accounts.

The main reasons people who are new to investing lose money in the stock market are anxiety and impatience. Afraid, they overreact. Generally, they do not have the knowledge, faith, and patience to wait it out through periods of fluctuation or stagnation. Anxious to get in when a stock is climbing, anxious to get out when it is falling, neophytes (and some experienced investors, too) sell near the bottom of a curve and buy near the top, exactly the opposite of the classic *buy low, sell high* formula for success.

It's Been Said
How poor are they that have not patience!
—William Shakespeare, *Othello*

But you don't have to fit the pattern of the "typical" beginner. In today's financial marketplace, it's not necessary to enter alone and proceed at the risk of making costly errors because of your unfamiliarity with the business, its language, and its method of operating. Instead, you can make your first forays into stock ownership by investing in mutual funds. If you choose this option, your money will be in the hands of a professional fund manager. Keep reading.

Choosing a Stockbroker

In 1975, the Securities and Exchange Commission (SEC) deregulated the stock brokerage industry. Until then, commissions on stock buying and selling were set by law; everyone paid the same rate no matter what company handled the transaction. After deregulation, brokerages became a more competitive business, and split into two camps.

Most of the well-established brokerage houses continued to pay working brokers by commission. And commission rates stayed high. Brokers still were motivated to encourage their clients to trade frequently, because the amount of trading they handled determined their incomes.

Then new firms began to open in the '70s. They were called *discount brokers* because their fees for trading were vastly lower than those charged by the older firms. Brokers in the new discount firms were, and still are, paid a straight salary, thus eliminating the motivation to encourage clients to trade.

In today's marketplace, it is absolutely essential to shop around for a stockbroker. Ask about fees and services before committing to do business through any stock brokerage firm. And don't hesitate to change if you are dissatisfied. Remember: This is a business that involves **your** money. The higher priced companies maintain that they provide more personal service, more research, and more professional advice to their clients. The discount brokers maintain that they have just as much information available to their clients but *without* a commission-dollar motivation to encourage trading.

"And what **is** the cost of trading?" you ask. If we told you, 10 people could say we were wrong on 10 different days. Let's just say that a "full-service" broker might charge up to 10 times as much as the lowest-priced broker on the same trade. It's a competitive marketplace out there, and it changes from month to month, sometimes from day to day. Watch advertisements in financial newspapers and magazines, watch the financial television channels, and call brokerage houses and ask them to send you material on the services they provide and at what cost.

> **Thin Ice**
> Some self-named *financial planners*, *financial advisors*, or *financial consultants* who work in their own offices (independent of the large brokerage firms) choose to be paid for their advice by commission. If they also belong to broker/dealer networks that have products to sell, the motivations behind their advice may not be as pure as the driven snow.

Stock Mutual Funds

Like money market mutual funds, stock mutual funds are pools of money invested to achieve a certain goal. Each fund is managed by a fund manager; some of these managers achieve a kind of star quality, being known by name and performance record throughout the industry.

All mutual funds ultimately must answer to examination by the Securities and Exchange Commission. When the funds offer shares to the public, they must reveal, in a published prospectus, data on the fund's earnings, its operating expenses and other fees, and its rate of trading (called *turnover*) in the fund's investments.

Often, all this either puts investors to sleep or stimulates anxiety attacks. But there may be hope on the horizon. As of the summer of 1995, eight companies are participating in an SEC-approved project to simplify mutual fund prospectus presentation. The project will make 24 fund profiles available in clear, readable language. The experiment runs for one year before reevaluation. Let's hope the results are good.

As you begin to get into mutual funds, be aware of the tremendous variety available to you. Some funds invest in stocks only, some in stocks and bonds, and some in combinations of investment vehicles—including real estate and precious metals. Be sure you know exactly where your fund's money will be invested.

With Goals in Mind

Every fund has a name, and many names are intended to give clues to the fund's goal by including words such as *growth, aggressive growth, income, growth and income, blue chip, balanced, emerging market,* and so on. Within the structure of goal pursuit, however, fund managers have a vast number of choices, which they freely sample to achieve the diversification that is both a safety net and a money maker. A stock fund holding shares in 25 companies would be considered small. A fund of 100 companies is not uncommon, and some funds hold even more.

Some mutual funds pursue their goals by balancing stocks with other investment vehicles. Their diversification, therefore, is not only among the different companies and industries sold on the stock market but also among many types of investments that have no relationship to Wall Street whatsoever (bonds, real estate, and gold, for example). In these funds, a general decline in the stock market may well be protected against by profits in the bond market. This additional safety net, however, often means lower returns than in exclusively stock funds.

At the other end of the spectrum are the specialty funds, sometimes known as *sector funds*. Most financial analysts consider these funds more risky because their limitation to specific industries essentially wipes out the mutual fund advantage of diversification. If that industry performs poorly, the fund performance will follow. Precious metals funds and real estate funds are among the more common specialty funds.

When looking for a fund, you might notice words such as *international*, *global*, *world*, or *worldwide* among fund names. Generally, international funds invest outside the United States only, whereas global, world, and worldwide funds may include both domestic and foreign investments. Are you interested? Many analysts consider these funds to be high risk. Others say that foreign markets are where the growth potential is, pointing out that two-thirds of the world's investment opportunities are outside the United States.

> **Gray Matter Alert**
> Don't choose a mutual fund on the basis of the promises in its name. Some names are misleading and some funds are neither investing nor performing as their names imply. Read the prospectus! Here are five points to identify: 1) the summaries of shareholder transaction expenses and annual fund operating expenses, 2) investment objectives, 3) investment policies, 4) tax consequences, and 5) the policy to redeem shares.

To Pay or Not To Pay

And finally, fees! All the 6,000 odd funds out there can be classified into one of two categories: *load* or *no load*. No-load funds are free of commission charges, whereas load funds come with up-front commissions. Both load and no-load funds, however, have operating expenses. Annual expenses for running a fund are deducted before returns are paid. Most fund expenses hover at around 1 percent per year, some can be found for as little as .5 percent, and a few even lower. They are available through major discount brokers such as Acorn, Columbia, Janus, PIMCO, Schwab, Scudder, T. Rowe Price, and Vanguard, to name only a few. Two of the largest brokerage houses, Dreyfus and Fidelity, sell both load and no-load funds.

Load funds require you to pay a commission when you purchase them. The actual amounts of the commissions vary, typically from 4 percent to 6

> **Thin Ice**
> Beware of salespersons selling "no-load" funds that are no load only if you keep them for five or seven years. If you sell before the given time, you'll be charged a fee, which sometimes is called a *back-end load* or *deferred sales charge*. High operating fees also may be hidden in the pages of the prospectus.

percent, but sometimes as high as 8.5 percent of the amount you invest. Some brokers argue that the performance of load funds is better than no-load funds. But that question is open to debate.

Load funds have operating fee structures similar to no-load funds. So take commissions and fees into account when evaluating your expected return. Some, but most certainly not all, load-fund brokers are Alliance, American, Dean Witter, Franklin, Kemper, Merrill Lynch, Nuveen, Oppenheimer, PaineWebber, Prudential, Putnam, Smith Barney Shearson, and, of course, Dreyfus and Fidelity. This is big business. Even if you're a novice in the marketplace, you probably recognize almost every name.

Extra! Extra!

Mutual funds got started way back in the 1920s, but began their climb to current popularity in the '70s. Since government regulation was put into effect with the passing of the Investment Company Act of 1940, no stock mutual fund has ever gone belly up. Of the approximately $2 trillion now invested in mutual funds, about one-third is invested in stocks.

Marketplace Language You Must Know

Whether you decide to invest in mutual funds or choose to buy stocks on your own, there are many words specific to the financial marketplace that you must know. Let's run through some of them before we get into the various investing styles:

➤ **Common stock:** Units of ownership, also called *equity shares*, in a public corporation. Shareholders typically have voting rights in the selection of directors and are entitled to dividends on their holdings. Common stock is traded through brokers at market price and has a theoretically limitless price.

➤ **Preferred stock:** Owners of preferred stock usually do not have voting rights on company matters. They are, however, entitled to receive dividends before the holders of the common stock. If a company is liquidated, preferred stock claims are satisfied before common stock claims. Preferred stock dividends are set at the time the shares are issued and cannot go up, as common stock dividends might. Common stock usually has more potential for appreciation.

➤ **Dividends:** The distribution of earnings to shareholders. The amount is decided on by the board of directors and is usually paid quarterly. Dividends must be declared on federal income taxes in the year they are received.

➤ **Price/earnings ratio:** The price of a stock divided by its earnings per share for the latest four quarters is called the *trailing P/E*. This figure is listed along with a stock's price and trading activity in daily newspapers. The *forward P/E* is based on an analyst's prediction of earnings for the coming year. The higher the P/E, the more growth investors are expecting. Stocks with P/Es of more than 20 usually are fast-growing, young companies; these stocks are far riskier than stocks with lower P/Es.

➤ **Dollar cost averaging:** A method of investing that could help to prevent both anxiety-motivated and greed-driven reactions to movements in the market. The investor decides on a fixed amount of money that will be invested in given stock at preset intervals. When the price of the shares is low, the investor buys more; when the price of the shares is high, the investor buys only the shares that can be purchased with the allotted money—in other words, fewer shares. The theory is that the overall cost is lower than it would be if a constant number of shares were bought regardless of price. This strategy also is called the *constant dollar plan*. See Table 10.1 for a demonstration of how dollar cost averaging works.

Table 10.1   Investing $5,000 through a Dollar Cost Averaging Plan

Month	Money Invested	Share Price	Number of Shares	Total Shares Owned	Current Market Value
Jan	$ 500	$50	10	10	$ 500
Feb	$ 500	$45	11	21	$ 945
Mar	$ 500	$40	12	33	$1,320
Apr	$ 500	$45	11	44	$1,980
May	$ 500	$55	9	53	$2,915
Jun	$ 500	$48	10	63	$3,024
Jul	$ 500	$44	11	74	$3,256
Aug	$ 500	$50	10	84	$4,200
Sep	$ 500	$53	9	93	$4,929
Oct	$ 500	$50	10	103	$5,150
Nov	—	$52	—	103	$5,356
Total	$5,000	$48 (avg)	103	103	$5,356

Investing $5,000 at one time and holding for 10 months.

Month	Money Invested	Share Price	Number of Shares	Total Shares Owned	Current Market Value
Jan	$5,000	$50	100	100	$5,000
Nov	—	$52	100	100	$5,200

➤ **Cyclical stocks:** Stocks issued by companies whose fortunes are tied closely to the ups and downs of the economy. The trick is to *sell* when the stock is hot and *buy* when it's cold... which is much harder than it reads on paper.

➤ **Growth stocks:** Investments for people who want to sell higher than they bought to make a considerable profit. Usually, the corporation in question has shown higher than average gains in earnings over the past year or more and is expected to continue to do so. Most so-called growth stocks are the more risky investments in the marketplace. They tend to have high price/earnings ratios, and few pay dividends.

➤ **Income stocks:** Better known for providing steady dividend income than for actual or potential capital appreciation. Generally, income stocks are from companies that are well established.

➤ **Futures:** These are not ownership in stocks at all. They are contracts to buy a certain commodity at a stated price on a given date. You do this if you believe the commodity will be worth more on that future date than you are agreeing to pay for it on the present day. And then, of course, you sell immediately and pocket the difference. In fact, futures are a kind of betting and are **not** recommended for beginning investors.

➤ **Call options:** Give buyers the right to *buy* a certain number of shares of a stock at a named price before some named date—usually three, six, or nine months in the future. Buyers pay a fee, called a *premium*, for this right and forfeit the fee if they do not purchase the stock. When investors buy a call option, they are betting that the stock will go up in price. For example, John buys a call option for 100 shares of The Cattery Inc. at $60 when the stock is selling at $60. Two months later, the stock is at $68. He exercises his option to buy 100 shares at $60 and immediately sells at $68. Instant profit. But it doesn't always work out quite so well! Working with calls is considered high-risk investing and is best left to the pros or very rich amateurs who can afford to lose as often as they gain.

➤ **Put options:** Give buyers the right to *sell* a specified number of shares at a named price before a named date. Holders of put options are betting that the price of the stock will go *down*. For example, Nancy buys a put option for 100 shares of Doggone

Inc. at $50. Two months later, she sees that the stock has hit $36. She then can buy 100 shares at $36 and exercise her put option to sell them immediately at $50. Nice! But this is a *story*! It does happen like this, but not as often as most people would like to believe. If the stock goes up instead of down, Nancy's put option is worth nothing and she loses the money she paid for it. Playing with options, like playing with matches, is not recommended for the inexperienced.

Aggressive Investing

The aggressive investor is one who wants to make money through maximum growth. These investors choose stocks with high P/E ratios, where risk is inherent in the investment.

Often, many investors and, perhaps more important, many fund managers, are interested in the same growth stocks at the same time. Demand drives the price ever higher. But the climb is always tenuous at best. A rumor, one quarter reporting below expectations, or a glitch in the economy can send the price plummeting.

If you choose to go for the big gains, be aware also that aggressive investing is plagued by fad pressure—what's hot and what's not... are you one of those people who know? Can you sense a change in the air? Will you get your "sensing" early enough to get out before the hot air goes out of the balloon?

Growth is easier to achieve in smaller companies—sometimes called *emerging* growth companies—but the risk also is higher. Some large companies with sales of more than $1 billion still are considered growth companies, even though the oxymoron *blue chip growth* often is applied and is probably more appropriate.

Whether you choose aggressive investing on your own or an aggressive growth or growth mutual fund depends both on your personality and your stage of life. Most advisors suggest aggressive investing for younger people who have many years before retirement to compensate for a bad choice or a bad year. However, some young people, especially those raising families, simply do not feel comfortable with risk or cannot afford to take risks. In contrast, some older people have money beyond their anticipated needs and feel quite comfortable in the aggressive growth or even the speculative marketplaces.

> **Power Word**
> **Blue chip** describes the common stock of nationally known companies with long histories of growing profits and dividend payments. These companies are regarded as well managed, with quality products and services. Many are so well known that we recognize them by their initials: AT&T, IBM, GE, and GM, just to name a few. Blue-chip stocks often are relatively high priced and low yielding. But they are considered safe investments.

Investing for Income

Many investors think immediately of bonds whenever the goal of income is mentioned. And bonds will do it, as we'll tell you in the next chapter. But there are excellent income stocks and income-stock funds, and they have some advantages over bonds.

The interest rate on a bond usually is fixed. But a stock might raise its dividend year after year. A solid stock with a good history of paying dividends also might respond to the market and inflation by climbing in price. (And, then again, dividends and prices *could* go down in bad times, too.)

Income stocks seem to have an inverse relationship with bonds, although both are influenced by the direction of interest rates. When interest rates fall, bonds are less appealing and high yield stocks are more appealing. As a result, stock prices tend to go up. When interest rates rise, bonds are more appealing and high yield stocks attract less attention, with a corresponding fall in prices.

Investing in the stock market for income is considered a conservative strategy. Generally, most advisors suggest that some portion of every portfolio be maintained in income stocks—more for older people and less for younger people.

Turbulence

The speculative investments at the top of the financial pyramid are not recommended for beginning investors or even experienced investors who are seriously interested in saving for retirement. If you want to try them despite the warning, bring to this sector of the marketplace only the money you might take to Las Vegas or Atlantic City.

Commodities are bulk goods such as precious metals, grains, and other foods. They are traded on the commodities exchange. Futures trading, as we mentioned, is one of the most risky adventures in the marketplace. This marketplace also can be very rewarding if your blood pressure, self image, and relationships can tolerate the level of anxiety.

> **It's Been Said**
> *One thing we learned in farming is that you never rely on one source. The more sources you have, the more educated your decisions.*
> —Carnell Korsmeyer, Member, Beardstown Business and Professional Women's Investment Club

Unnoticed and out-of-favor stocks are other risk adventures that often appeal to bargain hunters, sometimes bringing excellent returns. Have you spotted a stock with a low P/E ratio (less than 10) and you think the company deserves better? You anticipate a turnaround in earnings and you think the price of the stock will shoot up. Maybe time will prove you right. And maybe not.

New issues are another dangerous opportunity. Known as IPOs (*initial public offerings*), they are the first stocks to be sold when a privately held company "goes public." Sometimes the prices soar on the first day of trading and, then again, sometimes the response of the public is less positive, especially over the long haul. These stocks are speculative because the company has no history in the public arena.

Finally, *penny stocks*. They sell for less than $1 as IPOs and sometimes ride up as high as $10. But they are as volatile as Mexican jumping beans. You'll find them traded "over the counter" in local markets—usually in Denver, Vancouver, or Salt Lake City. *Over the counter* means the trading is done by brokers by phone and computer just as government and municipal bonds are traded. The fact that a stock trades over the counter does not necessarily mean it has increased risk.

Sources for More Information, Advice, and News

Just in case you haven't noticed, financial advice is everywhere! Books, newspapers, magazines, newsletters, videos, software, CDs, the Internet, television, radio, and your mailbox bring you free-for-the-asking (and sometimes without asking) information from trade associations and brokerage houses. If we tried to include every one, this book would be a good deal heavier than it already is, and nobody wants that. So here's a selection. Once you get into doing financial research, you'll see that one thing leads to another, and you'll soon be virtually surrounded by information.

Investment Clubs

If you think you might enjoy working with your friends and neighbors to make money, we recommend that you read *The Beardstown Ladies' Common-Sense Investment Guide*, by The Beardstown Ladies Investment Club with Leslie Whitaker. These uncommonly successful people will tell you how they did it and how to put together and run your own club.

You also can get advice on developing a club by contacting the *National Association of Investors Corporation* at 711 West Thirteen-Mile Road, Madison Heights, MI 48071. Or, call (810) 583-6242.

Newsletters

Hundreds of newsletters are available, covering all aspects of investing. Before you subscribe, check out the book that rates the top 120: *The Hulbert Guide to Financial Newsletters*, by Mark Hulbert. Later, even if you choose among those not mentioned in the book, you'll have some standards to evaluate by.

Magazines

Just stop at a newsstand. There are shelves full! Among the best known: *Business Week, Fortune, Forbes, Kiplinger's Personal Finance, Financial World, Money,* and *Worth.*

Newspapers

Five nationally available papers present detailed financial information: *Barron's National Business and Financial Weekly; Investor's Business Daily;* the *New York Times; USA Today;* and the *Wall Street Journal.*

Radio

A number of all-business news stations exist, such as WBBR in New York City. Several business programs are also aired on networks across the nation, such as Business Radio Network. Marketplace and Sound Money air on National Public Radio.

Television

CNBC is a 24-hour cable channel specializing in business and financial news. CNN Business News has two morning shows and one in the evening. PBS offers three shows: *Nightly Business Report; Adam Smith's Money World;* and *Wall Street Week, with Louis Rukeyser.*

Online Services

In this electronic age, you "dial in" to these services with your computer's modem. They make very current information available electronically, and the industry is growing rapidly with more services coming up all the time. Among those available are CompuServe, Dow Jones News/Retrieval, Prodigy, and Signal.

Software

This field is growing fast also. If you want a comprehensive listing of software to help you choose stocks that fit your goals, consult the *Individual Investor's Guide to Computerized Investing,* available from the American Association of Individual Investors, 625 North Michigan Ave., Chicago, IL 60611; (312) 280-0170.

Periodical Reports

For detailed information on individual companies, you might sample *Value Line Investment Survey, Standard & Poor's Stock Reports,* and *Moody's Handbook of Common Stocks.* For mutual fund performance, check Morningstar and Lipper Analytical Services.

The Least You Need to Know

➤ There is less risk in buying stocks for long-term investment than in buying to trade frequently.

➤ You can buy stocks through full-commission brokers or through discount brokers.

➤ Most mutual funds offer the small investor the security of a diversified portfolio.

➤ Mutual funds come in load and no-load varieties. *No load* means no commission fees.

➤ If you don't learn the terminology of the marketplace, you could easily find yourself in a situation you don't want to be in.

➤ Different investment styles bring different results—know what you want!

➤ There's a lot of investment information and advice available. Do use it.

Bonds—Your Money Earning Money

Think bond.

OK, what did you see? Probably either Sean Connery with a *femme fatale* double agent or one of those nice crisp government card things with a picture of Jefferson (or somebody with a wig) that you got from both sets of grandparents at your junior high school graduation.

Well, there's lots more, folks! The federal government sells many, many types of bonds in addition to these familiar savings bonds. States and cities also issue bonds. And foreign governments. Corporations too! And some bonds come in denominations that require more than one comma to separate all the zeros. Yes, bonds are *big* business!

Lending to Make Money

If you don't want to get into owning a business or an interest in a business, and you don't want to do more work to earn more money, you might consider letting your money earn money. When you buy bonds of any type, you are lending money with the expectation that it will be paid back, with interest. Most financial planners recommend bonds as a good source of retirement income and as a generally conservative investment. There are two ways that you can make money with bonds: collecting the interest and buying and selling bonds.

Collecting Interest

Bonds are a *fixed-rate instrument*. The interest rate is locked in at whatever it was when the bond was first issued. So if you choose to buy and hold this investment, you'll know your rate of return. On most, but not all bonds, you'll get that return twice a year when interest payments are made. Which leads to your next question, "For how long?"

It's Been Said
I'm not so concerned about the return on my money as I am about the return of my money!
—Bernard Baruch, 1870-1965, American businessman and statesman

Generally, most bonds fall into one of three classifications, although there is no hard-and-fast rule here. *Short-term bonds* can run to about five years. *Intermediate-term bonds* typically mature within seven to ten years. *Long-term bonds* mature in 20 years or more. But a bond theoretically can be sold for any prescribed length of time. So, of course, you could have a long, intermediate-term bond for 14 years or a short, long-term bond for 18 years. The number of years to maturity is very important, however, because that's when the IOU is up. In other words, it's when you are scheduled to get your *principal* (the money you invested) returned!

Selling the Bonds You Hold

If you get impatient with collecting interest and want your principal back, or if you need it for some sudden emergency or need (like buying a boat), you can sell your bonds. Whether you get the face value of the bond, more than face value, or less depends primarily on the national economy at the time. The value of your bond in the market-place is determined by how much money someone else thinks he or she can make on the investment. The essential rule of bond investing is this: *Bond prices move in the opposite direction of interest rates*. If interest rates are up from the rate at which your bond was issued, your bond will be worth less. If interest rates are down, your bond will be worth more.

Does that sound confusing? Think of the 30-year Treasury bonds issued at 13 percent in the early '80s. No one gets 13 percent now! But all those investors who bought 13 percent Treasuries are still collecting 13 percent a year paid semiannually.

Now if someone wanted to sell a $10,000 Treasury with a 13 percent coupon (interest) rate, he or she could sell the bond for more than $10,000, even though almost 15 years of interest already has been collected. Why? Because the buyer of the bond will get the $10,000 face value on the 30-year maturity date and also will have collected 13 percent interest per year until then. That high interest rate is what the new buyer pays for.

Does that sound fabulous? Hold on before you run out to buy ten 30-year Treasuries at $10,000 each. Interest rates right now are relatively low. But let's say that you're conservative and just want steady income. So you buy one. By 1999, interest rates are up around 11 percent. And you want your money. Well, you can't get it for more than 25 years. So, you'll sell your bond, right? Yes, but who will want it when new issues are available at 11 percent? The person who buys it will pay you much less than the $10,000 face value. Enough less, thousands less (maybe less than half!), so that getting $10,000 at maturity will make up for the low coupon rate. Or some bond traders might buy it thinking to make a profit by selling it for more than $10,000 when interest rates plummet to 5 percent.

Is your head spinning? Bonds can be one of the most stable, simple investments, or one of the most volatile and complex. Even buying them is more complex than most other investments, because you can go right to the source issuing the bonds, deal with a specialized bond broker, or even work through some banks and other financial institutions. Often, different types of bonds have different vendors. Part of getting into this investment arena is learning where and how to buy.

Fortunately, there's help for the asking. The industry group that represents brokerage firms, dealers, and bond-trading banks has several publications available. Contact the Public Securities Association at 40 Broad Street, 12th Floor, New York, NY 10004-2373 or call (212) 809-7000. Pamphlets also are available from a not-for-profit group whose stated purpose is to educate the public about bonds. They also keep statistics about defaulted bonds. Contact the Bond Investors Association at 6175 NW 153rd Street, Suite 229, Miami Lakes, FL 33014 or call (305) 557-1832.

Extra! Extra!

Despite the fact that bonds are the most common lending instrument traded in the securities marketplace, there are no bond markets as there are stock markets (NYSE, AMEX, and so on) around the world. Bonds are traded by dealers who communicate by telephone and computer. There is no separate commission charge for buying and selling. Instead, bond dealers make money by taking a portion of the spread between buying and selling price. The amount of the cut can differ from one dealer to another. Shopping around for the best deal is highly recommended.

Bond Mutual Funds—Numbers Power

Because the face value of many bonds is in the five- and six-digit range, investing in bonds had been considered the province of the wealthy. Then came the '80s, with volatile interest rates; junk bonds; and, most important, the growth of bond mutual funds. Today, you can invest in bonds through mutual funds with small amounts of cash. You also can move into and out of funds without huge cash penalties.

Gray Matter Alert
Bond dealers don't like small orders. Many simply won't trade unless you have $25,000 in hand. Those that do take small trades charge more. This is a marketplace that favors the large institutional traders. If you want to buy bonds without large fees, use a bond mutual fund or deal directly with the U.S. Treasury through Federal Reserve banks and branches or through the Bureau of Public Debt at 1300 C St. SW, Washington, DC 20239.

Like stock mutual funds, bond funds have goals. These usually are tied to maturity; some funds specialize in short-term bonds, some in intermediate, some in long, and some in mixed bonds. Then add the risk factor. Some funds go for the safe instruments, which usually have lower rates of return, while others go for *high-yield* bonds (a.k.a. junk bonds), which promise to pay more interest but also have a higher default rate. And some funds choose to mix and match. The gambling funds usually are called *aggressive*, and those that stay with known entities without a lot of trading are called *passive*.

There are several advantages to bond mutual funds. Besides saving on those inflated small-trade fees imposed by dealers, funds enable the individual investor to participate in diversification. As in the stock market, diversification increases security.

OOOOH...

Power Word
In the financial marketplace, **default** means the failure of a debtor (the bond issuer, for example) to make on-time payments of interest and principal. When there is a default, bondholders may make claims against the assets of the bond issuer. But if the issuer has gone belly-up, chances of getting your principal back are non-existent or, at best, slim indeed.

Bond funds also can supply a steady income for retirement. As we said, most bond interest is paid twice a year. If you're counting on that income to meet everyday expenses, there can be a lot of half year left at the end of the money. A bond fund portfolio can mean a monthly dividend check.

One disadvantage of bond funds is that you never see a maturity date. (Except in zero coupons, but we'll get to them in just a bit.) Bond funds constantly reinvest the proceeds from sold and matured bonds back into more bonds. So, in terms of your principal (the money you used to buy bond fund shares), the bond fund becomes more like a stock fund because you must sell your shares in order to get your investment back. And remember: Interest rates up, bond prices (and bond fund prices) down; interest rates down, bond prices (and bond fund prices) up. There are both load and no-load funds available. There also are funds that buy only taxable bonds and funds that buy only tax-free bonds.

Ratings—Not a Popularity Contest

Because bonds are IOUs, it stands to reason that you might want to run a credit check before turning over thousands of dollars and getting a promise recorded in a computer in return. Several credit rating agencies exist in the bond market. Moody's and Standard & Poor's are the largest, and their ratings are widely available, even in local libraries.

A company's or a government agency's *bond credit rating* is an evaluation of its ability to pay back its debts. Most bond credit ratings are expressed with a letter grade. AAA is usually the highest and most creditworthy. The grades then proceed downward through AA, A, BBB, BB, B, CCC, and so on. BBBs through Bs get progressively more risky. Cs and Ds are often in arrears or default and have little or no market value.

Thin Ice

The term *coupon rate* comes from the coupons that used to be attached to bonds. The bearer of a coupon would be paid the interest stated—hence the name *bearer bonds*. But check for authenticity if someone tries to sell you a bond certificate with coupons attached. Bearer bonds have not been issued since 1982. Today, bonds are *registered*, which means that you get a certificate with your name on it, or *book entry*, which means that the computer takes care of everything.

From the United States Treasury and Friends

Our government is one of the great borrowers of the world—maybe the universe. It also is considered one of the safest, surest, best bets in the investment industry. There are trillions of dollars worth of outstanding Treasury securities in the marketplace, and more are being sold every month. All have virtually no risk of default.

We talked about T-bills and U.S. Savings Bonds in Chapter 9 because they generally are regarded to be in the category of liquid assets and are considered an alternative to cash. Treasury securities with terms of one to ten years are called *notes*. Those with terms of more than 10 years are called *bonds*. Treasury securities are available in denominations ranging from $1,000 to more than $1,000,000. All federal bonds are exempt from state and local taxes, but you do pay federal income tax on the interest that is paid to you in the year that you receive it.

Thin Ice
Even though Treasuries are considered risk-free of default, you *can* lose money if you decide to sell them before maturity at a time when interest rates are up. If the rate change has been significant and you are selling early in the term, you can lose a major portion of your principal. The longer the term, the more sensitive the value of a bond is to interest rate changes.

Almost all Treasury bonds are *noncallable*. Now that doesn't mean that you can't call them whatever names you like if they disappoint you. It does mean that if interest rates go down—from 13 percent to 6 percent, for example—the government is *not* allowed to pay off the bond early (a trick that some corporations and municipalities use regularly). Treasury bonds keep paying their original interest rate right up to their maturity date. Great income and great for resale value when rates are down.

Just a tad more risky than the no-risk Treasuries are the bonds issued by a whole bunch of federal-government-backed agencies. With the slightly higher risks come slightly higher interest rates. You'll probably recognize some of these agencies—names like Fannie Mae, Ginnie Mae, and Freddie Mac—as tied to the secondary mortgage marketplace. But you might be surprised at some other agencies that are issuing bonds. For example: the United States Postal Service and the Small Business Administration.

Municipal Bonds

Issued by states, counties, cities, towns, and other taxing authorities, municipal bonds are very popular bonds that are totally free of federal income taxes. Also, in most states, the

OOOOH...

Power Word
A **call** in the *bond market* is very, very different from a call in the *stock market*. In the stock market, a call is an option to buy. In the bond market, it's the right to redeem outstanding bonds before their date of maturity. The first date for a possible call must be named in every prospectus that has a call provision.

bond holders who live in the state issuing the bonds do not have to pay state and local taxes on the interest earned. But a few states—Illinois, Iowa, Kansas, Oklahoma, and Wisconsin—exempt the interest from some in-state bonds, but not all. Most states do impose taxes on the interest earned by residents who buy bonds issued by other states. The exceptions are Alaska, the District of Columbia, Indiana, Nevada, South Dakota, Texas, Utah, Washington, and Wyoming—all of which do not tax any munis. Check out the map to see whether your state lets you out of paying taxes on municipal bonds. And remember, if you own munis and you move to a new state, your interest may be subject to taxation.

How does your state tax interest on municipal bonds?

States that tax the bonds issued by other states and some bonds issued by the state and sold to its own residents

States that tax only bonds issued by other states

States that do not tax bonds issued by other states or their own bonds

Because municipal bonds are not taxable by the federal government, they often are referred to as *tax-free munis* (pronounced *mew-knees*). When bonds are not taxable by the residence state, they are called *double tax-free bonds*. And when they are also not taxable by a city or locality, they are known, naturally, as *triple tax-free bonds*. The higher your federal, state, and local tax bracket, the more appealing munis become. For an investor in the 28 percent federal tax bracket, a tax-exempt yield of 6 percent is the equivalent of 8.33 percent on a taxable bond.

It's Been Said
We at Chrysler borrow money the old-fashioned way. We pay it back.
—Lee Iacocca as Chairman of Chrysler Corp.

Corporate Bonds

Corporate bonds are more risky than government bonds because corporations can fold up and blow away. Because of the higher risk, corporate bonds pay higher interest rates. It's not unusual for a corporate bond to yield 2 to 6 percentage points more than a Treasury of the same maturity.

Gray Matter Alert
There's sometimes an unpleasant surprise in store for bond investors. When interest rates drop, many corporations redeem their bonds early. This practice nips in the bud what would have been a high-yielding investment. However, some corporations offer a 10-year guarantee against early redemption. Ask your broker about *call protection*. It's a plus.

So if you want the most security you can get on the corporate bond market, you want to choose bonds from corporations that are doing well and are not likely to go bankrupt. This is when you should get very familiar with bond-rating agencies like Standard & Poor's Corporation, and take their advice seriously. Or choose a good mutual fund that specializes in corporate bonds.

If you want to play the investment game with one foot in bonds and one foot in stocks, you might consider *convertible bonds*. These bonds pay a fixed rate of interest and are convertible into corporate common stock when the stock reaches a certain price, known as the *conversion price*. The conversion price always is set higher than the price of the common stock on the day the convertibles are issued. It might be as little as 15 or 20 percent above, or it might be 50 percent or more above. When and if underlying stock hits the conversion price, the convertible bond can be changed for a specified number of common stock shares. This rate of bond-to-stock exchange is called the *conversion ratio*. Most advisers consider a good convertible a solid investment.

Junk bonds, on the other hand, are considered high risk and speculative. Their proper name in the brokerage industry is *high-yield bonds*, but because of the scandals in the '80s, everyone calls them junk bonds. They usually are rated in the B range, sometimes trying to move up to A, sometimes having fallen down from A. Because of their higher risk, they have to pay higher interest rates in order to get anyone at all to buy them. Yes, you can make money on high-yield bonds. But you also can lose your entire investment.

Zero Coupon Bonds

By now you know that, in the bond marketplace, *coupon rate* means interest to be paid. So why would anyone want to buy a bond with a zero coupon rate?

Because the bonds are issued at a deep discount. What you actually pay for the bond is far less than the face value. The return on your money is the gradual increase in the bond's price as it nears maturity. If you hold the bond to maturity, you receive the face value.

The most common and safest of the zeros are the Treasury bonds. Like all other Treasuries, they are backed by the full faith and credit of the U.S. government. Treasury zeros are known formally as *separate trading of registered interest and principal of securities*. If that makes no sense to you, don't worry, you'll never hear it. Everyone calls them *STRIPS*.

Other sources of zeros are mutual funds, corporations, and municipalities. Which brings us to the hitch in this great investment: taxes. Although you don't receive semiannual interest payments on zeros, the growth of your investment toward face value is considered interest earned by the federal government. (The IRS calls it *accretion*.)

Are you confused? Think of Series EE savings bonds as a kind of zero. You buy them at a discount of 50 percent off face value. You don't receive interest payments while you hold them, but you pay taxes on your interest earned when you redeem them.

The IRS is not so lenient on the accretion of other zeros. Even though you don't receive a penny in interest payment each year, the IRS says you must pay taxes on the imputed (meaning *credited* here) interest. Contact the IRS for a schedule telling you how much interest you must report each year.

Having to pay taxes on money not yet received has pushed many people who like zeros into tax-free municipal zeros, where no tax payment is ever required. Another tactic is to stash your zeros in a safe place. A place where the hand of the government won't go, that is. Yes, a tax shelter.

For those who hold zeros in an IRA, a Keogh, or another tax-deferred retirement savings plan, the payment of taxes on imputed interest is *not* required. You pay taxes on the increase in value when you withdraw the money from your account—usually, well into retirement. Most investment advisers consider zeros a good investment if you want to be sure that you will have a certain amount of money at a certain time—in time for college tuition or retirement, for example.

Something a Little More Adventurous, Please

Bored? Maybe you'd like a little foreign adventure. You can buy foreign government bonds and bonds issued by foreign-based companies. Yields usually are higher, but so are the minimum denominations of the bonds, which means you need more money to buy them and, if you're lucky, that big investment will bring you a better return than you might get elsewhere. This arena is not for beginners. Even experienced investors get butterflies in their stomachs as they watch currency fluctuations.

If you are determined to take a world tour in bonds, you can avoid the high denominations and the high cost of dealers' fees for buying individual foreign bonds by investing in a mutual fund that specializes in foreign bonds.

The Least You Need to Know

➤ When you buy bonds, you lend your money with the expectation that it will be paid back, with interest.

➤ You can sell most bonds before they mature.

➤ Change in the value of a bond on the resale market is inverse to interest rates. Rates up = bond prices down; rates down = bond prices up.

➤ Many bond mutual funds are available. Their advantages are diversification, lower dealer fees, and ease of selling and buying.

➤ Bonds come in taxed and tax-free varieties.

➤ Some bonds are more risky than others. Be aware of the ratings.

Chapter 12

Real Estate—Your Hands-On Money Maker

In This Chapter

➤ The personality traits you'll need

➤ What makes real estate a good investment

➤ What makes real estate a difficult investment

➤ Five kinds of property with tips and comments

➤ The "other" kids on the block—REITs & RELPs

Let's say you have $25,000 invested in bonds and another $20,000 in stocks.

And what do you have to show for it? Nothing. Not even a gold-edged certificate. Everything is in your broker's computer.

This makes some people nervous. They don't care that the liquidity is great or that you can get your money out quickly if you need to. They want an investment they can point to, work on, and manage.

Well, there's real estate. It's big, solid, and touchable, and it's usually right there in town or close by, waiting, maybe even beckoning. It can bring in steady income through rentals, or it can bring in big bucks through profitable sales. Some investors see it as a perfect money maker.

We agree and disagree. It's often a money maker. It's rarely, if ever, perfect. And, contrary to popular thought, you sometimes can lose money in real estate. This is not everyone's pot o' gold, but for those willing to put in the time and effort, it can pay off handsomely.

Are You the Type?

Many financial advisors are so focused on following "the markets" that they never suggest buying real estate as a long-term investment for both growth and income. But then again, maybe the reason isn't just that stocks and bonds are their only fields of interest. Maybe most financial advisors don't advise people to invest in real estate because they know it takes a certain kind of personality to increase the odds of success in this arena. Let's go over some traits that real estate investors should have:

➤ **Risk taking:** The numbers involved with real estate investment ownership often have six digits on two fronts (the purchase price and the mortgage), five digits on several others (rental income, maintenance, taxes, improvements, and so on), and a whole lot of juggling among all those digits on the day-to-day front. The prospective investor must be able to deal with strings of zeros following along after every dollar sign.

➤ **Decision making:** The decision is not just to buy or not to buy. Real estate investment requires decisions on improvements, maintenance, tenants, managers, financing, and more. Plus few of these are yes/no decisions. Most involve need evaluation, compromise, cost/value analysis, time/value analysis, and aesthetic and environmental considerations.

It's Been Said
When I build something for somebody, I always add $50,000,000 or $60,000,000 onto the price. My guys come in, they say it's going to cost $75,000,000. I say it's going to cost $125,000,000, and I build it for $100,000,000.
—Donald Trump, reported in the *New York Times*, July 1, 1986

➤ **Commitment:** Unlike activity in the financial marketplace, you can't get in and out of a real estate purchase in the same week. In fact, it's often hard to get in and out within the same year and make a profit. Once you execute that contract, you've got to be willing to stay for the long haul.

➤ **Logical and rational evaluation:** Real estate investors must put aside their personal tastes and preferences when considering property.

Comparable values, carrying costs, projected income, maintenance costs, taxes, and other *numbers* must take over as decision-making criteria. You should never buy a property because you "love" it; there's no place for love in investment real estate.

➤ **Attention to legal matters:** Zoning regulations and building codes affect every real estate project. Beyond these compliance matters, there's the title search, the deed, title insurance, closing costs, CC&Rs (conditions, covenants, and restrictions), and enough other terms to fill a whole book. If you intend to invest in real estate, you'll more than likely need the help of a lawyer and an accountant.

➤ **Organization and management skills:** Of course you'll have to keep track of who has paid the rent and when mortgage payments and taxes are due, but management requirements also extend to knowing what's going on in the local and national economies in order to plan for the improvement or sale of certain properties.

➤ **Imagination and creativity:** The successful investor can look at a place that has languished on the market because of poor decorating or a generally run-down appearance and imagine it clean and sparkling. He or she also can look at a gasoline station that has gone out of business and see a donut shop.

➤ **Patience, tact, and self control:** You might think real estate investment deals with property, but *people* use property. As a landlord, you need well-honed interpersonal skills.

➤ **Negotiating skills:** The most successful investors believe that no asking price is ever firm and that *no* never means *absolutely not.* They walk softly and save their best offers for the last stand. It's a skill and an art that must be developed.

The Pros for Real Estate Investment

Just about everyone who knows *Gone With the Wind* remembers the advice of Gerald O'Hara to his daughter: "Land is the only thing that matters, Katie Scarlet. It's the only thing that lasts."

Of course, he was right. But as you can see in Table 12.1, there are several other good reasons to invest in real estate. Let's go over them a bit.

Table 12.1   Real Estate Investment

The Pros	The Cons
Potential for both income and appreciation	Non-liquid investment
Control over management	Management required
Security/indestructibility of the land	High degree of specific-to-the-investment knowledge required
Investment can be leveraged Sweat-equity potential	High cost of the investment

There's Potential for Both Income and Appreciation

During the soaring '70s, the sales pitch in most real estate offices included well-worn statistics showing that every real estate purchase was a hedge against inflation. In fact, in the '70s, real estate was actually far outpacing inflation. Today, it's still out in front by a nose in most parts of the nation. In the years between, however, it's been on something of a roller-coaster ride in many areas.

Over the century, real estate has been one of the best investments for financial growth available to the general public. Averaged nationally and over time, its return is neck and neck with stocks. Real estate, however, has had a more even upward curve, without the high peaks and low valleys of the stock market. Except—and there's always an except, isn't there? Except in some parts of the nation where real estate's sudden drops and swings would make the market curves look smooth. Ask people from Texas, California, and Connecticut.

Gray Matter Alert
If you're concerned about losing some of your Social Security benefits because you might exceed the maximums on earned income in the early years of your retirement, stick with real estate! The income from rental units or from the sale of property is *not* counted as earned income. More in Chapter 14.

Besides the general trend of the real estate marketplace, there is always the potential that the appreciation of a particular investment property will either far outpace the average or drag behind it. So much depends on the original price, location, condition, and use of each individual parcel of land or building. And so much depends on national and local economic conditions. The sale of a carefully selected purchase, held over some years and well maintained, could buy you that second home in a warmer climate or the boat or RV you've been dreaming of for your early retirement years. Economic bad luck or a poor selection of property could keep you in debt and working to support that debt for years.

And there's still more! Except for raw land, which does not usually generate monthly or even annual income, most real estate purchases can be structured to provide positive cash flow if that is the investor's goal. A multi-family house or a small apartment building can help to close the gap between your pension income and the money you'll need to continue in your pre-retirement lifestyle.

You Have Control Over the Management of Your Property

Unlike the stock market, where your ownership interest is an infinitely small portion and you have no say in the day-to-day decisions of company management, you as a landlord are the boss. You can hire and fire, seize opportunities or remain passive, buy or sell. It's all up to you alone, or you and a small group if you form a partnership.

There Are Tax Advantages

Property depreciation regulations in the federal tax code have helped many entrepreneurs and investors look forward to a merry month of May for many decades. The breaks are not quite as good now as they once were, but they're still significant. If you invest in real estate, you will, of course, have a good accountant. It's quite likely that he or she will save you a good deal of money.

It's Been Said
I heard my father say he never knew a piece of land [to] run away or break.
—John Adams in his *Autobiography*

You also can postpone paying capital gains taxes when you sell your investment properties if you put the proceeds into another investment property of a similar kind. *Similar kind* is open to some interpretation. Again, your accountant will help.

Consider Security and the Indestructibility of the Land

For taxation and depreciation purposes, land is considered indestructible. Of course, there could be an earthquake or a volcano, but let's not get technical! The land won't disappear, and the buildings on it are as permanent a fixture as humans can create. Title to real estate is recorded in municipal records offices, it's virtually impossible to steal a building, and destruction of buildings can be protected against with insurance.

There's the Possibility of Leveraged Investment

When real estate is appreciating rapidly, you can increase the return on your investment by *leveraging*. Here's how it works. Suppose that you buy a $200,000 piece of property. You put $20,000 down and get a mortgage loan for $180,000. Your rental income provides a positive cash flow for five years. Then you sell for $260,000. So you made $60,000 on a $200,000 investment, right?

Not quite. After commissions on the sale, closing costs, and repayment of the mortgage, you do find yourself with $60,000 cash. But, in fact, you made that $60,000 on a $20,000 investment (your down payment). In other words, you tripled your money in five years!

It's not quite that simple, but this example is indeed how leveraging works. If it sounds appealing, talk with your accountant or a good financial advisor.

There Might Be Sweat-Equity Potential

Sweat-equity is the value added to a piece of property because of improvements made by the owners through their own work efforts. Real estate investment is still a field where you can work for yourself. If you are competent in the skills required for repair and refurbishing, you can save thousands of dollars while increasing your property's resale value.

The Cons Against Real Estate Investment

With so many positives, why isn't everyone rushing out to buy real estate investments? Well, as always, there are a few little hurdles on the track to riches.

Thin Ice
One of the greatest dangers to the novice investor is overestimating his or her competence in the repair and refurbishing department and underestimating the amount of work that must be done and the cost of supplies. *Always* get professional estimates *before* buying.

It's a Non-Liquid Investment

"Non-liquid"—that's the first thing they say, all those people who caution you about diving into real estate. "It's not easy to liquefy your real estate assets. Invest only money you don't need. Be careful."

And they're right. Real estate is a non-liquid asset. But most cautionary advisors forget to tell you that real estate is also the best collateral for loans in virtually every lending marketplace. It's true that you may not be able to sell quickly, but you could well get emergency money rather quickly through the mortgage marketplace.

It's Management Intensive

Very true. If you don't have the time, the interest, the personality, and the skills to manage your investment property, it's possible to hire managers. But that will cut into your return and, perhaps more important, decrease your control. Don't get into real estate thinking it will be easy money. That's rarely true. On the other hand, attention, commitment, and hard work are usually well rewarded.

It Requires a High Degree of Knowledge

Yes! Yes! The need to understand not only the real estate field in general but the requirements of each specific investment is probably the main reason more people don't get into this money-making investment. But remember, you don't have to learn everything at once! You can start with an investment type that you feel comfortable with such as a fixer-upper or perhaps a multi-family home. After a while, you might buy another. Later, you might get a group together to buy an apartment building. That's how it usually goes—knowledge and experience add up to create the successful investor.

Extra! Extra!

Unless you live in at least a fairly large city, you might not find a great deal of information on investing in real estate at your local library. Information *is* available, however. Many publishers bring out books on real-estate-related topics every year. Call and ask for their catalogs. Trade and professional organizations—like the National Association of Realtors, the National Association of Home Builders, and the Urban Land Institute—offer a vast number of books and booklets, some free.

It Requires a Huge Initial Investment

The amount of the down payment necessary to buy investment property often frightens away prospective investors. And it's true; you can't just deposit $500 a month, and even $5,000 usually isn't enough to get you started. But the down payment requirements may be less than you think.

You've certainly heard of government-backed programs through the FHA and VA that help you get into real estate with little or nothing down. These are primarily home-buying programs, but who's to say you can't start out by living in a multi-family house? (Usually an excellent investment vehicle, by the way.) And there is a program that covers investment property with nothing down, and in some cases, more mortgage than the purchase price if certain repairs are included. It's a HUD-insured program called 203K. You can get information about it through your local HUD office or through the lending institutions that participate.

Gray Matter Alert
Almost unknown before the 1980s, mortgage brokers and mortgage bankers now originate more than 50 percent of home mortgages and many investment mortgages. Because they work with many lenders and have hundreds of different mortgage programs available, they often can save you time and money, not to mention make your wish come true. Your local real estate agency can provide the names of several good brokers and other sources of financing.

Mortgage money is readily available as we write this, and many lenders are out there competing for your business. Keen competition means more creative loan packages. Shop around—it might be easier to get into real estate investment than you think.

Although mortgage money is available, it is not without cost or effort. Besides the interest you must pay, there will be a mortgage application fee, appraisal fees, credit check fees, and possibly points. All of which could add up to several thousand dollars out of your pocket.

Points are the lender's way of making the loan more profitable. One point is one percent of the amount being borrowed. Points are paid before or at the closing.

Besides money, you also must spend time on the mortgage application process. And you must be certain that you and your prospective property meet the qualification guidelines established by the lender. A mortgage broker or the lending officer at your bank will help you.

What You Can Buy

Real estate is like a country fair with many, many booths. What you choose to play at depends on the prizes being offered, your perception of your skills, the amount of the wager required to play, and the size of the crowds around the booths. The picking decisions are all yours:

➤ **Fixer-uppers:** They're everyone's entry dream. Find a run-down house in a good neighborhood, fix it up, and sell it for a big profit. Sometimes it works, but good fixer-uppers are not as easy to find as you might think. Before you sign a contract to buy one, be sure you estimate not only fix-up costs, but also fix-up time. The longer it takes to complete the refurbishing, the less profit you'll make, because you'll be making mortgage payments and paying taxes. You should try to buy the property for at least 15 percent below market value. A good real estate agent helps you to determine current fair market value.

➤ **Vacation homes:** Many people buy second homes in vacation areas where they hope to retire someday. This can be a good investment, especially if you can pick up some annual income from rental—either big bucks during prime season or sustaining income during off-season. (Check on federal tax reporting rules with your accountant. They're a bit hairy and determine whether your property can be classified as a second home or merely an investment property.)

Condos can be a fine investment in the vacation marketplace if they are in communities that are well run and desirable. Check the deed restrictions, however, to be certain that you can rent for profit. In those communities where vacation rental is common, the condo management often handles all the details. Some resort condo associations operate on a rental pool basis, so if your unit is available, it shares in the profits even though it might not be occupied as much as some others.

➤ **Residential rental properties:** This is a big category including condos, single-family houses, multi-family houses, and apartment buildings. Before purchasing, be sure that you get a rental history and an accounting of operating costs for at least the past two years. Consider how much mortgage and taxes will cost per month. Consider repair, maintenance, and management costs. Add up your projected income from the property, and then subtract expected costs. Do you come up with a positive number? If you don't, do tax advantages make the investment still appealing? It's a very good idea to have a good accountant if rental property is your investment of choice.

➤ **Commercial and mixed-use properties:** Few beginning investors have the money or the knowledge to jump into commercial real estate. It has all the complications of residential rental property with much higher price tags and some bonus features like net, and net/net, and net/net/net leases thrown in. It also has a lot more sensitivity to the state of the local economy.

If you think commercial property might be for you one day, consider starting with a mixed-use property. You know, the dentist's office and the donut shop on the main floor and two residential rental apartments on the second floor. These buildings are far less costly than strip malls, and the mixed use provides a diversity that can be a bit of insurance against long vacancy.

➤ **Land:** Many people think that if you buy land you'll be wealthy someday. Actually, undeveloped land is one of the riskiest investment vehicles at the real estate fair. It is slow to sell, its future value often is dependent on what is developed around it, zoning regulations can change its potential use (both for better or worse), and environmental concerns often require extensive and expensive testing and planning before a building project can be approved.

Land rarely brings in any income, so your investment is a bet on appreciation. It also is difficult, if not impossible, to take out a mortgage on raw land, so you can't even borrow against your invested money. Land is the longest of long-term, non-liquid investments.

REITs and RELPs

Neither REITs nor RELPs are hands-on real estate investments. But they are based in the real estate marketplace, so we might as well mention them here.

REITs Are More Like Stocks

Real estate investment trusts (called *REITs* and pronounced *reets*, rhymes with *beets*) are companies, usually publicly traded, that manage a portfolio of real estate investments with the goal of earning profits for shareholders. *Equity REITs* buy, sell, and manage income-producing property. *Mortgage REITs* lend money to developers or buy mortgages on commercial property. Some REITs (called *hybrids*) have a mix of equity and mortgage holdings.

REIT shares are traded just like General Motors. The IRS considers them portfolio income, not real estate income. Mortgage REITs are somewhat more risky than equity REITs and have a somewhat better return. Currently, 7 percent is considered good on an equity REIT.

Be careful that you're not misled by the name of these investment vehicles. Don't assume that REITs have all the security of the little house you just bought around the corner. Many REITs went under in the '70s.

RELPs Are More Like... Well, Like Themselves!

A real estate limited partnership (RELP) is an organization of investors led by a general partner who manages both the money and the project. The limited partners lend their money to the general partner by buying shares in the RELP. There often are high sales charges and other buying-in fees—sometimes as much as 10 percent—and there are annual management fees—usually 2 or 3 percent. The limited partners hope to get high annual returns from rents and high capital gains when the limited partnership is dissolved (usually a scheduled date in less than 10 years).

Sometimes they do, and sometimes they don't!

Smaller limited partnerships generally are regarded as a non-liquid investment. When there is the opportunity to sell shares, it is usually at a deep discount. Some general partners promise to buy you out if you're dissatisfied, but don't expect to get all your money back.

There are two types of limited partnerships: the *specified*, which tells you in advance which properties it will buy, and the *blind pool*, in which you trust the general partner to buy whatever will bring the best return. Many of the fish in the blind pools have been seen floating belly up over the past decade.

It's Been Said
*The law locks up both man and woman
Who steals the goose from off the common,
But lets the greater felon loose
Who steals the common from the goose.*
—Anonymous English Poet, probably early-19th century

In truth, a limited partnership isn't really much of a partnership at all. The limited partners have no say in the day-to-day management of the investments. They also are not liable for the acts of the general partners and cannot be pulled into a bankruptcy if the partnership fails. Theoretically, the most a limited partner can lose is the money he or she invested. General partners have a lot more at risk and many lost a great deal in the '80s, sometimes after legitimate efforts, sometimes not. Unfortunately, there has been a good deal of corruption and mismanagement in this investment vehicle.

Large, public, limited partnerships called *master limited partnerships* (MLPs) are sold through brokerage houses on the stock exchanges. Unlike their smaller cousins, the MLPs are a liquid investment, if a risky one. Besides real estate, they can be formed to invest in agriculture and livestock; Broadway musicals, plays, and other productions; cable TV; multi-million-dollar movies; leveraged buyouts; oil and gas; and almost anything else that might appeal to venture capital. We do not recommend MLPs for the beginning investor or even for the seasoned veteran who wants to secure his or her retirement.

The Future of Real Estate

Real estate is one of the oldest investments to be traded in our culture. There have been great fortunes made in it, there have been losses, and there have been great scams and abuses. In these last decades of the 20th century, however, regulatory agencies have become more aware of the effects of property development on the environment. As a result, there will be fewer opportunities to "steal the common from the goose."

It is still likely that the biggest profits will be made by the biggest investors. But no matter how many Wal-Marts want to come into town, there always will be opportunities to make money in real estate for the individual investor.

This is a country of property owners. Where there are owners, there also are sellers and buyers. If you have what it takes; do your homework; and buy, manage, and sell wisely; real estate can be your road to a very comfortable retirement.

But that doesn't mean you should ignore all the other investment opportunities we've discussed. Remember that there is greatest safety in a diversified portfolio.

The Least You Need to Know

➤ Real estate investment demands risk taking, decision making, commitment, logical and rational evaluation, attention to legal matters, organization and management skills, imagination and creativity, patience, tact, self control, and negotiating skills.

➤ The pros for real estate investment are potential for both income and appreciation, control over the management of the investment, tax advantages, security and the indestructibility of the land, and the possibility of leveraging and sweat equity.

➤ The cons against real estate investment are non-liquidity, the fact that it is management intensive, the need for specialized knowledge, and the need for a large initial investment in most cases.

➤ There are many types of real estate investments available that require different levels of skill, commitment, and cash.

➤ Although their investment vehicles are real estate or real estate secured, the process of investing in REITs and RELPs has few similarities to the real estate investment process.

Chapter 13

Stretching Your Pension Dollar

In This Chapter

➤ How to find out what you can get

➤ Such beautiful tax shelters!

➤ Vehicles on the road to retirement

➤ When you must start collecting and why

➤ Borrowing power, survivorship options, and legal recourse

Bet you can't guess who sets the maximum limits on your pension. No, not the company you loved so dearly and worked for so, ahhh, devotedly. It's your Uncle Sam! Federal law has established the maximum pension that can be paid to an individual. Adjusted periodically for inflation, the current limit is $120,000 a year.

"Aw shucks!" you say. "That's a limitation that just doesn't bother me a bit."

Ok, you're like most of us and will be getting less than the federal max. So what can you do? Just make sure that you'll be getting every penny you're entitled to. And whenever you can, try to stretch those pennies into extra dollars.

Knowledge Is Power

Step One: Get the information. The Employee Retirement Income Security Act (ERISA) gives you the right to get from your employer a *Summary Plan Description* regarding the company's pension plan. That document includes information about the type of plan and how it works, your options for collecting benefits, the rules for participation, the accrual of benefits, how and when you are vested, and your opportunities for other benefits. Check for each point.

ERISA also establishes your right to request (and get) your individual benefits statement. Those benefits include your monthly pension income plus any extra, such as company-paid medical insurance or life insurance.

Request your benefits statement often—even as much as every year when you do your financial reevaluation. It tells you your benefits to date and your projected benefits. This is essential information. After all, how can you plan where to go if you don't know where you are! Contact your pension plan administrator or your company personnel department.

Grab Those Employer Contributions!

Many employers have "wised-up" during the past decade. They figure that if *you* don't care about saving for retirement, why should they? Presto! Defined contribution plans are in.

OOOOH...

Power Word
Compound when paired with **interest** has nothing to do with chemical elements. **Compound interest** means that interest is paid on both principal and the interest that already has been earned. So interest is paid on interest, and more interest on that interest, and so on. With modern computers, it can be done by the minute! Quarterly is more common.

Defined contribution plans cost the company less money than defined benefit plans. One of the reasons for this savings is that the amount of the company contribution often is tied to the amount of the employee contribution. And would you believe that more than 25 percent of employees who have 401(k)s available to them don't contribute! And many, many more employees don't contribute the maximum they are allowed.

If you're one of these non-contributors or under-contributors, you'll probably get a severe attack of I-Wish-I-Had-Knownitis when you realize the tremendous benefits of tax-deferred investments. But don't just sit there and cry—change! Unless you're absolutely on the brink of retirement, you still can benefit from employer contributions to a tax-deferred retirement account.

Extra! Extra!

ESOPs (Employee Stock Ownership Plans) sometimes are available in addition to, as well as part of, tax-deferred retirement savings plans. The employer contribution here is usually (1) a deep discount on purchase price, (2) matching your purchase with some proportion of shares from the company, (3) in lieu of a bonus, or (4) as a part of a profit-sharing plan. Depending on your company, an ESOP could be a good deal. But remember: Experts recommend that only a small portion (5 percent or so) of your retirement savings portfolio should be in your employing company's stock.

The Joy of Tax Deferment

Maybe they're not *the* best, but tax-deferred retirement savings accounts are certainly one of the best tax shelters available in the United States today. Depending on the type of account available to you, some portion of your income may be eligible to be deposited pre-tax each year, thus reducing your taxable income. As long as the money remains in your retirement account, it is not subject to taxation. Interest compounds on that money, and it is not subject to taxation. Investments made with that money appreciate, and the gains are not subject to taxation. You pay taxes only when you withdraw money from the account. Check out the charts here to see the effects of compounding and tax deferment.

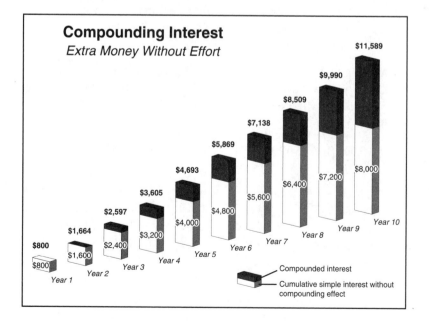

Compounding Interest
Extra Money Without Effort

$11,589
$9,990
$8,509
$7,138
$5,869
$4,693
$3,605
$2,597
$1,664
$800

$8,000 — Year 10
$7,200 — Year 9
$6,400 — Year 8
$5,600 — Year 7
$4,800 — Year 6
$4,000 — Year 5
$3,200 — Year 4
$2,400 — Year 3
$1,600 — Year 2
$800 — Year 1

Compounded interest
Cumulative simple interest without compounding effect

If you have $10,000 invested at 8 percent, after 10 years you'll have $18,000 if you're paid simple interest, or $21,589 if you're paid compounding interest. Compounding interest earned you $3,598 more!

This chart shows the value of your IRA's tax-deferred advantage. This example assumes a $2,000 annual contribution for 10, 20, and 30 years, a 31 percent tax bracket, and a constant earnings rate of 10 percent annually.

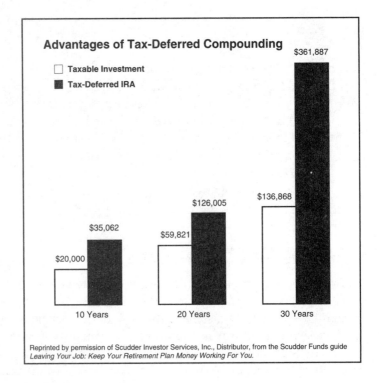

Reprinted by permission of Scudder Investor Services, Inc., Distributor, from the Scudder Funds guide *Leaving Your Job: Keep Your Retirement Plan Money Working For You.*

Tax-Deferred Vehicles

It's almost like being at one of those new, huge, multi-manufacturer "auto-marts." Everywhere you look, there's a different model—everything from Cadillacs to Subarus. And the extras and options! You need a laptop to keep track.

Well, maybe we're exaggerating just a little. But you get the idea. There *are* a good number of tax-deferred retirement plans available in this country. To tell the truth, however, most people's choices are limited by their employment, just as most people's car purchases are limited by their incomes.

It's the "other stuff"—the extras, specifications, warranties, and so on—that are mind-boggling.

OK, stop the metaphor! *What* are we talking about? In two words: *government regulations.* There are so many EITHER/ORs, Ifs, If AND WHENs, and other contingencies in pension law that making choices, whenever there are choices, can be very difficult. And yet the government requires compliance and doesn't accept "I honestly didn't know" as an excuse.

So we're going to introduce you to the most common tax-deferred vehicles. When you finish this section, you'll know them by name, but certainly not intimately. To accomplish that, you'll need a good financial advisor. Come to think of it, even with an advisor you probably won't want to get *intimate*. Just knowing what to do when will be quite good enough, thanks. So here they are:

➤ **IRAs (individual retirement accounts):** If you earn money in a given year, you can contribute up to $2,000 to an IRA. A married couple, both working, can have two IRAs, each for up to $2,000. A married couple with only one spouse working can contribute up to $2,250. Withdrawals before age 59 1/2 are subject to federal income taxes plus an additional 10 percent penalty tax. There also are income and employment pension plan limits for tax deductibility of the contribution. Once you have an IRA, there are some limitations on your choice of investment vehicles, but a wide choice still remains, including mutual funds. For more information, call the IRS at (800) 829-3676 and ask for publication number 590 titled, you guessed it, *IRAs*.

➤ **401(k) plans:** The name comes from the tax code number that describes it. These are defined contribution pension plans for companies in business to make a profit. The plan allows you to save up to $9,000 a year or 20 percent of your salary, whichever is lower. The amount you contribute to your plan is not counted in computing federal or state income taxes. Some employers match your contribution or a portion of it. For more information on the administration of these plans, you should talk with your company benefits representative.

➤ **403(b) plans:** These are similar to 401(k)s, except that they apply to not-for-profit companies. There are some slight differences in income limitations and investment opportunities, however. So, of course, you should talk with your employee benefits representative.

➤ **SEP-IRAs (simplified employee pension—individual retirement account):** These are the government's answer to complaints from self-employed individuals and owners of small businesses about not having government support for pensioning. The self-employed individual or employee sets up his or her own IRA and the employer may or may not contribute to it. The rules are the same as for regular IRAs, except for contribution limits. In a SEP-IRA, the contribution limit is currently 15 percent of the first $150,000 of earned income or $30,000, whichever is less.

OOOOH...

Power Word
Keogh is not really a word, it's a name. These pensions plans were named after U.S. Representative Eugene James Keogh, who first suggested them in the House. Keogh is pronounced *key-oh*.

➤ **Keogh plans:** Since 1962, self-employed individuals, whether full-timers or moon-lighters with another job in someone else's company, have been able to sock away retirement savings with tax-deductible and tax-deferred dollars. Individuals who start small businesses also can set up a Keogh plan for their employees. Both defined benefit plans and defined contribution plans are available. Yes, it's much more complex than the SEP-IRAs. Company owners and high earners, however, can get some extra benefits. Withdrawal requirements and penalties are the same as for IRAs. Contribution limits in 1995 were 25 percent of the first $150,000 or $30,000, whichever is less. You'll need legal and tax help to set up one of these.

Thin Ice
Although investing money that is already in a tax-deferred retirement account in annuities, cash-value life insurance, or tax-free bonds is allowed, it's not a good idea. Because these investment vehicles already are tax-free or tax-deferred, they are better held outside the retirement account. Invest your retirement account money in vehicles with the potential for better returns.

➤ **Annuities:** Whether through your employment or on your own, you can put as much money as you want each year into an annuity. That's right, no limits and the money grows without taxation. But the amount you deposit is *not* deducted from your reported earnings. Annuities are purchased through insurance companies. They are considered a safe haven for future-oriented savings but with limited returns. More about them in Chapter 17, "Protection for Your Possessions."

Some of the larger fund managers like Dreyfus and Fidelity are working with insurance companies to offer *variable* annuities. A variable annuity puts your principal into the stock market, and therefore its return is responsive to the economy and the performance of the selected portfolio. It is just as risk oriented as any other mutual fund or stock purchase. Tax-deferred is its big advantage.

You Can't Save Forever

You say your great grandfather lived to 101 and your great grandmother, now 102, is the leader of the walking group at the Alpine Air Retirement Community? So you figure you'll just keep working until about 85 or so and just keep stashing money away in your tax-deferred retirement account.

Sorry! Your friendly IRS says, "No way!" You must begin making regular withdrawals from your retirement account by April 1 of the year after you reach 70 1/2. The amount you must withdraw is based on the estimated life expectancy of someone your age.

But there are some loopholes here. You also can base your minimum required distribution on the combined life expectancy of you and a beneficiary. If the beneficiary is your spouse, you use your actual ages. However, if the beneficiary is someone other than your spouse (a child or grandchild, for example), the age difference between you and your beneficiary cannot exceed 10 years for calculating purposes.

Take a look at the IRS table for life expectancy. To estimate how much you must begin withdrawing at age 70 1/2, find the age of your beneficiary across the top, and then find your age on the left. The point where the two columns meet is the remaining years of your joint life expectancy. Now find out exactly how much you have in your IRA or other tax-deferred pension account and divide that balance by the life expectancy figure you came up with.

> **Thin Ice**
> It's a good idea to check with a tax advisor before you actually start withdrawing money at age 70 1/2. If the IRS thinks you have not withdrawn enough money, it will impose a horrendous tax penalty. The IRS will take 50 percent of the difference between what you withdrew and what they think you should have withdrawn.

You can withdraw the amount you came up with in equal annual payments until the money runs out, or you can recalculate each year. Recalculating will lower the required withdrawal amount, because each year that you live, you extend your life expectancy. Upon your death, your beneficiary can take all the cash immediately, continue withdrawing it at your rate, or withdraw it at a new rate based on his or her life expectancy.

Estimating Life Expectancy for IRA-Required Payouts After Age 70 1/2

Your age	Age of Beneficiary	60	61	62	63	64	65	66	67	68	69	70	71	72	73	74	75
70	16.0	26.2	25.6	24.9	24.3	23.7	23.1	22.5	22.0	21.5	21.1	20.6	20.2	19.8	19.4	19.1	18.8
71	15.3	26.0	25.3	24.7	24.0	23.4	22.8	22.2	21.7	21.2	20.7	20.2	19.8	19.4	19.0	18.6	18.3
72	14.6	25.8	25.1	24.4	23.8	23.1	22.5	21.9	21.3	20.8	20.3	19.8	19.4	18.9	18.5	18.2	17.8
73	13.9	25.6	24.9	24.2	23.5	22.9	22.2	21.6	21.0	20.5	20.0	19.4	19.0	18.5	18.1	17.7	17.3
74	13.2	25.5	24.7	24.0	23.3	22.7	22.0	21.4	20.8	20.2	19.6	19.1	18.6	18.2	17.7	17.3	16.9
75	12.5	25.3	24.6	23.8	23.1	22.4	21.8	21.1	20.5	19.9	19.3	18.8	18.3	17.8	17.3	16.9	16.5
76	11.9	25.2	24.4	23.7	23.0	22.3	21.6	20.9	20.3	19.7	19.1	18.5	18.0	17.5	17.0	16.5	16.1
77	11.2	25.1	24.3	23.6	22.8	22.1	21.4	20.7	20.1	19.4	18.8	18.3	17.7	17.2	16.7	16.2	15.8
78	10.6	25.0	24.2	23.4	22.7	21.9	21.2	20.5	19.9	19.2	18.6	18.0	17.5	16.9	16.4	15.9	15.4
79	10.0	24.9	24.1	23.3	22.6	21.8	21.1	20.4	19.7	19.0	18.4	17.8	17.2	16.7	16.1	15.6	15.1
80	9.5	24.8	24.0	23.2	22.4	21.7	21.0	20.2	19.5	18.9	18.2	17.6	17.0	16.4	15.9	15.4	14.9
81	8.9	24.7	23.9	23.1	22.3	21.6	20.8	20.1	19.4	18.7	18.1	17.4	16.8	16.2	15.7	15.1	14.6
82	8.4	24.6	23.8	23.0	22.3	21.5	20.7	20.0	19.3	18.6	17.9	17.3	16.6	16.0	15.5	14.9	14.4
83	7.9	24.6	23.8	23.0	22.2	21.4	20.6	19.9	19.2	18.5	17.8	17.1	16.5	15.9	15.3	14.7	14.2
84	7.4	24.5	23.7	22.9	22.1	21.3	20.5	19.8	19.1	18.4	17.7	17.0	16.3	15.7	15.1	14.5	14.0
85	6.9	24.5	23.7	22.8	22.0	21.3	20.5	19.7	19.0	18.3	17.6	16.9	16.2	15.6	15.0	14.4	13.8

Source: IRS Publication 930; Publication 575

The IRS table for life expectancy.

Withdrawing Money from Your Pension Plan

As we've already said, withdrawing money from your tax-deferred pension plan before age 59 1/2 usually means a 20 percent tax withholding and a 10 percent tax penalty. There are, however, some exceptions to this penalty rule:

1. You could die. Then your beneficiary or estate will get the distribution without penalty.

2. You could become permanently disabled. Then you could tap the fund without penalty.

3. You could choose to have the amount that is to be distributed paid to you in equal annual installments based on the life expectancy for the age at which you begin withdrawals.

It's Been Said
My problem lies in reconciling my gross habits with my net income.
—Errol Flynn, actor, 1909-1959

If you don't opt for one of these three choices but you still want or need to get your hands on some of that money, you can withdraw and pay the penalties or sometimes you can borrow against your accumulated assets. Most 401(k) and 403(b) plans allow you to borrow up to 50 percent of your account balance or $50,000 (whichever is less). Usually, you have five years to repay the loan and the payments are made through payroll deduction. Your company usually charges you an interest rate a little better than you would get in the open market.

Pension Plan Survivorship Options

Some company pension plans offer married employees the opportunity to arrange for continuation of pension payments to their spouses if the employee pre-deceases. Plans range from 100 percent of the employee's scheduled payment until the death of the spouse down to 50 percent. In most cases, choosing this joint and survivor annuity reduces the amount of pension payment from what the employee would have received without the survivorship option. Ten percent is a common reduction.

Before making the decision to opt for joint and survivor annuity, you should consider your financial position, the income needs of the single spouse, his or her emotional need for the security of a pension, and the "cost" in terms of the reduced annual payment. There are arguments pro and con. We'll talk about term life insurance as an alternative in Chapter 17.

Early Retirement—Voluntary and Otherwise

The '90s have been the age of "the offer." Corporate downsizing and *outsourcing* (using consultants and specialty firms to do specific jobs once done in-house) have stimulated the "easing out" of older and usually higher paid employees. Some have gotten the *golden parachute*, a severance package rich enough to guarantee a soft landing into retirement. Others have complained that their severance made them feel as though they had been thrown out of a moving truck.

The severance packages of companies differ. And even within the same company, not everyone gets exactly the same deal. Negotiating can sweeten the pot. Get as much as you can.

If you feel that you have been forced out of your job solely because of your age, or if you feel that the company's retirement incentives discriminated against older workers, you may have cause for legal action. Ask your attorney about the federal Age Discrimination in Employment Act (ADEA) and the Older Workers Benefit Protection Act (OWBPA). If you feel that you were discriminated against as an individual, you can file a complaint with the Equal Employment Opportunity Commission. We'll give you more details in Chapter 15, "Work—It Can Be Fun."

Before you leave your company, be sure you know what your vested pension benefits are. If your pension allowance is to be distributed to you in a lump sum, be sure you roll it over directly into an IRA without ever receiving the check in your name, or you will be subject to federal and possibly state income taxes.

Then decide whether you want to try to go back into the employed work force, start a business of your own, or revel in your retirement.

The Least You Need to Know

> ➤ Your employer is required by federal law to give you a written summary of your pension benefits.

> ➤ When a pension plan includes the offer of matching funds from your employer, take as much as you can qualify for.

> ➤ Tax-deferred retirement plans are one of the best tax shelters available in America today.

> ➤ The most common tax-deferred pension vehicles are IRAs, 401(k)s, 403(b)s, SEP-IRAs, and Keoghs.

➤ You are required to begin taking distribution of your tax-deferred pension savings at age 70 1/2.

➤ Money withdrawn before age 59 1/2 is taxed and penalized; however, the fund sometimes can be borrowed against.

➤ If you are forced to retire early, you may have legal recourse in federal court.

Chapter 14

What You Can Expect from Social Security—Maybe

In This Chapter

➤ How to find out what you'll be getting

➤ The benefits of early benefits

➤ Incentives to start collecting a little later

➤ When Social Security is like an insurance policy

Ah, the age of Social Security! That golden time when (after paying in every week of your working life) you can expect the government to start paying you. But will it work? What do you deserve? What can you really expect?

The thoughts of all Americans facing retirement were probably most vividly collected by Jesse Jackson when he cried, "I cast my bread on the waters long ago. Now it's time for you to send it back to me—toasted and buttered on both sides."

And no one wants that toast burned! So let's take a look at Social Security from *your* point of view.

Oh What Will My Benefit Be?

Although their booklets do include some ballpark estimates of your benefits according to your age and current income, the Social Security Administration doesn't publish any handy tables that will tell you exactly what you'd get if you made *x* number of dollars at a certain age. That's because each person's benefits are calculated individually, according to the amount of income earned and the number of years worked. In other words, your contributions (taxes paid) are a major factor in determining your benefits.

Thin Ice

Check on your standing with Social Security, *often*. For tax purposes, employers are required to keep earnings records for only four years. If your income is not reported or recorded, or if it is reported but recorded incorrectly, and the adjustment period has passed, you won't be able to correct the effects of the error on your benefits. The Social Security Administration will go back only three years to make changes regarding employment income.

But like pensions, Social Security benefits are not limitless. To put some perspective on your pie in the sky, the maximum amount that can be paid to a person aged 65 in 1995 is $1,199 a month or $14,388 a year. This figure is adjusted every year, however, so don't count it as a hard number if you're figuring for the future.

The best way to find out where you stand with Social Security is to ask them. As we mentioned in Chapter 4, you can call them at (800) 772-1213 to request a benefits estimate. They will send you, free, a computer printout that will give you a year-to-year breakdown of your earnings, the amount of Social Security taxes you have paid, and the current-dollar estimate of the retirement benefits you will receive.

Why Not Start Collecting Early?

Right now, 65 is the age at which a person can start receiving full benefits, but as we all know, that age point will be raised gradually. (There's a table in Chapter 2 if you want to check again when you'll be eligible.) For those who just can't wait, however, it's possible to start receiving benefits as early as age 62. Naturally, the benefit is a bit reduced. Take a look at Table 14.1 to get a feel for the effects of the reduction.

It's Been Said

He who is of calm and happy nature will hardly feel the pressure of age.

—Plato in *The Republic*

Should you consider the earlier and reduced pension? That depends on a lot of things: your health, your lifestyle, your desire to stop or continue working, your financial security, and the health and age of your spouse and other dependents.

Many analysts recommend the earlier benefits for those who can afford it. They point out that it will take between 12 and 20 years before the early-start retiree and the full-benefits retiree get even. Which means that if you wait until you're 65, you will be at least 77 before you catch up in the funds-collected category with a person exactly like you who started collecting at 62.

Table 14.1 How Early Retirement Reduces Benefits for Retired Workers Born Before 1938

Retirement Age	Reduction in Benefits	Benefit If Full Benefit Is		
		$600	$850	$1,100
65	0%	$600	$850	$1,100
64.5	3.33%	$580	$822	$1,063
64	6.66%	$560	$793	$1,027
63.5	10%	$540	$765	$990
63	13.33%	$520	$737	$953
62.5	16.66%	$500	$708	$917
62	20%	$480	$680	$880

Source: Social Security Administration

Rewards for the Late Collector

But who knows what the future holds. Maybe in your sixties, you'll be full of vim and vigor with no desire to stop fighting dragons. Or maybe you'll be calm and perfectly happy in your work as a florist, or a chef, or a writer for that matter, with no longing for the golf course or the TV couch-and-chips drop-out. So you'll want to keep right on working full time until you're 70 or maybe 80. "Who needs Social Security!" you say.

"Great!" says our government. "We'll reward you."

For every year you don't claim your Social Security benefits between the ages of 65 and 70, those benefits are increased. Check out Table 14.2 for an idea of increases for those approaching retirement in the fairly near future. If you don't find your birth year in the list, be patient. These figures are always being revised. When you get into your fifties, just ask the Social Security Administration. They'll be happy to supply you with new percentages. And right now, the computer printout of your individual benefits estimate that we mentioned earlier will include a figure for retirement at 62, at 65, and at 67. With this estimated projection, you can get a sense of the increase.

Table 14.2   Annual Increases in Benefits for Delaying Retirement Past Normal Retirement Age Up to Age 70

Year of Birth	Annual Percentage Increase
1917-24	3.0%
1925-26	3.5%
1927-28	4.0%
1929-30	4.5%
1931-32	5.0%
1933-34	5.5%
1935-36	6.0%
1937-38	6.5%
1939-40	7.0%
1941-42	7.5%
1943	8.0%

Source: Social Security Administration

Why Not Collect Benefits, Work Full Time, and Stash Away the Loot?

No, you can't have your cake and eat it too. At least not until you reach age 70. Uncle Sam has limits on how much younger retirees can earn and still qualify for full benefits. In 1995, those who are under 65 can earn $8,160 a year without reduction of their scheduled annual benefits. Those who are 65 to 69 can earn $11,280. Once you hit 70, however, you can earn as much as you like and still collect full scheduled Social Security benefits.

"Whoa!" you say. "Isn't there a freedom to work, or something like that? How can the government set limits on how much I can earn at a certain age?"

They do it by withholding the benefits. For people under 65, $1 will be withheld for every $2 earned above the stated maximum. For people 65 to 69, $1 will be withheld for every $3 earned over the maximum. In any given year that you think you will earn more than the limits, you are required to give the Social Security Administration an estimate of what you think your earnings will be.

The Special Monthly Rule

For one year, usually the first year of retirement when things are often unstable at best, the Social Security Administration will allow you to collect benefits for any month you are retired and meet income limits regardless of your annual earnings. In other words, there's a monthly, not an annual, limit. So you could collect for lean months in January and February even though you make five times the limit in March, April, and May. But be careful because the Social Security Administration counts your wages in the month you *earn* the money, not the month you are paid.

In 1995, the limits are $680 in a month if you're under 65, and $940 in a month if you're 65 through 69. There are also rules and limitations for the self-employed. When you're ready for the exact figures for your retirement, call Social Security at (800) 772-1213.

> **Thin Ice**
> If you earn above the limit and also receive some Social Security benefits in any given year, you *must* report your earnings to the Social Security Administration by April 15. This report is in addition to your federal income tax return. And there *is* a penalty for not filing the annual report on time!

What Are Wages?

Our government is very specific about what it considers "wages" that count toward your limit. They count total yearly earnings, including all wages and self-employment income. Wages include bonuses, commissions, fees, vacation pay or pay in lieu of vacation, cash tips of $20 or more a month, severance pay, and certain noncash compensation such as meals or living quarters. They count gross wages, not take-home pay. And they even count wages from a job where you don't pay Social Security taxes.

Some Income Doesn't Count

There is a silver lining, however. The following types of income do *not* count toward the earnings limit:

➤ Investment income (unless you are a securities dealer)

➤ Interest

➤ Social Security benefits, Veterans benefits, or other government benefits

➤ Annuities

➤ Capital gains

➤ Gifts or inheritances

➤ Rental income (unless you are a real estate dealer or you rent a farm to someone and take an active role in the production or the management of production of farm commodities)

➤ Income from trust funds

➤ Sick pay after the sixth full month you last worked or were paid after your employment ended

➤ Moving expenses

➤ Travel expenses

➤ Jury duty pay

Lurking Taxes

Yes, there's still more. Even after you reach age 70, you still might feel a tax bite that affects your Social Security income. High income individuals and couples are subject to taxes on a portion of their benefits—sometimes as much as 85 percent. If you're among this "lucky" group, you should certainly have a financial advisor and a tax accountant.

Surviving Spouse Benefits

This is where Social Security is almost like an insurance policy. The standard benefit of the surviving spouse of a retired worker is 100 percent of the deceased spouse's benefit. But in order to receive full benefits, you must wait until you (the surviving spouse) reach age 65. If you don't want to wait that long, you can start collecting as early as age 60. Be aware, however, that at age 60, you only get 71.5 percent of the deceased spouse's benefit.

You also should bear in mind that you *cannot* collect both surviving spouse benefits and your own individual benefits. If your individual benefits, based on your work history and contributions, are scheduled to be greater than the survivor's benefits you would receive, you should apply for benefit payments in your own name.

If surviving spouse benefits are greater than your own, you can collect them even if you are a divorced spouse. Your marriage to the deceased person had to have lasted at least 10 years and you cannot be married to anyone else at the time you start collecting benefits. If there was an intervening marriage that has since ended, however, you still might qualify. Check with the Social Security Administration 800 number or a local office.

In addition to surviving spouse benefits, there is a small death benefit payable to help defray the cost of funeral expenses. In 1995, it is $255 and can be paid to the surviving spouse or to a child. You must apply for it by phone or in person at a Social Security office.

> **Gray Matter Alert**
> If you are widowed and have begun collecting surviving spouse benefits, you need not fret about a new love in your life. You will not lose your benefits if you remarry.

Disability Benefits

So you think income tax, tax-deferred retirement accounts, and Social Security rules and regulations are as nerve-racking as a 1,500-piece jigsaw puzzle picturing a spider web? Just wait until you try to sort out disability benefits. Even the Social Security Administration writes:

> Because disability is one of the most complicated of all Social Security programs, we recommend that you call or visit Social Security to ask for a free copy of the booklet *Disability* (Publication No. 05-10029).

Having warned you about the paperwork, we'll just add that disability benefits can provide life-sustaining income to a family faced with medical catastrophe. The disabled person may not be the only one eligible to collect benefits. Under certain conditions, the spouse and children of the qualified benefit recipient can qualify for benefits of their own. Also, if a person is disabled, he or she can qualify for surviving spouse benefits as young as age 50.

> OOOOH...
>
> **Power Word**
> **Disability** has a very specific definition in the Social Security Administration. It means a physical or mental impairment that is expected to keep you from doing any substantial work for at least one year. (If you can earn $500 in a month, that is considered "substantial" work.) A condition that is expected to result in your death also is considered a disability.

Extra! Extra!

If you must dispute a claim with the Social Security Administration and hire an attorney to represent you, be aware that the attorney cannot charge you according to whatever going rate the market will bear. The fee must be approved as reasonable by the Social Security Administration or by the court. If your attorney asks for an up-front fee or a retainer, federal law requires that the attorney keep the fee in an escrow account, pending the approval of the fee that will be charged. If the case involves the collection of past-due benefits, the approved fee usually will be 25 percent of the amount collected on your behalf.

What If the Program Is Restructured?

Well, there *will* be cuts and restructuring. It already has begun, as we've mentioned in earlier chapters. And everyone in the government is nervous about it. Senator Bill Bradley (D-NJ), when as Chairman of the Senate Finance Subcommittee on Deficits, Debt Management, and Long-Term Economic Growth, responded to the question *What happens if we don't confront the retirement crisis?* in a *Money* magazine cover feature on retirement (October 1994). He replied, "We're going to wake up one day and see that the S&L crisis was small by comparison."

Bradley went on to say, "We must boost our national savings or settle for a poorer future."

What Senator Bradley sees as necessary for the nation also is necessary for each individual. We must think in terms of saving and investing for our old and very old age. It is very unlikely that Social Security will disappear, although its benefits might be reduced for the wealthy. But we must all remember that it is a program designed to supplement income, not to make retirement a carefree picnic.

The carefree picnic part is the responsibility of each of us, individually.

The Least You Need to Know

➤ You can get a record of your Social Security taxes paid and a current-dollar estimate of your future benefits by calling the Social Security number: (800) 772-1213.

➤ You can start collecting a reduced benefit at age 62.

➤ Your future benefits increase for each year between age 65 and 70 that you do not file for Social Security benefits. There are no increases after age 70.

➤ Between ages 62 and 69, there are limits on how much you can earn without decreasing your Social Security benefit payments. There are no limits after age 70.

➤ Benefit payments are available for surviving spouses of qualified workers and for people who are disabled.

Chapter 15

Work—It Can Be Fun

In This Chapter

➤ Some famous words on working

➤ What to do if someone says you're too old

➤ Retiring and getting re-hired

➤ Part-time and partnership opportunities

➤ Why *not* open a bed 'n breakfast or little business

➤ Getting educated for new horizons

Retirees get money without working! They used to call it "mailbox" income, all those checks from the pension, the investments, Social Security, the annuity, even the coupon refunds. But for many people, only the coupon refunds come in the mail nowadays. Real cash seems to travel electronically. Think what it will be like in the 21st century!

"Gosh, it will all be invisible," you say. "There will be nothing to hold on to."

Fear not! Even if the mail becomes an advertising medium and the concept of "check" disappears, we'll still have the good old tradition of getting paid for work. And even if that money spirits in electronically, its spending power will still be real. *Wages!* Quaint word. But we bet they'll still call it that. And you will get the *stub* in the mail.

Some of us will need wages from working for the comfort and security we want in our retirement, at least while we're still young elders. Others, with plenty of other mailbox income, will still go out each morning to earn wages, because... Well, let's talk about it.

Why Work?

Many people, rich and poor, educated-to-the-nines and simple, famous and infamous, have voiced answers to that question. When asked why she started writing her now famous humor column, Erma Bombeck replied, "I was too old for a paper route, too young for Social Security, and too tired for an affair." (Reported in *Time*, July 2, 1984.) The British economist John Mayard Keynes expressed our entrepreneurial stirrings in a more metaphorical voice in his *A Treatise on Money*, where he wrote, "The engine which drives Enterprise is not Thrift but Profit."

As their retirement dates approach, many people are working at peak performance, and feeling fine physically too. So quite naturally they think, "Why not take in a little more money?"

Whether you work for an employer or start a business, whether you choose to live better today or stash it away for the future, more money is probably the chief motivator. Ava Gardner probably said it all when she was asked why she came out of retirement to appear in a prime-time soap opera. "For the loot, honey, for the loot." (Reported in *People*, June 10, 1985.)

But there are more rewards than just more money. Some retirees choose to work for the mental stimulation. Harold Geneen, former Chairman of IT&T, said "I'd hate to spend the rest of my life trying to outwit an 18-inch fish." (Reported in the *New York Times*, November 18, 1984.)

It's Been Said
Work banishes those three great evils, boredom, vice, and poverty.

—Voltaire

Working continues the socialization you have been accustomed to throughout your life. You have a reason to get up at a certain time, to dress well, and to go somewhere. Usually, you work with a mixed-age group so you don't get wrapped up in the concerns of your generation alone. And there's always those juicy bits of conversation around the water cooler. In a word, work keeps you *young!*

Age Discrimination

"Hold on," you say. "That's a nice rosy picture, all those quotes and all. But let's get real. Not everybody that wants to work, can work. Some of us get either kicked out or squeezed out of our jobs. Some of us can't get jobs. Haven't you heard that nobody wants to hire managers in their fifties, not to mention manufacturing and construction workers or regional sales reps?"

Yes, we've heard, and the problem is very real. There are state and federal laws against age discrimination, but the negative perception of older people working less well is actually a cultural thing. It's based on attitudes, and attitudes take longer to change than actions. So even if you're a youngish adult when reading this book, you'll probably have to fight age discrimination one day even if you've fought against it for years. When your children are aging, that might not be the case. Meanwhile, let's look at what you can do:

Thin Ice

If you want to file an age discrimination grievance, you must file with the Equal Employment Opportunity Commission within 180 days. This is a strict deadline. You can contact EEOC by calling the nearest office listed in your phone book or their Washington headquarters at (202) 663-4264. Word is, though, that people who show up at the local office *in person* do better.

➤ **You can file a charge with EEOC.** You will be asked to give names, addresses, dates, and your version of events. The EEOC will investigate and attempt a conciliation before resorting to a case in court.

➤ **You can file a complaint with EEOC.** If you choose a *complaint* rather than a *charge*, you can ask that your name be withheld. It will be revealed to your employer only if you sign a release or by court order.

➤ **You can tip off the EEOC.** The EEOC has the power to investigate cases of discrimination even when no one has signed a formal complaint or charge.

➤ **You can file suit against your employer in federal court.** You must do this within 60 days of the date you file the charge with EEOC. Be sure you have an attorney.

➤ **You can file a claim with your state.** Most state laws also forbid age discrimination. If you choose to file in your state, the matter usually will be handled out of court through administrative hearings. This route almost always is less expensive than going to court.

Independent Contractor—Your Old Company or a New One

They call it *double dipping*—when you begin collecting your pension but go back to work full time doing the same job at the same company, but as an independent contractor. There are no set rules for pay; each person negotiates his or her own deal. Most often, however, an employee's salary, minus the value of benefits such as medical insurance, is transposed into an hourly wage. There are no paid vacation days, no sick days, no medical or other insurance, and of course, no retirement plan.

Be aware, however, that some companies do allow retirees to continue on their health insurance plans, sometimes without cost, and sometimes at a reduced premium. These lucky people have the cushion of their old company benefits while working as a "new person" without benefits in the same company. The financial gain is significant, and many retirees choose being an independent contractor as a good way to phase into retirement.

OOOOH...

Power Word
Outsourcing is a brand-new American word. First used in print in 1982, it means the practice of subcontracting work to outside companies or contractors. A company that is outsourcing is fertile ground for growing your independent contractor business.

If your old company has released you in a downsizing move, there might not be opportunities for continued work with them, at least not beyond a brief interval of a few months. You then might want to approach other companies in the same field because outsourcing is a growing corporate trend. Like every other business venture, however, you must expect to spend 50 to 70 percent of your time in the early months marketing your skills. Networking with people you knew in your old job is one of the best ways to establish contacts in your new role.

And finally, don't forget that you now are self-employed. You can open a SEP-IRA or a Keogh and shelter a good deal of your extra income.

Not All of the Time, Just Part of the Time

According the U.S. Census Bureau, of the more than 31 million Americans who work part time, approximately 4 million are age 55 or older. Are you surprised? Why are so many older Americans working at small jobs?

It's a combination of economics and convenience. Even though the wages for part-time work are usually relatively low, they do supply the pocket money needed for the joy of impulse spending (without guilt). Part-time employees have both time and money for hobbies, travel, and special interests without cutting into their long-term savings.

So where are the part-time jobs? Only a small percentage are advertised. Most successful part-time employees find their jobs through temporary employment agencies, networking, or by approaching an employer with a suggestion for improvement in the business and a resume of their skills. The easiest jobs to get are in commission-based careers such as finance, insurance, and real estate. For less technical work, try retail trade establishments and service industries. The illustration that follows shows a regional comparison of job availability and its growth or loss in the past 12 months.

Gray Matter Alert
If both husband and wife are collecting Social Security, each spouse can earn the maximum allowed without affecting benefits. A retired couple aged 63 and 66 in 1995 can earn $8,160 and $11,280, respectively, before losing any of their Social Security income.

Studies show that young adults (college students) and people over 55 hold a much larger proportion of part-time jobs than any other age group. If working part time is an important part of your retirement plan, you might want to choose your retirement town with that in mind. Which means you might want to avoid college and university towns like Chapel Hill, NC and Flagstaff, AZ where you would be pitting your wisdom and maturity against the boundless energy of all those whiz-kids for what part-time work there is.

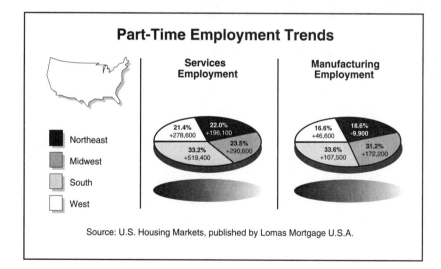

Part-Time Employment Trends

Northeast
Midwest
South
West

Services Employment
21.4% +278,600
22.0% +196,100
33.2% +519,400
23.5% +290,600

Manufacturing Employment
16.6% +46,600
18.6% -9,900
33.6% +107,500
31.2% +172,200

Source: U.S. Housing Markets, published by Lomas Mortgage U.S.A.

These charts show the regional shares in each part-time employment category as of March 1995, and the number of jobs gained or lost by each region in each category during the previous 12 months.

Partnerships—The Art of Splitting Responsibility

When most people hear the word *partnership*, they think of a business or a professional association. And, of course, you could start a business with a partner, contributing equally to start-up costs, covering for each other on vacations and time off, and dividing management and record-keeping tasks.

In another interpretation of partnership, some enterprising young retirees are joining together as a partnership to fill one full-time job. Employers like the deal because neither retiree is a "full-time" employee and, therefore, neither is entitled to expensive benefits packages. Meanwhile, the company has two people who know the work. What an efficient and inexpensive backup system!

The retirees, on the other hand, have extra income at a good hourly rate, someone to share responsibility with and count on if there's a problem or an emergency, and plenty of time to enjoy the leisure activities they've been anticipating in retirement. These part-time partnerships are usually at a professional level (dental hygiene, real estate, or paralegal services, for example), and finding another person with the necessary skills and credentials may take some time. Once you do so, however, you should job-hunt as a team.

Can You Imagine? They Started a Bed 'n Breakfast!

Finding a large, rambling, old (and preferably run-down) house in a desirable location and transforming it into a thriving and fantastically profitable B 'n B is one of the most common retirement fantasies of people in their forties and fifties. Before you start imagining yourself in a flowered apron holding a platter of warm blueberry muffins, there are some important points to consider:

➤ **Your investment:** Most houses large enough to generate significant income and located in desirable areas are not cheap. The most important factor in profitability is location. While other buyers might be put off by needed repairs, few will fail to recognize the value of location. Starting this business can mean a significant cash investment. And remember, a large house with extra bathrooms for "guests" is definitely a non-liquid asset.

➤ **You and local laws:** Will the community's zoning laws allow you to open your B 'n B? You should find out even before you make an offer on a property. And what about food? Are the breakfasts you can serve limited because you can't be considered a restaurant? Will you be subject to community Health Department inspections? And will you have enough parking space to keep your guests off the street?

➤ **Your start-up costs:** You can't give your guests your kids' old *Star Wars* towels with the frayed edges. You'll need big, fluffy (and clean) towels, excellent-condition sheets and pillowcases, pillows in various degrees of firmness and non-allergic qualities, good mattresses, and breakfast ware (including coffee pots) for each group of guests. You'll also have to get remodeling estimates for the house and, of course, your maintenance of the place will be beyond question. And don't forget the extra insurance you'll need.

Gray Matter Alert
For more information on franchises and a catalog of books and pamphlets, contact the International Franchise Association at 1350 New York Ave. N.W., Suite 900, Washington, DC 20005, (202) 628-8000.

➤ **You in your home:** The personalities and lifestyles of the people who own and live in a bed and breakfast can make or break the enterprise. Some people genuinely love meeting guests from all over the country, sometimes all over the world, and thrive on innkeepership. Others resent the invasion of privacy and the demands of serving, caring for, and catering to guests. Marketing your business and keeping records also make demands on personal time.

How About That Little Business?

The statistics are grim indeed. Somewhere between one-third and one-half of the more than 200,000 new businesses that are started each year fail before the end of their first year. At the five-year point, only one in five is still in business.

Why? Most experts believe the answers are lack of research and lack of funding. People start up without knowing the competition, without market research, without an accurate estimate of operating expenses, and sometimes without adequate training in the field. Many businesses also are started on the proverbial shoestring and can't survive the start-up marketing costs and the waiting time needed to develop a clientele.

Gray Matter Alert
When considering a new business, get in touch with SCORE—the Service Corps of Retired Executives. Your local library will have a list of members in your area. These knowledgeable people will help you, free of charge, to estimate costs and time commitments and point out areas of concern.

The franchises (there are hundreds—think Burger King, Midas Muffler, Century 21) help with establishing the business, training, and name recognition. But most are expensive to buy into and often require a longer commitment than many retirees are willing to make.

Some retirees have gathered in small groups to form partnerships to buy into a franchise. If you consider this move, be certain to get your own lawyer, not just the service provided by the franchiser.

Extra! Extra!

If you start a business that needs a building, you probably should get a mortgage rather than invest a great deal of your retirement savings. You might run into some credit discrimination based on your age, however. The federal Equal Credit Opportunity Act (ECOA) makes this discrimination illegal.

If you do encounter problems, contact the Federal Trade Commission at Sixth Street and Pennsylvania Ave., N.W., Washington, DC 20580, (202) 326-2000. They have several booklets available and can direct you to the area of banking supervision most appropriate to your complaint. Among them are the Comptroller of the Currency, the Federal Reserve System, the FDIC , the Federal Credit Union Administration, and, of course, the Department of Justice.

You also can check with your state Attorney General's office to see whether your state has laws against credit discrimination. But be sure to get your own lawyer. When you do get a mortgage, have it written so that failure of the business and foreclosure on the mortgage cannot affect your personal savings and other assets.

Off We Go Into the... Ah, Another Career?

You say you always wanted to be a pediatrician? And here you are, age 53 and holding a considerable inheritance. Could you? Can you?

Your government says YES! Since 1979, federal law does not allow colleges, universities, and other institutions of higher learning that receive federal aid (and most do) to discriminate in admissions because of age. Medical schools protested, but the Department of Health and Human Services has specifically stated that they will not be allowed to set age limits on admissions.

Naturally, what's good for our doctors is good for the nation. If you want to embark on another career that needs specialized education, go for it. You can even get the same student aid, if you need it, that is available to 19-year-olds. Talk with the school's financial aid officer.

You say you're more interested in vocational training? Well, that's available too. If a program gets any federal aid, there can be no discrimination. You might even be eligible to receive training and work experience in programs financed by the Comprehensive Employment and Training Act (CETA).

A New Meaning to Work

When you were competing for those promotions and watching your backside at the same time, you probably didn't find work much fun. But take away that stress and the financial need also. Now work might look more appealing.

Before his death at age 96, Frederick Hudson Ecker, former Chairman of Metropolitan Life, said "I don't think anybody yet has invented a pastime that's as much fun, or keeps you as young, as a good job." (Reported in the *New York Times*, March 20, 1964.) Maybe he was right.

The Least You Need to Know

➤ Work can be a pleasure, especially when the pressure to compete and perform is off.

➤ Age discrimination is illegal and there's a lot you can do about it.

➤ You can go back into the workforce as an independent contractor or as a part-time employee.

➤ Bed 'n Breakfast innkeeping and all other new business ventures have risks as well as rewards.

➤ College and career program admission cannot be refused because of age.

Part 4
Covering Your Assets

Now that you've read through three parts of this book and are about to jump in with great retirement financial planning, things should be looking pretty rosy for the future, right?

*Well, maybe. But don't stretch out on the couch just yet. If the assets you accumulate during your working years are going to help support you through your retirement years, you've got to **keep** as much of them as possible. And the keeping is not always easy. There are definitely intergalactic-sized vultures out there just waiting to swoop down and grab some of your stash.*

Although we can't provide you with lead-lined safety boxes for your assets, we can give you advice on how to protect them from the usual end-of-the-century threats and even add some tips on how to come out ahead financially. We'll cover getting the most out of your home, laws that protect your holdings and some that threaten them, taxes and tax tips, and finally how to avoid those white-collar thieves and scam artists who try to persuade you to part with your money.

Home! The Biggest Asset for Most People

OK, we know you're tired of those old clichés: *the American dream, the biggest single investment most people will ever make,* and even *it's never too late to feather your nest.* Maybe you're ready for the island condo dream. Maybe you'd like to cash in on the biggest investment you ever made so you can get into another investment or two. Or maybe it's time to stop feathering your nest and let it start feathering you. Whatever your retirement goals, if you're a homeowner, you've got to stop thinking *home* for at least a little while and evaluate the place where you live as a piece of property—one of your assets.

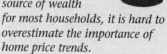

It's Been Said
Because home equity remains the single largest source of wealth for most households, it is hard to overestimate the importance of home price trends.
—Alan Greenspan, Federal Reserve Board Chairman

What You Have in It Depends on What It's Worth

You may be saying to yourself, "Hold on! I put $50,000 down so I have $50,000 or maybe a little more in it!" Or perhaps you're thinking, "Hey, wait a minute! I paid off my mortgage. I know exactly what I have in it!"

Only partly right. You do know what you put in as a down payment and what you paid off, but these numbers are not usually accurate indicators of what you'll get out of the property when you sell it. What it's worth (the market value of your home) is determined by the highest price a ready, willing, and able buyer will pay and the lowest price you, the ready, willing, and able seller will accept. That figure changes with home price trends. It is almost certainly different from the amount you paid for the property.

Gray Matter Alert

Sales comparison is a universally used residential appraisal method. It's also the one method where *you* may be able to influence outcome. Ask your appraiser to discuss with you the nearby, recently sold properties that will be used as comparables. Point out specific facts or features that might have lowered the selling price. Many important items that everyone in the neighborhood knows about never get written into the comparables data sheet!

So is this really the biggest (and best) investment you've ever made? Let's find out. The correct real estate term for *what you have in it* is *equity*. To determine your equity, take the market value, subtract the total amount of outstanding loans on the property, and *voila*! That's it.

Except for one little detail. If market value is the highest price someone will pay and the lowest you'll accept, how can you get a fix on that dollar figure *without putting your home on the market*?

It's easier than you might think. There are two methods that usually work quite well. One will cost you somewhere between $200 and $500 or more. The other is free.

The Appraisal

A professional appraisal is the costly method. If you are determined to get one or if you must (for probate, divorce, or other legal requirements), your first problem is finding a professional appraiser. Some larger real estate firms have appraisal departments or appraisal specialists. You can also find the names of independent real estate appraisers mixed among the art, antique, and jewelry people under *appraisers* in your Yellow Pages.

But if you want someone who knows your area and knows value in residential properties (and this *is* what you want!), ask the bank that services your mortgage loan to give you the names of the appraisers they use in your area. If you should have any trouble getting names from your mortgage holder, stop in at a real estate broker's office near your home and talk with the friendly folks you'll find there. Every day, the sales agents deal with mortgage brokers and lenders who deal with appraisers. They should be able to put you on a good track.

The CMA

Real estate agents will also offer you the free service that may serve your purposes better than an appraisal. It's called a *competitive market analysis*, or sometimes a *comparative market analysis* (but always CMA for short). Real estate brokers will do a CMA free because it provides them with an opportunity to meet with prospective sellers. If you can sit through sales pitches from three different brokers, you'll get an up-to-the-minute comparison of your property with everything like it that has sold in the area during the past year or more, including the actual selling prices and the number of days on the market. You'll also get information on every single property similar to yours that is currently on the market. And you'll get a recommended asking price and a probable selling price.

But wait! You don't want to sell, you just want to calculate your equity. Why bother with *three* CMAs? Why not just one?

You can go with just one if you like. But remember, even though the computer will call up the properties, calculate the ratio of comparisons, and print the data, the CMA is still one agent's *opinion* of market value. If you get three professional opinions in real estate, you can bet you'll get three different opinions. So get three, average them out, and you'll be pretty close.

Get Rid of That Mortgage!

"Pay off your mortgage as soon as you can!" You've read it in newspapers and magazines and you've heard it on radio and television, not to mention your parents' little proddings. It's good advice.

In fact, there are all kinds of numbers to support paying off your mortgage in the least possible time. At 7 percent, you'll pay interest of $61,789 to pay off a $100,000, 15-year loan. If you pay it off in 7.5 years, however, you'll only pay $28,479 in interest—a whopping big savings of $33,310! On the other hand, if you pay off your loan over 30 years, you'll pay $139,511 in interest—more than doubling what you borrowed.

The longer you take to pay off a mortgage, the more it costs.

Mortgages Cost Money

Pay off in: Interest on a $100,000 loan at 7% annual interest

Pay off in:		
7.5 years	$$$$$$$	$28,479
15 years	$$$$$$$$$$$$$$$$	$61,789
30 years	$$	$139,511

Interest: 0 $10,000 $20,000 $30,000 $40,000 $50,000 $60,000 $70,000 $80,000 $90,000 $100,000 $110,000 $120,000 $130,000 $140,000 $150,000 $160,000 $170,000 $180,000

OOOOH...

Power Word
Amortization is the gradual paying off of your mortgage debt over a scheduled period of time. You can ask your lender to give you an amortization schedule so you'll know exactly where you are. You also can get it updated each year if you make extra payments.

If you're committed to a 30-year mortgage, you can still save money by making extra payments toward the principal. Paying just an extra $25 each month can save you more than $25,000 over the life of the loan.

Besides the numbers, there's also that warm fuzzy feeling you get while thinking about a retirement with all your equity at your disposal and no monthly mortgage check to write. And if you pay off the loan well before your retirement date, you can take the amount of the check you would have written to the bank each month and invest it in a stock or bond mutual fund that can help bring in some extra cash after you stop collecting a paycheck.

Or Maybe, Don't Get Rid of That Mortgage

There are some very good reasons why you might *not* want to pay off your mortgage, even if you win your state lottery or get that promotion to CEO that you've been anticipating for years. You're probably thinking that we're going to mention the loss of the home interest tax deduction. We are, and more too.

➤ During the years that you are at maximum income, you should do some serious number crunching to determine the overall tax effects of paying off your mortgage.

If you're at all unsure of your number-crunching abilities, this may be a good time to consult with an accountant or tax attorney.

➤ You should not pay off your mortgage if the value of your home is flat or decreasing. Rather than put your extra cash into a diminishing asset, make your regular mortgage payments and invest your extra money where it will bring a greater return. If the rate of inflation is high, you also may want to continue to make mortgage payments that have been determined in cheaper dollars.

➤ You might pay down, but you should not pay off, your mortgage if you think you might need short-term loans in the near or distant pre-retirement future. Think about college costs, a wedding or two, that boat, or perhaps a stupendous month in Australia. Home equity lines of credit (which are really *second mortgages*) are among the least expensive forms of short-term credit. They are especially easy to get if you have substantial equity; however, they are not available if you do not have a first mortgage on your property.

> **Thin Ice**
> Don't pay off your mortgage thinking that you can get a new one on the same house whenever you want. *Cash out loans* (mortgages that draw cash out of a house that is owned free and clear) are often wrapped in troublesome red tape for youngsters under 62. You'll also have to qualify all over again.

A RAM Could Be Your Cash Cow

Here's a different program to keep in mind today that can help you a few years down the road. The *reverse annuity mortgage* (RAM) is a program for seniors that provides them with added income at a time when they need it most. Although you might see the possibility of a RAM only far in your future, this special mortgaging might just be a help to your parents *right now*. A bonus!

RAMs enable homeowners age 62 or older, without a mortgage or carrying one with a small balance, to draw on the equity in their single-family, principal residence without selling it. That equity can be in the form of a cash lump sum, in monthly install-

> **It's Been Said**
> *Social Security just wasn't enough. This mortgage check helps!*
> —Jeanne Kelly, a Callahan, Florida widow in her seventies

ments, in a line of credit, or in some combination of all these methods. The line of credit is especially popular because it gives homeowners a comfortable "cushion" to meet a financial emergency.

More than comfort—for some retirees, a reverse mortgage can mean the difference between keeping and losing one's home. The loan can be a life saver for the homeowner with few or poorly performing other sources of retirement income. If you will have no pension, for example, you particularly might want to consider this program.

How It Works

If you have a RAM, instead of making a mortgage payment to the lender each month, the lender pays you. And, also unlike conventional home loans, the lender adds interest, closing costs, and any other charges at the end of the loan, so you don't have to pay those charges at the beginning or during the course of the mortgage.

The loan, including all those related charges, is payable when the homeowner sells, moves, or dies. However, interest charges can never run up to an ultimate cost beyond the value of the home.

Heirs can pay off the loan if they want, or they can refinance it into a regular mortgage if they qualify for such a loan.

The lender bases the amount you can borrow on your age, the amount of equity in your home, and the interest rate the lender is charging. There are a variety of reverse mortgage programs from which to choose. The best way to get the broadest selection is to work through a mortgage broker rather than a bank or other conventional lender.

There are no income requirements for a RAM. The money received is not taxable because it is considered proceeds from a loan and not income. It also does not affect Social Security or Medicare benefits.

When you have a RAM, you still own your home and are responsible for paying your real estate taxes and insurance, and for handling repairs. You cannot lose your home with this mortgage unless it is for a reason any other homeowner might—by not paying real estate taxes, for example.

Down Sides?

Yes, there are a few. The RAM loan, like any other, is expensive, often written at a higher interest rate than conventional mortgages in the area. Also, unless you pay off the mortgage, you cannot leave your home free and clear to your heirs. Studies have shown, however, that most adult children prefer that their parents be able to stay in their homes, if that is what they want, and know some financial security.

If you'd like to know more, your local U.S. Department of Housing and Urban Development (HUD) office, listed in the phone book under *U.S. Government* can give you a list of reverse mortgage lenders in your area. Also, the American Association of Retired Persons offers the free booklet *Home-Made Money, a Consumer's Guide to Home Equity Conversion.* Call AARP at (800) 424-3410.

The "Over 55" Tax Exemption

Not all tax news is bad. Sometimes, the IRS wants to *give* you something—and this gift is not a bill or a summons, either.

If you are a married couple, one of you is 55 years or older, and you have lived in your present home for at least three of the preceding five years, you are entitled to a tax break when you sell the home. The first $125,000 of profit on your home will be tax exempt. If you are single, that amount is $62,500. You do not have to buy another home to claim this deduction.

Note that this is the first $125,000 of *profit* that is tax exempt. The check you are handed at the closing is not necessarily what you will be taxed on. You can deduct the money you spent over the years on major improvements to the house. (Save every receipt!) The amount left after those deductions, and any others pointed out by your accountant, is taxable as profit. Here's where you are allowed that $125,000 exemption.

> **Thin Ice**
> Be sure that you take your "over 55" tax exemption at the time you are making the biggest step down in home price. If you take only part of your allowance (say $100,000 out of the $125,000), you're done. You can't go back on your next home sale and claim the $25,000 you missed out on.

Now, the IRS is not known for its generosity and this is a one-time-only gift. If you have taken the exemption, and perhaps marry or remarry years later, you can't take it again, even if your new partner has never claimed that deduction.

When an Empty Nest Drains Your Money

Take a look around your home. You might be able to put *it* to work for you. Empty rooms can bring in extra walking-around money or big bucks.

Consider Tenants

If your children have moved out and you find the house too big and expensive, but you like both it and the neighborhood, think about converting part of that space to a full rental apartment ("full" meaning with a kitchen). Your house can earn from $3,000 to well over $10,000 a year in rent, depending on where you live.

As the owner of a two-family house, you'll enjoy some tax benefits, too. For example, repairs and improvements to that rental unit are tax deductible. Also, the apartment's share of over-all fix-ups and upgrades can be deducted. So, if you spend $5,000 for a new roof, and rent one-third of your house, you can deduct one-third of the cost of that roof against your rental income.

You will need to be certain there is a need for an apartment like yours in your neighborhood or community. Even though you have an ordinary new or older home, you might not do well with this plan if there are several new apartment complexes in the vicinity. Renters are likely to prefer the pools, tennis courts, and other bells and whistles of the newer construction.

However, if there is a scarcity of rental units of any kind where you are, you might be in business no matter how mundane your place. Also, if you live in an old or historic district and can offer an apartment with interesting architectural detail such as mantels, moldings, parquet floors and the like, then you have a viable property in any rental market. Another rental attraction is a waterfront, golf course adjacent, or other view.

Check your local zoning office to be sure you *can* convert your home into a multiple-family dwelling, however. If local laws say no, you can appeal for a variance, which is an exception to some specific point or points in the zoning law. It may or may not be granted by the zoning board of appeals.

A point to consider here: You could be allowed a variance, even in a strictly single-family residence neighborhood, if you want to create a separate apartment for a parent or other close relative. Often called mother/daughter houses or in-law apartments, these dwellings usually revert to single-family status when the parent moves or dies.

Shop around for the best terms in borrowing money for the conversion. A home equity loan, of course, is one option.

Newspaper classified advertisements can give you an idea of the rents that apartments similar to yours are bringing. You can find tenants yourself, or turn the whole business over to a real estate agent, who will usually charge you one month's rent as a commission.

Roomers—Permanent and Occasional

Maybe you can't convert space into an apartment, or maybe you'd prefer renting just an unused room and its own bath, or at least a bath that's close by. Zoning laws for a one-roomer are usually lax, if they exist at all.

Power Words

"Roomer? Heavens above," you cry. "Breakfast and dinner every day... no way." You've got the wrong word. A **roomer** does not take meals at your place. It's a **boarder** you must feed.

The "roomer" solution to the too large, too costly house can work well into retirement, when the local branch of your state's Department on Aging will assist you in finding a roomer, or even a house sharer. Perhaps by then you'll have more than one room you'd like to let.

You can rent to a roomer year round, of course, but you might prefer having the house to yourself at times. Then go with an occasional roomer, such as a college student who will be there only during the school term.

If you can offer a private bath, contact the Human Resources Department of companies within a short drive from your home about renting occasionally to visiting branch office co-workers or other corporate guests. Some of them—women especially—prefer a private home to a motel for safety's sake.

Do you live close to a hospital with its many visitors to patients and offices? Contact that administration office too. Are you near a popular tourist attraction? A seasonal little theater? All offer opportunities for occasionally letting rooms at your place.

Check the classified advertisements under *Rooms for Rent* for an idea of what to charge. Keep in mind what you have to offer that others don't.

Doing Business at Home

If you sell refrigerators for a living, you might skip the next few paragraphs. If you're engaged in any other occupation that requires your presence in a store, plant, office, or similar facility, you also can read ahead.

But if your work at all lends itself to working at home, you can save an appreciable amount of money annually by moving your work into your home.

The self-employed in some specialties are the most likely choices for in-home work, but there's another growing group of home workers: those who tele-commute. They are salaried, but they are permitted to spend all or part of the workday at home, communicating by computer with the office and clients.

The former toilers can save anywhere from $200 to $2,000 or more each month in rent by abandoning office space in town and moving home. Both groups will save on commuting costs, restaurant lunches, and probably the expense of a business wardrobe.

What Will the Neighbors Say?

You don't care, you say? You should. They can be your biggest obstacle to working at home successfully.

Most towns have zoning laws that either allow or prohibit home businesses in some neighborhoods, but often they are directed at the obvious: converting the front of the house to a beauty salon, for example. No local official is going to bother someone who is giving piano lessons, a traditional home business.

It's the folks in your immediate neighborhood who, becoming angry, are likely to call your home business to municipal attention. They might just do that if you:

➤ Alter the exterior of your home, which they feel will compromise property values.

➤ Have too many people coming and going at one time.

➤ Have your customers' cars getting in the way of *their* on-street parking.

➤ Engage in any kind of business that increases the noise level in the neighborhood. A quiet little business with no sign and no more than one client at a time usually causes no distress to the folks on the block.

More Tax Talk

Yes, there are tax advantages to working at home. This is a continually changing area, however. Briefly, the requirements: Your business must have a profit motive to qualify for a home office deduction, your home must also be your primary business location, it must be used to meet clients if that is a part of your trade, and it must be a separate area of your home—not the dining room table.

With a home business, you can deduct a percentage of your utilities, property taxes, and repairs to the house and depreciation of your business area from your taxes. Then there are the regular business deductions you are allowed, such as telephones, office supplies, advertising, and the like.

Gray Matter Alert
Look for a good chair, desk, and computer work station for your home office since you'll be spending a lot of time there. You are entitled to tax deductions for some office furnishings too.

If you are planning to move fairly soon, here's a tax tip. Consider closing down your home office and converting the space back to residential use at least one year before you move. If you sell with the office intact, you may have to pay capital gains tax on the portion of your profit in the home equal to the portion of space occupied by the office.

For more information about home offices and taxes, contact the Small Business Administration office in your area and call the IRS at (800) 829-1040. Both offer lots of printed materials on the subject.

How to Sell—For Maximum Profit With Minimum Pain

OK, it's bottom-line time. You're tired of managing the cash flow from your home; now you just want to get your cash out of it. So you'll sell it, of course. But it's not quite as easy as putting up a stall in your local Saturday flea market.

➤ **Setting the price is the most important part, and you should get professional help.** Just as we suggested in the section "What You Have in It Depends on What It's Worth," get three CMAs from local Realtors. If you want to sell quickly, set your price to compete favorably with your competition. If you want to try for top dollar, set your price on the high side and see how the market responds.

➤ **Should you list it with one of the real estate brokers who did those CMAs?** You could, but you don't have to. You don't owe anything to the nice agent who spent so much time admiring your garden. This is business, and doing CMAs is a part of the real estate business.

➤ **If you have a yen to try a *For Sale By Owner* strategy, give it a go.** Sometimes you'll pick up that ready buyer who hasn't been able to find anything until your house came along. Do remember, however, that most buyers expect FSBO houses to sell at off-market prices. "After all," they think, "the seller is saving all that commission!"

➤ **Do not work at this FSBO stuff more than six weeks.** After that time, you will have exhausted the supply of buyers-on-the-verge and you will benefit immensely from the services of professional real estate agents. Choose one who works full time out of an office that is close to your home and that sells a lot of properties similar to yours in style and price.

> **Gray Matter Alert**
> Intangibles affect value. Make a list of everything you like about your house. Is it close to commuter routes? Do windows catch both sunrise and sunset? Is it within walking distance of a great coffee shop? Discuss the list with your real estate agent. Create a *What We Love About This House* flyer to leave on the table for prospective buyers.

➤ **Dress your home for success.** Exterior painting (if your house needs it) will bring the greatest return on money spent. In fact, if you do the job yourself, most surveys agree that it will increase the value of your home by 10 times the cost of materials. If you only want to do touch-up painting, concentrate on your front doorway area. Every buyer looks up and around that front door while awaiting entry. It's like kicking the tires on a used car.

➤ **Get it scrubbed and polished.** Inside, cleanliness is close to godliness (and more money). Wash up, pick up, and paint where necessary. Keep your color choices as neutral as possible, and avoid wallpaper if you can. A coat of fresh paint on the kitchen ceiling usually brightens that very important room.

➤ **Strive for spacious, light, and airy.** Try to take as many non-essentials as you can out of each room. Sometimes taking photos of the rooms will help you get a more detached perspective. Cross out the things that might be crowding the room—go ahead! Right on the photo. You'd be surprised at how much you don't see just because you're accustomed to things the way they are.

➤ **Negotiate like a pro.** When an offer comes in, put your head in control. Remember that this is a sales transaction, not the barter of a dearly beloved possession. Never say never. Don't raise your voice or slam anything (phone, door, table, or other). If an offer is far too low, reduce your asking price infinitesimally and tell the agent you will happily consider another offer closer to the property's true value.

➤ **Read that purchase contract.** If you feel uncomfortable with any of the fine print in the purchase contract or with any of the printed-in additions the agent or the buyers have made, you might want to consult an attorney before signing.

➤ **Keep in touch with the real estate agent or agents so that you can monitor the progress of the deal.** And try to remain flexible. Remember that the closing date on the contract is rarely the actual date of closing.

➤ **Celebrate!** (*After* you get that wonderful check.)

The Least You Need to Know

➤ The competitive market analysis (CMA) is the easiest and least expensive way to estimate the market value of your home.

➤ Paying off your mortgage early will save you mega-bucks, but check first with a financial advisor to be sure the time is right for you.

➤ After age 62, you can apply for a reverse mortgage.

➤ After age 55, there's a one-time home sellers' tax break available.

➤ Your home can be put to work earning money.

➤ When selling your home, location, price, and presentation are most important.

Chapter 17

Protection for Your Possessions

In This Chapter

➤ Keeping the house *and* collecting Medicaid nursing home support

➤ Passing on real estate without a blip

➤ Marriage and divorce—get it in writing

➤ Insurance issues you won't want to miss

Everyone has a nightmare now and then, but the money ones seem to carry over into morning. The catastrophic illness—what if they take my house? A suit for damages—will it wipe me out? Divorce—what will the ex-spouse take? Second marriage—will the children of the first marriage lose what should be theirs someday?

We can't prevent nightmares of course, but we can help you with answers to some of the money questions. There are many ways to protect your assets. What is right for you depends on what you have and how you want it protected. An attorney with a specialty, or at least extensive experience, in estate planning can be invaluable to you. No, more than invaluable—an absolute necessity. We'll give you more tips on choosing an attorney in Chapter 20, "About Lawyers."

OOOOH...

Power Word
Lien (pronounced *lean*) is a claim against property for money. In order to pass clear title when the property is sold, it must be paid off. A mortgage is a lien you take on voluntarily. A lien for Medicaid costs or a tax lien would be an involuntary lien.

The moves you have to make are not bold and daring forays into uncharted territory. It's all been done before, many times. But they *are* moves—you can't just wait for something to happen and then react. For protection, you must take some initiative before the nightmare happens.

Don't Let Them Get the House

Every state has the power to place a lien on your home to pay for the cost of nursing home care. In most states, that is not done until after a Medicaid recipient's death, and then only when there is no surviving spouse. If there is a surviving spouse, he or she is allowed to stay in the house without a lien and pass the property on to children or other heirs. Home for the spouse is considered an exempt asset. By federal mandate to the states, either spouse is allowed to transfer ownership interest in the home to the other spouse, even when already in a nursing home.

It seems the bureaucracy gets a little meaner when there is no surviving spouse, however. This is where you might have to plan ahead to save your property for the heirs you choose. The federal government has given to each state the option of taking your house before you die to pay nursing home care costs if you are single and enter a nursing home on Medicaid. The rules for *non-exempt* (which means the house is up for grabs) status for the house differ from state to state, so check with your state office on aging. If you can't locate the phone number by using your phone book or directory assistance in your state's capitol, contact the National Association of State Units on Aging at (202) 898-2578.

Extra! Extra!

Imagine this story. You're single, aged 68, and have just had major surgery, which forces you to enter a nursing home on Medicaid because you are income-eligible in your state. After the six-month waiting period, the state insists that your home be sold to pay nursing home bills. If you refuse to sell, the state threatens to terminate your Medicaid benefits. You need the benefits, so you say "yes" and the house is sold.

After a year of very slow recovery and extensive therapy, you're much improved—more than anyone expected. The doctors say you are ready to leave the nursing home. Problem is, you are homeless! That's right, the property is gone and you have no rights to get it back.

Could this really be your story? Changing the exempt status of a Medicaid recipient's home after six months isn't allowed in every state. As of this writing, the number is at 10 states and rising. Be aware, however, that the rules are always being changed. Find out where your state stands before it's too late!

Statistics on how many people will someday be in nursing homes vary and change as we all live longer. One commonly occurring prediction is that one in five people in their fifties today will need nursing home care. With stats like that, it's no surprise that long-term care insurance is a growing industry. Some companies now include it in their medical benefits packages, and others offer it as an option at some extra cost. If you do buy it on your own without a company plan, be sure the policy is renewable for life and doesn't have riders that exclude certain diseases (Alzheimer's, for example). Most policies do have pay-out limits, however. So you can count the insurance as a help, but not as the promise of total freedom from risk.

Even if you are (1) happily retired, (2) convinced you are financially secure, (3) don't think you will ever need to rely solely on Medicaid, and (4) don't intend to buy long-term care insurance, you still might want to take steps to move certain possessions, especially property, into ownership forms that will put them out of any creditor's reach, just in case the money does run out. One of these forms is the trust, which we'll introduce you to in Chapter 21, "A Will, Perhaps a Trust, and Other Legal Paperwork." The other is the joint tenancy. Read on.

Gray Matter Alert
More information about long-term insurance is available free in the booklet *A Shopper's Guide to Long-Term Care Insurance*. Contact: Publications Department, National Association of Insurance Commissioners, 120 West 12th Street, Suite 1100, Kansas City, MO 64105-1925; (816) 842-3600. Also read Chapter 23, "Paying the Bills."

OOOOH...

Power Word
Tenancy goes beyond renting. In law, tenancy means any interest or holding in property. There are many types, each affecting owners in different ways.

Check Out Your Tenancy

If you are single and want to protect your home from being used to pay the costs of a catastrophic illness, you can choose a younger person to whom you want to leave the house and make him or her a co-owner. Be sure, however, that your lawyer structures the co-ownership as a *joint tenancy*, not a *tenancy in common*.

Upon the death of one co-owner in a joint tenancy, ownership of the entire property passes to the other co-owner without becoming a part of the estate of the deceased. In tenancy in common, the deceased person's share is treated as a part of the estate and can be taxed. So choose joint tenancy. If you think you might use Medicaid for nursing home care someday, be certain your lawyer checks to see that the move doesn't go against the regulations in effect in some states.

Thin Ice

If you're single, a transfer of ownership interest to anyone within 30 months of applying for Medicaid will mean a disqualification from Medicaid until either 30 months pass or the nursing bills accumulate to the value of the property. You must think about transferring your home *before* you become ill or protecting it with long-term care insurance covering at least three years of care.

Keep It By Giving It Away!

A good way to protect your home from the costs of catastrophic illness is by giving it away. That's allowed by Medicaid if you do it at least 30 months before you enter a nursing home. And you can legally guarantee yourself the right to live in the property for the rest of your life and even collect any revenues generated by the property. How? It's called a *life estate*.

Gray Matter Alert

Few people lose sleep over the thought of losing their house to a faulty title—until there's a claim, that is. Title insurance is available nationwide and required by many lenders. You buy it as a one-time fee at the closing. It will protect you in court for the cost of fighting claims against your good title.

When your attorney sets up a life estate for you, the title to the property passes to whomever you choose while you are still alive. That means your chosen person then *owns* the property. You (and your spouse, if you have one at the time the life estate is created) will retain a legal interest in the property that enables you to use it until you, or both of you, die. Medicaid cannot place a lien on the property to recoup nursing home expenses because you no longer own the property. When you die, the property is not part of your estate and never goes to probate because ownership already was transferred. The provisions of the life estate simply end.

Other assets besides your home and real estate can be protected against catastrophic illness costs by giving them away or holding them in a trust. Laws differ from state to state, however, so it is essential that you discuss your plans with an attorney or estate planner.

Marriage Or Divorce + Property = Problems

The problems, however, are not without solutions. Many adult children worry when a parent falls in love again after retirement and the death of his or her spouse. Sometimes the retirees worry, too. Usually, however, a pre-nuptial agreement can set out on paper exactly who keeps what. Even in community property states where everything acquired during the marriage is considered jointly held, property owned before marriage remains in the individual name.

Most therapists and social workers advise the generations to talk together about estate planning long before the talk is "needed." Adult children are more likely to accept a new spouse if they know the dead parent's wishes are safely protected. Besides the pre-nuptial agreement, many retirees opt to create joint tenancies with their children or to put assets destined for the children into trusts.

Dividing up property is almost always a problem in a divorce. Be sure to get at least one professional appraisal, three competitive market analyses from real estate agents, or a combination of the two in order to determine fair market value. To get clear title to real estate, you probably need a *quit claim deed* from your ex-spouse. Check also to see whether the mortgage you held jointly can be assumed by you as an individual.

The division of other assets usually is negotiated through attorneys. Many divorcing individuals, however, also successfully use financial advisors to help get a fair distribution. Not a bad idea. Remember: Some holdings are definitely more valuable than others.

If you are divorcing at or near retirement, check your pension rights and your Social Security spousal benefits (they do not always end with divorce). And get *everything* in writing. Remember, most potential family battles can be prevented by some careful planning and by signatures to every promise. If you don't do that, the assets you wanted to pass on can be trampled to the ground by the fees and taxes of family infighting and government regulations.

It's Been Said
When elephants fight, it is the grass that suffers.
—African proverb (Kikuyu)

See You in Court

Although being sued may not be as often-recurring a nightmare as catastrophic illness among the elderly, those who experience it (often caught raiding the refrigerator at 3 a.m.) are from a much broader age range. There should, however, be no fear. You can insure against losing your life savings to a lawsuit.

The great majority of liability suits can be traced back to moving cars, and most states require liability coverage in auto insurance policies. Even if you drop your collision insurance because your car isn't worth fixing, you should continue to carry as much liability as you can afford.

Power Word
Premium in insurance circles does not mean top quality or a giveaway. It is the amount you must pay either monthly or annually for your insurance coverage.

"OK," you say. "But what about the UPS person who steps from the truck onto the skateboard in my driveway? What do I do if he or she ends up in the hospital with serious back injuries?"

We certainly hope that never happens, but kids will leave things in the driveway no matter how many warnings they get from Mom and Dad. They do other unbelievable things too!

You can get liability insurance against what might happen on your property as well as against what any member of your family might say or do. This is called an *umbrella policy* and usually is written as a rider on your homeowner's policy. The most common amount of coverage is $1 million, but you can get more if you want.

It's Time for Inventory

If you have a video camera, we have an excellent suggestion for putting it to good use—besides, of course, pictures of the kids, cats, dogs, new birds at the feeder, vacation spots, and so on. Use the camera to record your possessions. Go from room to room in your home; focus on each item of furniture, the silver and the china, the jewelry and paintings, the appliances, the rugs, the garden equipment, and even the workshop in the basement. Be sure you speak while you shoot, naming the item, telling its original cost, and stating its approximate current value. When you have recorded all your possessions, the videotape will become a part of your insurance records.

If you don't have a video camera, take still photos. Try to have someone in the family in most of the shots so that you can prove they were taken in your home. After the pictures are developed, mount them on pages that have written value estimates assigned to each item.

Keep the videotape or photograph records in a place separate from your residence so that fire, theft, or natural disaster will not affect them. The home of a friend or relative is adequate, although most people who keep a safe deposit box keep insurance records there. Also check with your insurance company to be sure your valuables are covered and that your homeowner's insurance coverage is adequate.

Take a look at the following illustration for an overview of homeowner's insurance coverage. *HO* on each policy type stands for *Homeowners*. The types of policies are pretty much standard throughout the industry, although the insurance industry, like all others, is subject to competition and change. For special situations such as floods and earthquakes, which are not covered by homeowner's insurance, separate policies or riders can be purchased through the insurance industry or from the federal government.

Your Homeowner's Policy - What Does It Cover?

From basic coverage to all risk, the insurance industry offers policies to fit your needs and ease your fears.

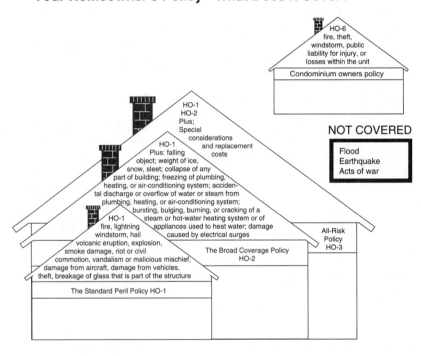

Life Insurance

There are entire books on life insurance. About the best we can do here, without overloading this book's capacity and maybe yours, is to point out a few of the major areas you might want to explore further.

Cash-Value to Pay Taxes and Burial Expenses

Although few financial advisors today recommend whole-life or cash-value life insurance because there are other ways to invest money that are equally safe with better returns, some people find it appealing. The major advantage of *cash-value* life insurance is the compounding, *tax-deferred*, of the dollars you pay in. Thus, if you cash in your policy in your sixties, you must pay taxes on the lump sum *only* if the total amount of cash value plus dividends exceeds the amount you paid in premiums over the life of the policy.

If you don't cash in a *whole-life policy*, however, upon your death, your heirs will get the face value of the policy to use tax-free for estate taxes, burial expenses, or whatever they need. Remember that life insurance benefits are not taxed.

Gray Matter Alert
Insurance companies are businesses, and some of them are in better shape than others. Company financial strength ratings are published by A.M. Best, Standard & Poor's, Moody's, Duff & Phelps, and Weiss Research. Choose your insurance carrier only from among the top-rated companies. A financial advisor can help you.

Another advantage of the cash-value life insurance policy is that you can borrow against the cash value over the life of the policy. You must pay a nondeductible interest on the loan, which is usually 2 or 3 percentage points above the prime lending rate, and the amount you borrowed is deducted from the face value payout until you repay the loan. But in all, it's a source of quick cash at a much better rate than a credit card.

Beside the standard fixed-interest rate whole-life policies, some other forms of cash-value insurance have become widely used. *Universal* life insurance promises to invest your money in money-market instruments. When rates are high, your returns are considerably better than the fixed-rate policies. *Variable* life insurance is somewhat more risky because your premiums are invested in stocks, bonds, or money-market funds. Usually the returns are much higher, but there's no guarantee that a depressed market won't cut those returns to the bone. *Second-to-die* insurance is a cash-value policy purchased by both husband and wife. It pays off on the death of the spouse who survives longer, which means that premiums are calculated on joint-life expectancy and therefore are usually lower.

Term Insurance Instead of Joint and Survivor Annuity

Term life insurance can be written for any length of time, although 1, 5, 10, and 20 years are the most common periods. The policy pays off only if the person dies during the term of the policy. There is no cash value.

So why buy it? The premiums are much lower than cash-value life insurance. Although you are not investing money for the future, a term policy provides security during a high-need period—when children are very young, for example. It pays death benefits that cover estate taxes and burial expenses, and it can provide security and income for a surviving spouse after retirement.

For those retirees who do not want to take a reduced benefit from their retirement plan in order to cover a surviving spouse through his or her lifetime, term life insurance is sometimes the answer. By structuring the plan so that the cost of the annual premium is no more than the amount of the reduced benefit, you can usually buy tens, possibly hundreds of thousands of dollars worth of life insurance. Upon the death of the insured, the money is paid to the spouse, tax-free. It then can be invested in an annuity or mutual fund. Unused money at the death of the remaining spouse can be passed on to heirs. This is a major plus over the pension plan survivor annuity, which leaves nothing.

> **Thin Ice**
> If you opt for term insurance, be certain that it is renewable and not subject to cancellation. Have the required physical exam done and reported on, the insurance in place, and the first payment made before the dependent spouse signs away his or her rights in the pension plan. Once the rights are signed away, you can't get them back.

About Annuities

The dictionary definition of *annuity* is "a sum of money payable yearly or at other regular intervals." But for most people, the term brings to mind a kind of life insurance that doesn't depend on death. Annuities are sold by insurance companies to people who want to guarantee regular income for certain periods of their lives.

There are two ways to purchase an annuity: *immediate* and *deferred*. Yes, the meanings are as simple as the words. For an immediate annuity, you pay in a large sum of money, and then begin immediately to collect regular-interval payments for an agreed-upon period of time—which could be for however long you live. If you want a deferred annuity, you pay in money over time, often much of your working life, and do not begin to collect your regular-interval payments until a deferred date in the future, usually after retirement.

When you purchase an annuity, you can specify how your money will be invested by choosing either the *fixed-dollar* option or the *variable* option. In the *fixed-dollar* annuity, the insurance company puts your principal into bonds or mortgages. Each year the company announces the fixed-return for the next year. Those returns are tied to interest rates and the economy, but most companies also have a guaranteed minimum. (Usually about 4 percent, but that could change.) Even though annuities with the fixed-dollar option are considered a conservative and "safe" investment, you should choose the company you buy from carefully. Ask for the track record.

Thin Ice

Don't get enticed by high teaser rates for the first year in fixed-dollar annuities. Those rates can (and probably will) go down. A *bail-out provision* in the policy allows you to pull out all or part of your money, without surrender fees or penalties if a new rate has dropped more than a percentage point from the previous rate.

Gray Matter

Annuities are a tax-deferred, not a tax-free, investment. When you begin receiving your checks, you must begin paying taxes on the "investment earnings" part of the payouts. The insurance company will tell you how much is the return of your original principal and how much are investment earnings.

With higher potential return and also greater risk, *variable annuities* allow you to choose a portfolio among stocks, bonds, and money-market instruments. The value of your annuity then will be tied to the investments you choose and the movements in each marketplace. It will certainly change over time and as the economy changes. A financial advisor can make available to you several publications that chart the success of variable annuities. Study them and get as much advice as you can. Then choose your company carefully because, besides investment risk, there often are fees and penalties for switching out.

How much you get per year from your annuity depends not only on the principal and the type of annuity, but also on your payout choice. The *10-year certain annuity* has the highest return because the insurance company knows exactly how long and how much it will have to pay. If you die before the 10 years are up, your heirs get the balance of your payments for the 10 years. If you live longer than 10 years, your checks will stop coming on the 10-year date.

If you think you might live more than 10 years but you'd like to protect your principal just in case you don't, you can choose a *life annuity with a 10-year certain term*. You'll get less per month than the 10-year certain annuity because the insurance company might have to pay you for a lot more than 10 years. But if you die before the 10 years are out, your heirs will receive your payments to the 10-year date.

If you choose a *life annuity*, the insurance company guarantees you payments for the rest of your life. When you die, however, there is no payment to a beneficiary.

Some married couples and some individuals who want to provide for a dependent choose a *joint and survivor annuity*. This plan pays until both the insured and the beneficiary die, but the amount of the payment usually is reduced when the insured dies first. By law, however, the reduction cannot be more than 50 percent of the amount for both people.

What To Do with an Inheritance

It could be overwhelming, all that money all at once. The worst thing you can do is spend it all immediately. So here are some suggestions for slowing down the process to allow for thinking time:

➤ **Don't worry about taxes.** An inheritance is not subject to income tax. Taxes are paid out of the estate before distribution. If you inherit real estate, the basis value for tax purposes is the appraised value at the time of inheritance. You do not pay taxes on the appreciation during the ownership time of the deceased.

➤ **Collect the check.** It probably will take at least several months before you actually get the money. If you still haven't decided what you want to do with it when it finally arrives, choose a money-market fund or a short-term CD. You might as well collect interest while you're thinking.

➤ **Use some of the money.** It's usually a good idea to pay off your high-interest debt—credit card accounts, for example. Tax-deductible debt, like your mortgage, usually can be left in place and the inherited money used for investment with better returns.

➤ **Save some of the money.** Get the value of that ready cash and emergency fund of liquid assets up to the equivalent of six months of salary, just in case. And max out on tax-deferred retirement accounts (401(k)s, Keoghs, and IRAs, for example) because you can use the inheritance money to smooth over the financially painful effects of the additional payroll deductions.

➤ **Invest some of the money.** Depending on your investor personality and your risk-taking ability, you can put some of the inheritance to work for your future. Buying an annuity that will pay off in your own retirement is the most conservative invest-ment. Stocks, bonds, or mutual funds can be selected to your taste or need. Real estate, if it appeals to you, can be both a source of annual income and an invest-ment. The inheritance could provide the large down payment that deters many people from this usually fine investment.

The Least You Need to Know

➤ Getting government help with nursing home costs requires careful planning at least 30 months in advance and has state-specific requirements for income eligibility.

➤ By creating a joint tenancy, you can take a piece of property out of your estate. Upon your death, it will pass directly to your person of choice.

➤ You can give away your home but keep the use of it for the remainder of your life. This is called a *life estate.*

➤ A financial planner can help to arrange a fair divorce settlement. Best to consult a lawyer for a prenuptial agreement.

➤ Certain forms of life insurance can be used to cover estate taxes and burial costs or to provide an annuity for the surviving spouse.

Chapter 18

The Tax Man Cometh

In This Chapter

➤ The federal government's tax bite can cut beyond retirement

➤ The impact of state taxes on your life and after

➤ Expatriates in retirement

➤ Services of your friendly IRS

Taxes—UGH! Hours and hours of committed time, pages and pages of endless detail. But this is a field where what you don't know can definitely hurt you *and* your heirs (financially, at least). So let us give you a brief introductory tour of Taxland. Then you should feel free to wander its back streets and buildings on your own or with a good tax advisor.

Our tour will be the equivalent of those guided city tours you take by bus—good for an overview but not enough time for real exploration. We'll try to point out what to look for on the federal and state levels, but do follow up on what you read. After all, you could hardly say you've seen Manhattan or Los Angeles after a three-hour tour.

Federal Taxes—The Jugular and Other Tax Points

All tax points are vulnerable—some just hurt more than others. The wounds of some bleed a lot more than others, too—all in that green stuff called money. The trick is to use prevention more than first aid.

Estate Tax

The federal government does not tax the money of a deceased individual twice, by taxing the deceased and then the heirs. So it imposes only an estate tax, which is placed on the net estate. (The *net estate* is the estate after expenses are deducted.) The amount of the tax is determined solely by the amount of the estate and is not influenced by the number of heirs or their relationships to the deceased.

Gray Matter Alert
Once you retire and begin to draw on your savings, be sure to tap *first* those assets that produce fully taxable income—CDs and money-market funds, for example. Leave tax-deferred and tax-free investments for use at a later time.

Estates of less than $600,000 are exempt from federal estate tax. Estates of more than that amount pay tax only on the amount that exceeds $600,000.

If your estate will be in excess of $600,000, there are many ways of sheltering some of the money from taxation. You are allowed to give anyone $10,000 per year without payment of taxes. In some cases, you also are able to structure asset ownership to avoid taxation. But this field is so complex that both financial advisors and lawyers see it as a specialty. Which boils down to: *Get help*. If you're a glutton for punishment, you can order and read IRS publication #448 called *Federal Estate and Gift Taxes*. The number to call is at the end of this chapter.

Income Taxes

As always, there's good news and bad news. The good news first. If you are 65 or disabled, you may be entitled to a tax credit of up to $1,125 each year. The amount of the credit will be limited, however, if your taxable income is more than $33,750 and you are single or the head of a household; $45,000 if you are married and filing jointly or a qualifying widow(er) with a dependent child; or $22,500 if married and filing separately. The IRS will calculate your credit for you, or you can get instructions along with a wealth of other tax information in publication #554, *Tax Information for Older Americans*.

Now the bad news. If your income is high, you may have to pay taxes on your Social Security benefits. The thresholds that determine taxation are based on what the government calls your *combined income*, which means your and your spouse's adjusted gross income (as reported on your Form 1040) plus nontaxable interest plus one-half of your Social Security benefits.

If you file a federal tax return as an "individual" and your combined income is between $25,000 and $34,000, you may have to pay taxes on 50 percent of your Social Security benefits. If your combined income is more than $34,000, you may have to pay taxes on 85 percent of your benefits.

> **Gray Matter Alert**
> The AARP Investment Program from Scudder has a free booklet available titled *The State Tax Laws: A Guide For Investors Aged 50 And Over*. For a copy, call (800) 253-2277.

If you file a joint return, you may have to pay taxes on 50 percent of your benefits if you and your spouse have a combined income that is between $32,000 and $44,000. If your combined income is more than $44,000, you may have to pay taxes on 85 percent of your Social Security benefits.

State Tax Laws Can Make a Big Difference

When you're about to retire and can live anywhere, the tax structure of a state can make it attractive or not so attractive. By choosing carefully, you can not only lower your cost of living by reducing taxation but also avoid taxes on your estate. Let's have a look.

Taxes After Death

All states have what is called a *pick-up tax*. This tax applies only to those residents' estates that exceed $600,000. The state is allowed to "pick up" a portion of the revenue paid for federal estate tax. This does not affect the total federal tax to be paid by the estate. In addition to their allowed portion of federal government estate tax, some states levy their own estate tax.

No state, however, has both an estate tax and an inheritance tax; and some states have neither. An *inheritance tax* is placed on the amount that an heir receives. It is based on the amount of the inheritance and the relationship of the heir to the deceased. Most, but not all, states exempt bequests to a spouse. To check out the policy in your state and compare it to some other states where you might consider living, take a look at the illustration called State Taxation After Death.

> **It's Been Said**
> *The art of taxation consists in so plucking the goose as to get the most feathers with the least hissing.*
> —attributed to Jean Baptiste Colbert, French statesman, 1619-1683

Where you die in the United States can affect the amount your heirs will inherit.

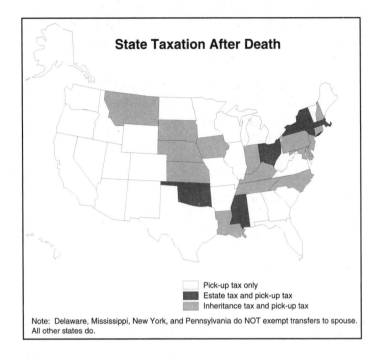

State Taxation After Death

Pick-up tax only
Estate tax and pick-up tax
Inheritance tax and pick-up tax

Note: Delaware, Mississippi, New York, and Pennsylvania do NOT exempt transfers to spouse. All other states do.

Income, Sales, and Property Taxes

All states except Alaska, Florida, Nevada, New Hampshire, South Dakota, Tennessee, Texas, Washington, and Wyoming have state income taxes. Of the exceptions, New Hampshire and Tennessee do levy a tax on interest and dividend income.

The states that do not have a sales tax are Alaska, Delaware, Montana, New Hampshire, and Oregon. Sales tax in other states ranges from 3 percent to 7 percent, but sometimes the effective rate is higher because it is combined with local sales taxes. In many states, prescription drugs and food are exempt from the sales tax.

All states have property taxes. There are several programs nationwide, however, that can help seniors with their property tax burdens. The most common are called the *Circuitbreaker*, the *Homestead exemption* or *credit*, and the *Deferral program*. Take a look at Table 18.1 to see what is in effect in your state.

Table 18.1 Easing Property Tax Burdens

	Circuitbreaker	Homestead	Deferral
Alabama		X	
Alaska	X	X	
Arizona	X	X	
Arkansas	X	X	
California	X	X	X
Colorado	X		X
Connecticut	X	X	
Delaware		X	
Dist. of Columbia	X	X	X
Florida		X	X
Georgia		X	X
Hawaii	X	X	
Idaho	X	X	
Illinois	X	X	X
Indiana	X	X	
Iowa	X	X	X
Kansas	X		
Kentucky		X	
Louisiana		X	
Maine	X	X	X
Maryland	X	X	X
Massachusetts		X	X
Michigan	X	X	X
Minnesota	X	X	
Mississippi		X	
Missouri	X		
Montana	X	X	
Nebraska		X	

continues

Table 18.1 Continued

	Circuitbreaker	Homestead	Deferral
Nevada	X	X	
New Hampshire		X	X
New Jersey	X	X	
New Mexico	X	X	
New York	X	X	
North Carolina		X	
North Dakota	X	X	X
Ohio	X	X	
Oklahoma	X	X	
Oregon	X	X	X
Pennsylvania	X	X	
Rhode Island	X	X	
South Carolina		X	
South Dakota	X		X
Tennessee	X		X
Texas		X	X
Utah	X	X	X
Vermont	X	X	
Virginia		X	X
Washington		X	X
West Virginia	X	X	
Wisconsin	X	X	X
Wyoming	X	X	

Circuitbreaker is a property tax credit where benefits are determined by both your income and by property tax payment guidelines. There are two types of circuitbreakers: the sliding scale and the threshold. *Sliding-scale* programs rebate a percentage of property tax liability. *Threshold* programs rebate the amount of property tax that exceeds a certain percentage of your income.

Homestead exemptions or *credits* reduces the property taxes on a homeowner's primary residence.

Deferral programs allow older or disabled people to put off paying property taxes until after death or upon the sale of their property. It's not entirely free, however. Usually, a somewhat below-market interest rate is charged on the taxes that are being deferred. The tax deferral and all accumulated interest usually is represented by a lien on the property.

Source Taxes

Ten states charge income tax on pensions earned within the state, even though an individual no longer resides in the state. The states are California, Connecticut, Kansas, Louisiana, Massachusetts, Minnesota, New York, Oregon, Vermont, and Wisconsin. So if you spent your life working in Wisconsin and then retire to Arizona, you will pay taxes on your pension to Wisconsin.

Intangible Tax

Some states levy tax on intangibles such as stocks, bonds, cash and bank deposits, accounts receivable, patents, and licenses. There's a wide variety in laws in this area, so you would do well to check with your state office of taxation.

Local Tax Breaks

Many municipalities allow people over 65 some credit or other tax relief in addition to state programs. The only way to get these benefits, however, is to ask for them. Which is really easy. Just stop in at the tax collector's office the next time you're in the vicinity of town hall.

Americans Abroad—They Still Pay Taxes, Sort Of

The United States, which was once a colony, now has many "mini-colonies" of retired persons living in various countries around the world. In fact, the Social Security Administration will mail your check to any country except Albania, Cambodia, Cuba, North Korea, or Vietnam.

"But why go so far?" you ask.

Some people go for the weather. Others for the buying power of the dollar. Some for tax benefits.

It's Been Said
America is my country and Paris is my home town.
—Gertrude Stein, American writer, 1874-1946

Gray Matter Alert
The IRS is willing to help you gather information about taxation while living abroad. You can call them at (800) 829-3676. Also might request two free publications: #901, *U.S. Tax Treaties* and #593, *Tax Highlights for U.S. Citizens and Residents Going Abroad*.

Here's how the tax situation currently stands. You will have to pay U.S. income taxes on your pension and your investment income and capital gains. If you're still earning foreign money after retirement in the U.S., however, you'll be interested to know that the first $70,000 per year of earned income is excluded from U.S. tax. Forty-three nations also have tax treaties with the United States that exempt you from paying taxes on the income you earn in that country. Medicare and private health plans do not usually cover Americans abroad, but residents in many countries can join the national health system for a reasonable monthly fee.

How To Deal with Your Friendly IRS

Not one single person at the IRS wears a black, floor-length cape while working. These are not the villains of 19th-century melodrama coming to take your money or your house. They are folks just like you whose job it is to enforce the law. And they can be very helpful.

Extra! Extra!

The IRS encourages you to let your fingers do the walking. Their *TeleTax* lines provide automated refund information (updated every seven days) and recorded information on 148 tax topics. The refund information is available Monday through Friday, from 7 a.m. to 11:30 p.m. The recorded tax topics are available 24 hours a day, 7 days a week. Except for a few major cities across the nation and several counties in California, the toll-free number is (800) 829-4477. If that doesn't work for you, call your local IRS office and ask for the TeleTax number.

If you want to talk with a living, breathing person about your tax questions, the IRS will happily accommodate you. Their *Tax Help* lines are open Monday through Friday from 7:30 a.m. to 5:30 p.m. As in the TeleTax lines, there are some local numbers, but from most of the country, call (800) 829-1040. No record is kept of any taxpayer's identity during these conversations.

For the hearing impaired, call (800) 829-4059 in all 50 states and the District of Columbia, plus the Virgin Islands and Puerto Rico.

Besides telephone service, the IRS has a network of one-on-one help and a number of educational seminars available. They also have extensive printed information and some audiovisual programs. For a list of everything, call (800) 829-3676 and ask for publication #910, *Guide to Free Tax Services*.

If you should face an audit, most experts recommend that you gather all your paperwork, records, receipts, and verifications and organize it all, exquisitely. Take it with you to the audit. Be sure your attitude is cooperative, not defensive or belligerent. Answer every question to the best of your ability, but don't volunteer extra information or make suggestions. And smile. It helps.

The Least You Need to Know

➤ Federal estate tax is imposed only on estates in excess of $600,000.

➤ Once you are over 65, you are entitled to a tax credit of up to $1,125 a year, depending on your income. The IRS will calculate your credit for you.

➤ If your income is high, you may have to pay income tax on a portion of your Social Security benefits.

➤ In addition to the allowed state portion of the federal estate tax, some states impose an inheritance tax, while others impose a state estate tax.

➤ Income, sales, and property taxes differ from state to state and will affect your cost of living.

➤ Most Americans living abroad can get Social Security checks sent to them. Their first $70,000 per year of earned income is free of federal tax.

➤ The IRS has an abundance of tax-assistance information available.

Chapter 19

Stay Out of Scam City

In This Chapter

➤ Retirees as the prime target of many scams

➤ Why some thieves say: forget housebreaking, use the phone

➤ Watch out for offers that seem too good to be true

➤ Pyramids can pinch—big time

➤ Heart and soul at risk—money, too

Webster's Dictionary defines *scam* as a "fraudulent or deceptive act or operation." Which means illegal, right?

Well, would you believe that here in the United States experts estimate that scams are a $100 billion industry (per year) with approximately $40 billion attributed to telephone work? With numbers that high, odds are your life will be touched by this "industry."

Thieves at the Turn of the Millennium

Everyone is susceptible. It doesn't matter whether you're young, mid-life, or elderly. But the elderly get the worst of it.

Power Word

No! That's probably the most powerful two-letter word in the English language. Just say it.

"That's strange," you think. "Wouldn't it be the young? After all, they're so inexperienced."

In theory, yes. But young Americans rarely have any money to spare. So the flashlight of scam thieves is most often focused on older Americans. It's like going to the silver bin. Unlike the young and even the mid-lifers, many retirees have plenty of assets, including freed-up IRAs, life-insurance payouts, mortgage-free homes, and squirreled-away cash. Many also are lonely and bored. More than a few are worried about having enough money to last for the rest of their lives.

Enter the thieves—courteous, well-spoken, patient, friendly, seemingly knowledgeable. Well-dressed too, when you see them. But scam-avoidance is another life situation where *knowledge is power*. So let's turn the spotlight on these ruthless people.

Reach Out and Touch Someone—By Phone

Many people who live in "advantaged" ZIP codes are so bothered by soliciting phone calls that they let their answering machines answer all incoming calls, or they look at their caller ID before answering a call. Enough calls do go through, however, to make tele-marketing one of the fastest growing businesses in the nation. Which is fine when the product is legitimate and the recipient of the call is genuinely interested. But thieves slip in.

Please Help Us

Beware requests for money. Someone calls you to say that Willy Sunday, or someone else whose name you recognize and respect, is in town to help the homeless. "Wouldn't you be willing to help show the community's support and make a small donation?" the voice asks. Or you get a call from someone who calls himself a representative of the Joint Commission of Chiefs of Police, and the voice tells you there's a campaign on to collect funds for the widows and orphans of officers killed while on duty. "Wouldn't you con-tribute to help the families of the people who died protecting you?" he pleads.

You don't have to say no just because the solicitation is by phone. In fact, you can be as polite and generous as you see fit. Just be careful. You can buy time and an added mea-sure of safety by making a pledge.

Any legitimate charitable organization will take your pledge and send you a written contribution statement. You then can pay by check or call them back and put the donation on your credit card. *Do not* give your credit card number to anyone who calls you to solicit money. If it's a scam, the callers can take your number and do a heap of buying before that next credit card bill arrives in your mailbox.

Just Call Us At...

"You're a winner! To claim your prize, just call us at..."

Beware the 900 number. This is a dead giveaway that scam artists are at work. If you call to claim your prize, it's likely to take them five to seven minutes to explain all the glorious details to you. When you realize that your "free" airfare to Maui can be claimed only in conjunction with a $300-a-day, 10-day hotel package, say "Thanks anyway" and hang up.

It's Been Said
The number 1 rule of thieves is that nothing is too small to steal.
—Jimmy Breslin, New York City journalist and street reporter, on NBC-TV, May 15, 1974

Did the scam artist lose? No, you did. You'll find a charge somewhere between $3 and $5 minute on your next telephone bill. With several people working the phone lines, Scams Unlimited can handle several hundred calls an hour—each at about $25 to $50. Good income for no service. Don't even bother to call those 900 numbers! If you've won a real prize, someone will call you.

We Only Need a Small Deposit

In another common scam, the callers tell you that you've won something or they offer you a sensational "deal" on a car or other big-ticket merchandise. But they need "a small deposit" ($300 and up) to secure your item. They understand that it's not safe to give credit card numbers over the phone, so they will send their courier to your home within the hour.

The offer of a courier or messenger to pick up a check is another indication of a scam in the making. By using the "courier," the proponents of the "offer" avoid federal investigators and, if caught, prosecution for mail fraud.

A common source of names for these scams are professional trade shows; consumer home, garden, or boat shows; and village fairs. It costs little to set up a booth offering some prize. Many people fill out the free entry blanks, and the scam artists go right to work as soon as the event closes. They're usually long gone before anyone complains.

Watch for Your Prize in the Mail

Letters announcing to the recipients that their names are among the million-dollar winners are so common that you see them in post office trash bins, unopened. The ones that say you've won a free vacation, a cellular phone, a 99-inch TV, or a five-carat diamond ring arrive somewhat less frequently, but are still familiar. Usually, these giveaways are sales schemes for timeshare or other real estate ventures. If you go, you'll get a prize of some kind, but expect several hours of sales grilling.

Gray Matter Alert
If it sounds too good to be true, it probably is.

Puzzles in the mail are another scheme. You send one in and two weeks later you receive notice that you won; you were indeed one of the few who did the puzzle correctly. You get a check for a few dollars. And a notice that for only $10 or so you can get into a bigger and better contest with bigger and better prizes. You can imagine how long this can go on!

As Advertised on National TV

Many retirees, some of whom are unable to get to the mall easily, become "addicted" to home shopping networks. The items sold are marketed with more than a fair share of hype ("there are only seven pearl necklaces left, and they're going fast!") and the prices are seldom bargains. While not exactly a scam, these shows can take advantage of homebound people.

Excess health insurance is another profitable commodity. Do you really need joint and muscle insurance? If you have Medicare and a supplemental policy, do you need to buy cancer insurance? The government says no and is cracking down on these money makers. But they're still out there.

Life insurance policies with no physical requirements and the promise that you cannot be turned down are another common offering. Bait 'n switch is usually the technique here, but if you hold them to their offer, you'll probably find out that the insurance is nowhere near as cheap as it was made to sound in the advertising.

We'd Like You to Meet...

Some of the most financially and emotionally devastating scams are worked in person. The great salesperson, the romantic companion, the helpful friend—we've all heard how others got taken, yet when it's happening to us, we sometimes overlook the obvious.

Come Share My Gold Mine

In Connecticut in the 1980s, two men created Colonial Realty (a holding company for a number of development projects) and promised investors excellent returns. Which they paid for a while, moving money from one project to another. Then the Tax Reform Act of 1986, a bad real estate market, and numerous bank failures brought down the house of cards (or perhaps houses of IOUs would be a more appropriate image). More than 18,000 investors lost a great deal of money. In 1995, each of the founders of the company received an eight-year sentence in federal prison. The state of Connecticut is still recovering from the effects of the scam.

Limited partnerships and joint ventures generally are considered risky business even when everyone is being absolutely honest. Throw in someone skimming or borrowing from Peter's money to pay Paul, and a crash is inevitable. Ask yourself, "If it's such a great deal, why the hard-line sales pitch?"

Extra! Extra!

In 1919, Charles Ponzi started a business in Boston. He promised investors that he would pay a 40-percent return on their money within 80 days. He paid them in full in 50 days. How? By that time he had sold to a second group of investors. Naturally, their pay-off dates were scheduled later than the first group. Ponzi then paid the first group with the money invested by the second. And he went out and found a third group. (It was easily a larger group, because word was out about the fabulous returns.) He paid the second group with the third group's investment.

The pyramid kept growing, each group, of necessity, being larger than the last, until he was found out by federal authorities. Those investors who were in his last and largest group lost virtually all their money. Ponzi was convicted of mail fraud and theft. The case was so famous that *Ponzi scheme* has become another name for *pyramid scam*.

Just so you'll feel good knowing that what goes around comes around, we'll tell you the end of the story. After serving time in prison, Ponzi was deported to Italy in 1934. He then moved to Brazil, where he died in 1949 with an estate of $75.

Currently being marketed in the United States and other countries are "business investments" that promise to bring in income through a method similar to the Ponzi scheme.

You are told that you can make a living selling a product to your friends and neighbors or you can make really big bucks by developing distributorships under your control. The idea is that you get a cut from the money made by each person that you convince to join the business. If those people, in turn, get their friends into the business, you get a cut of their profits also. And so it goes, on and on. It's like a chain letter. Also like a chain letter, this type of business venture doesn't create a lot of millionaires. Some people, however, do have millions of product samples stored in their garages and basements.

Let Me Show You a Better Place to Put Your Money

If you were an adult in the '80s, you'll probably recognize the name Lincoln Savings and Loan, where many investors lost their life savings. Most of them didn't know their money was invested in junk bonds. Bank officials had tempted their depositors with the promise of rates of return far greater than the CDs they usually held. Many people bought in thinking their investments were protected by the FDIC because they had been recommended by bankers.

Although not exactly a scam, another risky person-to-person deal occurs when someone is referred to a financial advisor who is actually making a commission by selling the products he or she recommends. When that product is a mutual fund, there is often a load (or fee). Other investments, such as annuities and limited partnerships, have large commissions at stake and heavy up-front fees.

Thin Ice
Just because you do business inside the walls of a bank does *not* mean that the money you invest is insured by the FDIC. Know what you are buying into. *Read the prospectus!*

If you are seeking a financial advisor, be aware that it is generally much better to pay a fee for service than a commission. Earning a commission when there is no other way to get paid for services can be a motivator too strong to resist, even though the financial advisor might know that the recommended investment is not the best choice under the circumstances.

Holier Than Thou

Back in the '60s, many parents worried that their children would be assimilated (or kidnapped) into pseudo-religious cults. Today, many "kids" of that era are worried that their parents will find a cult and join, after signing over all their assets.

Does that sound preposterous? It's happening. Lonely seniors are easy targets for scheming groups that promise security, love, and a better life in the beyond. Few stay in these groups very long, but by the time they leave, many already have signed over a good portion, if not all, of their assets.

On an even more personal level, traditional religions are also, unknowingly, the means for another type of thief to enter the lives of older people. Here's what happens. New people appear in the congregation. They are so friendly and helpful. They pay extra attention to the elderly. "Friendships" develop. Money changes hands. The new people disappear.

How Do I Love Thee...

This is the romantic version of "the new people in the church group." The scam thief befriends and begins to invite out the older person, who often is recently widowed. They "fall in love" and, often, the thief moves into the widow's or widower's home. When enough money to satisfy his or her goals has been accumulated, the thief simply isn't there one morning.

I'm Collecting For...

The door-to-door collector looks like an unkempt teen trying to help out whatever charitable group is marked on the cardboard container. If you feel you must contribute, ask for an envelope so you can mail in your contribution. If you must contribute on the spot, write a *small* check.

Door-to-door solicitors in most towns must get identity badges from the town officials. If you feel funny after the solicitor leaves your home, call the police station and ask if such a group currently is working in your area.

Seven Sensible Recommendations

Is it a jungle out there? Not really. Just be sensible, don't let your heart rule your head, and take the time you need to get some perspective on the situation. Here are some suggestions to help you:

➤ Never give a telephone solicitor your credit card number.

➤ If you are notified that you've won something, get all the details of what it is and when it will be delivered. Do not use a 900 number.

➤ Do not allow yourself to be pressured to buy. If someone tells you that you could lose the deal if you don't act fast, just remember that there's always a new deal.

➤ Before you give anyone your money to invest, be sure you know what he or she plans to do with it. Get a prospectus and *read* it.

➤ If the lifestyle of a group appeals to you, ask for a trial run of one year. You can put your money in a trust if you must join without assets. If the group won't let you in without your money, their motives might not be spiritual.

217

➤ If you lend money, have a loan agreement written up by a lawyer. You should have a credit check done too.

➤ Before you allow anyone to move into your home, get references. Where were they a year ago on this date?

Where To Get Help

If you think you have been the victim of a fraud, call your state Attorney General's office. You also can get help and information on protecting yourself from the National Fraud Information Center. They operate a special telephone line weekdays from 9 a.m. to 5:30 p.m. at (800) 876-7060.

If you would like to check out the credentials of a securities broker or firm, you can call the North American Association of Securities Administrators at (202) 737-0900.

There are several places to get information on cults. Call the Cult Awareness Network at (312) 267-7777; the International Cult Education Project at (212) 439-1550; or the Maynard Bernstein Center for Cult Education at (213) 852-1234.

And, of course, call your local police department!

The Least You Need to Know

➤ Scams are a big (and getting bigger) industry in the United States.

➤ If you are asked to make a donation by a telephone solicitor, do not give out your credit card number. Ask for a statement in the mail. You then can send a check.

➤ Beware of 900 numbers. They are very expensive and often are tip-offs to a scam.

➤ Never give money to a courier or messenger sent by a telephone solicitor.

➤ Bait and switch is a common travel and health scam.

➤ Sudden and unusual "friendships" from people new in your community can be the beginning of a scam.

➤ Cults can play upon everyone's need to belong.

Part 5
Law and Medicine—What You Absolutely Have to Know

Weaving throughout your retirement planning—and becoming even more important in your life after 65—will be concerns about health and legal issues.

*We can't help you much with health, if it's in the context of your feeling good (diet? exercise? less stress?), but we **can** give you an overview of the decisions you will have to make when it comes to healthcare—insurance choices, hospitals, options for chronically ill relatives, and similar concerns.*

About the law—here, too, your involvement will be stepped up over the years. After you have made your retirement nest egg and have learned how to invest it wisely, the next step is considering how to leave those assets to your heirs with as little cost as possible to them or you.

We realize not every section of Part 5 will apply to you at the same time in your life. You may never have to deal with some topics. But many of you no doubt find yourselves in the position of planning for your own retirement, while looking after parents or other older loved ones who are facing right now many of the problems and needs mentioned in these chapters. We hope these pages will help a few members of your family as those very special concerns arise.

Chapter 20

About Lawyers

In This Chapter

➤ When you will need legal counsel, and when you might get by without it

➤ Suggestions for finding a lawyer

➤ A variety of billing styles

➤ What makes for a harmonious lawyer-client relationship

The first thing we do, let's kill all the lawyers.—Shakespeare, *King Henry VI*

There. We got the most often repeated jab-at-lawyers phrase out of the way right at the start.

What is it about lawyers that makes it open season for potshots at that profession? Is it the endless pages of legalese that spring from the lawyer's office, where 10 words, many of them incomprehensible, are used to do the work of one, instead of the other way around? Is it the stratospheric hourly rates we hear about?

Whatever makes our national psyche tick in this regard, one point should be added. When we are in an attorney's office, waiting for advice that will help us with our crucial problem, then it's funny how more accepting we become of lawyers.

When DO You Need a Lawyer, Anyway?

You will need legal counsel more and more often as you move closer and then into retirement because more occasions will crop up for putting together some documents and reviewing others.

Because this book is about retirement, we will skip the need for a lawyer in auto-accident cases or other unrelated situations.

Generally speaking, in the context of subjects covered in this book, you will need a lawyer when

➤ You are buying and selling a house, but not always. In some states, house closings are handled by escrow companies. Also, if you have bought and sold a few times over the years, you probably can do it without an attorney, although you certainly will want one if you are offering financing to a buyer, or if you are buying a condominium or cooperative, with all that printed material to plow through.

➤ You are doing comprehensive estate planning.

➤ You or a relative is entering a continuing care retirement community.

➤ You are marrying or remarrying, and want a prenuptial agreement.

➤ You are divorcing.

How To Pick a Good One

If you want to check your cholesterol level, you don't go to your nephew's pediatrician. Similarly, if you want a lawyer these days, you are sometimes wise to look for one in the specialty you need.

In the old days, a lawyer, sometimes on a family retainer, saw a clan through problems in every area of its life—from the patriarch's business concerns to the daughter's ill-advised love life, to the son's gambling and the housekeeper's shoplifting incidents. These days, one sees that wide range of services only on *Masterpiece Theatre*.

It's Been Said
A verbal contract isn't worth the paper it's written on.
—Samuel Goldwyn

Today, you may well have a general attorney over the years for drawing up a will and reviewing some documents from time to time. But when you are about to place a relative in a nursing home, you will be in touch with that elder law attorney a few towns over. When you are buying a condo, you will call the fellow that friends told you about who handles so many of those purchases and is up on the local buzz about condo communities where you are. If, a few years down the road, you want to file an age-discrimination suit, you will look for a specialist in that area.

Some Special Services

Perhaps you will not be starting out from scratch looking for a lawyer. Maybe you are entitled to a prepaid legal service where you work, or perhaps you can join one. This is a company perk for many employees, working the way health insurance in the workplace does. The employer pays all or some of the cost. You could spend $10 or $12 a month—the cost of either unlimited consultations with a lawyer for one year, or a set number of hours of legal work—possibly, 50 hours a year.

A prepaid service can work well for much legal paperwork, and is also good for consulting about... well, to see whether you need a lawyer. Two cautions: Be sure that the legal company you will be using is experienced. All lawyers in that company should have been practicing at least five years. Also, do some fast math. If you will be paying $12 a month—$144 a year—you probably won't save on a prepaid service unless you have a somewhat busy life, needing legal advice more than rarely.

> **Gray Matter Alert**
> Although most prepaid legal services come through one's job, some retail stores and credit card companies now offer those plans to their customers.

You have no doubt seen the words *legal aid* frequently over the years. That service falls under the umbrella of the Washington, D.C.–based Legal Services Corp. Legal aid is free legal assistance for those who cannot afford to pay market rates for an attorney. There are income guidelines for using that service, although sometimes just being over the age of 60 is enough to qualify. Local legal aid offices handle a variety of cases, determined by the needs of that community. If you are in an area heavily populated with seniors, then a sizable chunk of those lawyers' work will be devoted to elder issues.

To find an office, check your phone book under *Legal Aid* or *Legal Services*.

Legal services cases closed in 1994.

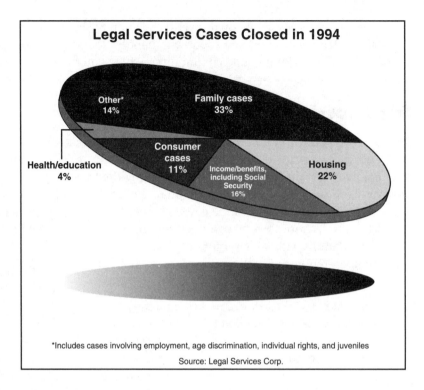

Legal Services Cases Closed in 1994

Other*
14%

Family cases
33%

Consumer cases
11%

Health/education
4%

Income/benefits,
including Social
Security
16%

Housing
22%

*Includes cases involving employment, age discrimination, individual rights, and juveniles

Source: Legal Services Corp.

Handling Referrals

If you are not using a prepaid service or a legal aid lawyer, the best way to find a good attorney is through recommendations of friends and work colleagues who have had experience with the services you now need.

That is a referral of a sort. Then there are professional referrals. You can call your local bar association for names they will offer, and you also might check with social service agencies in your community—especially those that deal with the subject matter you want to discuss with a lawyer. They might give you the names of attorneys who work for them occasionally, but who are actually employed by local firms.

The problem with both of the latter requests for a referral is that, although you probably will be given a few names of lawyers who specialize in what you have inquired about or those who have offices in your geographic area, you might just be given those whose names are the next to pop up on that office's list of referrals! Just because you are offered suggestions does not necessarily mean those lawyers carry an endorsement. You should talk with them before committing yourself—and your checkbook—to their service.

Interviewing Your Prospects

If you are considering any lawyer, from a friend's suggestion to a local bar association's referral, you will want to talk with that individual before assigning him or her your case. (We are not talking about a simple will here, but rather complete estate planning, or perhaps reviewing continuing care retirement community (CCRC) documents, up to actual trial work. We do not go into the latter in this book, but it might be a possibility for you some day.)

Call the lawyer and request a 20-minute talk on the phone. You will want to know how long he or she has been practicing and how much of that work is along the lines of what you need. You also should know whether the attorney will work on your case, or whether it will be assigned to an associate (if it will be handled by an associate, ask to meet the associate). Ask how the lawyer sees your particular case being resolved; how long that should take; and, of course, what types of fees are charged (fees are considered later in this chapter).

Overall, it is important that you like and have confidence in your lawyer. If you get negative feelings from your interview, keep looking.

There should be no charge for that brief chat, but you might want to ask when you call for your telephone appointment.

> **OOOOH...**
>
> **Power Words**
> **Associates** are fully qualified lawyers affiliated with a firm where they spend several years working and waiting to be tapped to become a **partner** there. **Paralegals** are trained in some legal work, but are not lawyers. They are usually heavily involved in research for particular cases within a firm. **Law clerks** might be lawyers, but more often they are law students working for a firm in an intern-like position.

A Growing Specialty: Elder Law

Noting how complicated life—and the law—can be as we grow older, some lawyers have formed a new specialty: *elder law*. Elder law attorneys specialize in the many issues facing older Americans, such as Social Security benefits, age discrimination, elder abuse and fraud, nursing homes, and more. Not every elder law attorney handles all these issues. They probably specialize in one or two of them.

The National Academy of Elder Law Attorneys (NAELA), the Tucson, Arizona-based professional association, was formed in 1989 and now has 350 member attorneys in 43 states who practice elder law. The number, of course, is growing.

Still, there may be no NAELA attorney near you at this time. You can ask around for a lawyer who specializes in elder issues, however. Follow the suggestions made earlier in this chapter for finding and interviewing an attorney.

225

Fees and Costs

Legal fees usually fall into one of three categories:

➤ You are charged a *flat fee* for the work to be done—$200 for a will, or $500 for a house closing, for example.

➤ You are billed at an *hourly rate*, which can run from $75 to $250. What is alarming about the hourly rate is that, boy, those hours add up quickly. Actually, it's the minutes that add up first, of course. You are likely to be billed for exactly the time you talk with your lawyer—every time. If that's a 10-minute phone call, you will be billed one-tenth of an hour. If the hourly rate is how your attorney wants to bill, ask for a ballpark figure of how much your work is likely to cost. If the lawyer does not want to be pinned down to an estimate, then look for someone else to represent you.

➤ There is also the *contingency fee*. Here, a lawyer handles your case, and if you lose, there is no charge to you. If you win, the attorney takes a percentage of your award (contingencies are used only when a monetary award is involved). That percentage can run from 25 to 50 percent, although in some instances you can negotiate for a sliding-scale fee so that if your attorney wins your case the very first day, with little effort, you pay less than if the case goes to trial two months later.

It's Been Said
I don't want a lawyer to tell me what I cannot do. I hire him to tell me how to do what I want to do.
—J. Pierpont Morgan

However you are paying, ask for an itemized bill listing all the services rendered by that lawyer and firm.

There are variations on these fees, such as an hourly fee with a cap, but they usually are bargained over by those with cases likely to run into many hours and dollars—certainly not smaller, one-time situations.

When talking about fees, ask about any extra charges as well. You probably will be billed for expenses such as long-distance phone calls, photocopying, fees for court documents, and the like.

What To Expect from Your Lawyer, and Vice Versa

You have a right to expect your lawyer to handle what is presented by you in a timely and fitting manner. Of course, that is assuming that what you ask is not illegal or otherwise impossible for that individual to accomplish. You also have a right to the following considerations from your lawyer:

➤ **Confidentiality:** Generally speaking, your lawyer should tell no one about your case. Confidentiality is important, because you need to be honest with your lawyer about details of your situation that could be damaging to you.

➤ **Loyalty:** Your lawyer should be working for just you, and not someone else on the opposing side. There should be no hint of a conflict of interest on your lawyer's part.

➤ **Communication:** You should be able to reach your lawyer when you have a good reason for a call. He or she should return your phone calls within 24 hours. Communication also means your lawyer should not mind explaining to you any points about your case that you do not understand. Don't let the legalese snow you. Ask for a translation!

Extra! Extra!

Can lawyers advertise? Until recently, they could not, but these days they are allowed to, as long as they follow certain guidelines. You probably have seen some advertisements on television and in the print media. Some firms, especially those specializing in auto injuries, advertise heavily, while many others still do not advertise at all.

What Your Lawyer Is Thinking

The attorney you engage has a mental list of what he or she expects from you, too:

➤ You should be open and honest with your attorney, so that he or she can represent you as solidly as possible.

➤ You should have confidence in your lawyer's ability.

➤ You should keep your lawyer posted on changes in your life—new address, new job, and so on.

➤ You should be realistic in your expectations. Maybe you are in the wrong, or maybe your case will just be lost. Don't immediately blame your lawyer.

➤ You should pay your bills promptly.

What To Do If You Are Dissatisfied with Your Attorney

Much here depends on the dissatisfaction. Are you angry because your lawyer has lost your case, or do you feel that he or she has acted in an unethical manner? You can contact your local Bar Association and the state offices that hold licenses to practice law where you are to inquire about a complaint. Your case may be submitted to arbitration. In serious instances, a lawyer can have a license suspended, or even be disbarred. Before you carry your complaint beyond your lawyer's offices, however, first try to come to terms with your attorney about your grievance.

The Least You Need to Know

➤ It is wise to line up a lawyer who can handle a house closing, review of certain documents, a will, and so on. But don't forget to consider a specialist if the need arises in your personal or business life.

➤ Interview any lawyer before engaging him or her, and be sure you will have confidence i that individual.

➤ Lawyers' fees can be high, but you might want to consider prepaid legal services if you can, or legal aid if you qualify.

➤ A successful lawyer-client relationship is a two-way street. Both sides have responsibilities and expectations. It would be wise to meet your lawyer's expectations—it could be important to the success of your case.

Chapter 21

A Will, Perhaps a Trust, and Other Legal Paperwork

In This Chapter

➤ The importance of having a will

➤ Your assets: probably more than you think

➤ The growing use of trusts

➤ The executor's role

➤ Making your last wishes known

You saw in previous chapters of this book how you can, by saving and investing wisely, build up a tidy estate to carry into retirement.

Then what? As it must to us all, death will come to those who have their financial affairs in order as well as those who, shall we say, decided to let the chips fall where they may. What a waste, if you have spent so many hours striving to build up your assets, to fizzle out when it comes to estate planning. That extra bit of work would enable you to pass those hard-earned assets on to whomever you want, and at the least possible cost (taxes and attorney's fees) to your heirs.

Do you see the wisdom of putting in just a little more time?

One more point: Some of this paperwork you might need at any time—while you are still alive, healthy, and perhaps even young. Not having it could pose a terrible dilemma for your nearest and dearest.

The Importance of Having a Will

Surveys show that only about two out of every five Americans have a will. If you fall into the "don't have" category, you should know that the state then will determine how your estate is divided, and that might be in ways you would not want. Think about it. For example, the state would likely give your spouse and children equal shares of your assets. Would that have been your wish?

Do you have young children? You will need a will to name a legal guardian who will raise them and manage their money if both you and your spouse die.

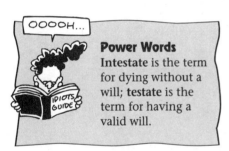

Power Words
Intestate is the term for dying without a will; **testate** is the term for having a valid will.

If your excuse for not having a will is "I don't really have much,"—uh-uh, that won't wash. You almost certainly have more than you think, and you surely have something. Even if you do not own a home, you probably have a car, household furnishings, possibly investments, and a savings and/or checking account, however meager. You also might have special items—furniture, some jewelry, antiques—that you would like to leave to specific family members or friends.

Your will sees that all of those wishes are carried out.

The Do-It-Yourself Will

A lawyer will charge anywhere from $100 to $500 to prepare a will, depending on your geographic area, the complexity of the document, and whether you are single or are having husband-and-wife wills made.

Thin Ice
Remember, you can only leave what you want to whomever you want if it is not owned jointly by you and another party, such as a spouse. Joint ownership takes precedence over a will.

You can do it yourself, with forms purchased at a stationery store for less than $20, from books to direct you, or with any one of a number of computer software programs costing around $50.

This can be a perfectly legal document but, as you might expect, there are a few words of caution for the do-it-yourselfer:

➤ **This works best with a simple estate.** If your estate is large and/or complicated, you are better off heading for a lawyer's office.

➤ **Read every word of instructions.** Each state has its own guidelines for wills, so there is no such thing as a generic, one-state-fits-all document. Books and software programs on this part of estate planning feature state-by-state requirements for wills.

Listing Your Assets

You also will need an inventory of exactly what comprises your estate. This will give you an idea of its dollar value, which can affect how you want it distributed.

List the location and numbers, where applicable, of your checking and savings accounts, insurance policies, investments, house deed, pension benefits, recent tax files, credit cards and their balances—everything that could be considered part of your financial picture and that your heirs will need to know about. Think really hard about this one. Here, too, you might have more income or savings than you think. For example, if you are an artist, writer, actor, or photographer, and have an agent representing your work, list him or her, too, because you could have funds coming in from that source in payment for past work.

Adding up all these amounts, less your current debt, will give you an *approximate* size of your estate (you also may have a car, some valuable effects, and other items you will have in your household inventory, suggested in Chapter 17).

Also put down the names, addresses, and phone numbers of your attorney, stockbroker, accountant, retirement benefits plan administrator, and any other financial consultant. Note where you have a safe deposit box and—this is important these days— list any computer passwords.

Gray Matter Alert
Don't forget your pet in your will. Your heirs might not care about that fur face the way you do. You might want to allocate a sum of money or a percentage of your estate for pet care to the individual who will take in the animal. You also might want to look into certain humane societies that will, through a trust, agree to keep and support your pet for life.

If You Have an Executor (Or Are One)

An estate's executor (you might see *executrix* used sometimes for women in that position), named in a will, locates and preserves all the assets of the estate, pays all appropriate bills and taxes, and then distributes what is left according to the terms of the deceased's will. Specific duties depend on the laws of that state and whether the deceased died testate or intestate.

You can choose anyone you like as an executor, but you should be sure that that individual has agreed to take on the job. The executor usually is paid a small percentage of the total estate as a fee for his or her work.

When It's Your Turn to Assume That Role

If you are named executor for someone else's estate, you can use your judgment about whether to engage a lawyer. They are usually unnecessary with a simple estate, but if you feel overwhelmed by the job ahead of you, an attorney could help guide you through an executor's responsibilities.

Some tricky parts of the job: finding all of the deceased's assets; putting a dollar value on some of them, such as antiques; and making sure you allow time for creditors to come forward before you distribute assets to the heirs. If you underestimate bills, you could wind up with them, unless you can convince the beneficiaries to return some of their money (and good luck on that one).

A Living Trust: Is That Best for You?

When you have a valid will, any assets that are not automatically transferred to others (such as real estate jointly held), must go through probate.

Probate is supposed to be the orderly transfer of property from you to your heirs. During the probate period, the court determines the validity of your will, the property in your estate is listed and valued, and taxes or other debts are paid from the proceeds of the estate. When that is completed, the remaining property is distributed according to your wishes.

This used to be the only way to see an estate transferred from the deceased to his or her heirs through a will. But probate precludes use of many of the tax breaks available these days. It is also frequently time consuming and can be expensive (probate usually costs about one percent of an estate, but costs sometimes can run 8 percent or more if there are many heirs fighting, a lot of creditors, or other complications).

Nowadays, about 40 percent of those planning their estates choose living trusts. You can use these trusts to transfer property—real estate, stocks, and other assets—to heirs without going through probate, and taking advantage of all tax benefits.

A trust also allows you more latitude in how you dispose of your assets—if you want to pass your money on to your children from a marriage, while omitting your present spouse, for example. You can do that with a trust, but you are likely to have a problem with a will. Also, a trust offers management of your assets if you become incapacitated, allowing whomever you designated to step in and make decisions for you.

Finally, a point that could matter to you: A trust is not open to public scrutiny the way a will is. No part of it will ever become public the way it would with a will in probate.

A *revocable living trust* allows you to spend, sell, or give away your assets while you are still alive. You can change its conditions at any time before death. Its biggest benefit: It is a good way to avoid federal estate tax while still retaining control of your assets.

An *irrevocable trust*, which is less popular, allows you to make a "gift" of property while still alive, forfeiting all control of it, in order to receive an exemption from federal estate taxes. One possible problem here for you: Once this trust is established, it is impossible to revise. So be careful you don't give away too much too soon.

> **Thin Ice**
> Be wary of buying a living trust from a door-to-door salesperson or a telemarketer. You can pay a high fee and still have a document that is not valid in your state. It's wiser to spring for a lawyer in this situation.

So Will It Be a Will or a Trust?

For some, after talking with a lawyer about their own particular situation, the answer will be both. A cooperative apartment, for example, cannot be included in a trust, so if you own one, you will need a will, at least for that property.

In the main, if you have a relatively small estate—say, less than $60,000—you might want to go through probate. Your heirs are likely to have that estate settled within a month at minimal cost. If you are relatively young, too, you might opt for a will based on cost. As mentioned, that will be just a few hundred dollars, while a fee to set up a living trust can run $1,500 or more.

> **Gray Matter Alert**
> If you are planning to move to another state after retirement, you will have to review all your estate documents with a lawyer there. Some of them, as they are presently written, will be ineffective according to the laws of your new state, and will have to be revised.

However, if your estate is worth more than $300,000, you probably will want to consider a trust. You certainly will if it is worth more than $600,000 (that's per individual, not per couple), when the federal government steps in for a sizable tax hit.

Talk to a lawyer familiar with trusts, and perhaps an accountant, too, who will be up on current tax laws, to see the varying ways you can save with these instruments.

How Power of Attorney Can Help in Difficult Times

If you become incapacitated—with Alzheimer's disease, for example—someone will have to handle your business and personal affairs. To avoid family disputes, especially the kind that can arise with a second marriage and grown children from an earlier union, it is wise to have a durable power of attorney. That allows your designated individual or individuals (you might want a backup person named, too) to act on your behalf if you cannot do so yourself. The *durable power of attorney* is not to be confused with the *healthcare power of attorney*, which covers decision-making only as it pertains to health matters.

As mentioned earlier, a living trust usually provides for another trustee besides yourself, and that person can handle your affairs if you are not able to do so.

Burial Expenses and Funeral Directives

Those who can't bear to think of their mortality long enough to make a will are not likely to cope with the mere idea of planning the true end of it all. But *you* are knuckling down to all of the aspects of estate planning here, which includes a burial or funeral or... well, read on. And even if all you do is read, you will at least know what paperwork is likely to be involved at this stage of things. It would be better for everyone, though, if you are able to muster some of these documents together.

A life insurance policy usually covers burial costs, or you can have them paid from savings. If you are of retirement age, beware of scamsters wanting to sell you a prepaid funeral. They prey on this age group assuming, often correctly, that these folks want to be sure they have arranged for this part of their lives the way they have taken care of all other matters. Yes, it certainly is wise to purchase a cemetery plot ahead of time, but there is no reason to pay for a funeral in advance. Even if you plan to engage a funeral director who has handled several family funerals, and you trust that individual, you still would be better off having that "funeral money" earning interest for you in an investment while you are alive.

Some aspects of death and a funeral you *can* plan ahead for:

It's Been Said
It was a cough that carried him off; it was a coffin they carried him off in.
—Inscription on a Mississippi tombstone

➤ Deciding about burial, choosing a funeral director and cemetery plot, and inquiring about future care for that plot.

➤ Looking into cremation. This option is increasingly popular because it is less costly than burial (averaging between $500 and $775, versus a typical $3,000 to 4,000 for coffin burial, not counting the cost of the plot). You can decide whether the remains will be buried in a cemetery, interred in a mausoleum, returned to a member of the family, or disposed of in some other manner of your choice (yes, like the often-heard-about scattering over the sea).

➤ Leaving detailed instructions for your funeral and other papers, such as information for your obituary and names of those you want notified after your death.

➤ Making sure your wishes relating to a funeral and burial are in one place and can be found easily by your next of kin. Include addresses, where appropriate, and receipts, such as for a burial plot.

Where to Keep All Those Important Papers, and a Few Others

You can store important papers in a safe place (such as a fire-proof box) in your home, but never put the original in a safe deposit box, which could be temporarily sealed after your death. Give copies of appropriate documents to your attorney; executor; trusted family member; and, in the case of a living will and healthcare power of attorney, your doctor. Be sure the person you most want involved knows where to find funeral instructions.

You can't forget about all those documents once you have filed them. It is good to review them every year or two, making changes as they occur in your life.

Whew! You're probably relieved to see you're at the end of this chapter. Good job! You finished reading it! Can you carry that fine work one step further now, and implement these suggestions?

Gray Matter Alert
Unmarried companions especially need to have their wishes on paper when it comes to a funeral (and everything else regarding their estate, for that matter). Sometimes it is assumed that parents or another close relative will plan the funeral. If you want other arrangements, you will have to tell the family or, better yet, put your wishes in writing and have them accessible.

The Least You Need to Know

➤ Minimal paperwork in estate planning is having a will drawn. Don't underestimate the importance of that document.

➤ After talking with a lawyer, you might opt for a trust instead of a will, or perhaps a trust *and* a will.

➤ A trust offers tax benefits and other advantages over a will, and means the estate does not have to go through probate court.

➤ List your assets so you will know what you will be leaving to heirs in your will. This will remind you of special bequests and give you an idea of the overall value of your estate.

➤ Your assets probably number more than you think, if you do a diligent job of thinking about and marking them down.

➤ Looking ahead to funeral wishes and related documents will assure you that your true "last wishes" will be carried out.

UM... WHY DON'T YOU TELL ME WHERE IT HURTS.

Chapter 22

Medical Care Choices

In This Chapter

➤ Looking for a doctor, perhaps a specialist

➤ How to select a hospital

➤ Making your wishes known in the event you become seriously ill

➤ Choices in healthcare for the terminally ill

There is probably no one out there who would deny that healthcare today is complicated, continually changing, frustrating, and expensive. However, there are areas where we can exercise some control. We do not feel so powerless once we know that Congress, doctors, hospitals, and healthcare plans are not making *all* our choices for us. So let's call the shots where we can, right?

One point will stand out in this chapter and in Chapter 23: You will see that managed healthcare is not only growing in importance, but seems to be the way healthcare will be administered in the future. If you've wondered what healthcare is all about, read on.

How To Find the Right Doctor

You will, of course, be looking for a new physician if you move out of your immediate area after retirement. But even if you plan to stay on Oak Street after age 65, you may want to switch doctors or look for a specialist you haven't needed before. Or forget about when you retire—maybe you want a different physician right now. How do you start?

First, a word of explanation. In managed care programs, you do not, of course, have the freedom to choose any physician at all. What we are talking about here is the type of health insurance that does allow choices.

Of course, the best recommendation is the tried-and-true referral from a friend, family member, or other person who is pleased with his or her doctor. You also can get names from the nearest hospital or the area medical association. If you know any nurses in a social context, ask them, too. And, if you have just moved, you can ask your new neighbors, or even the real estate agent who sold you your new home.

Before you begin calling those referrals, give a few minutes of thought to just what kind of physician you want. Knowledge of medicine is only one criterion. Do you prefer the kind of doctor who is very serious—who not only investigates your specific complaints, but also looks to see what other ailments you might have? Or, all things being equal, do you want a doctor to adopt a lighter tone, a sort of "don't worry" approach? Do you want him or her to be the voice of authority—not thrilled with too many questions or too much input from you—or would you prefer being able to participate in your own healthcare decisions?

Extra! Extra!

Here's a suggestion if you live in a metropolitan area that has a city magazine. Most of them publish an article every couple of years titled something like *The 20 Best Doctors in Town*. Reading over that list can help you choose your own physician, particularly a specialist. Call the magazine's back-copy department and ask if they have published such an article and how you can obtain a copy. Note: Sometimes those magazines run articles on the best hospitals, too.

Next, check to see that your one or two possibilities are licensed and certified by calling your state medical association. You might also call your state licensing agency to see whether any complaints have been lodged against that individual.

Call each doctor and say you are a prospective patient. If that doctor won't take your call for an introductory chat, don't keep trying, but just move on to the next name on your list. You probably wouldn't have been happy with that individual anyway.

When you do speak with the doctor, note whether you feel comfortable with him or her even in the few minutes you are talking.

When it's time for your first appointment, here are some other points to check:

➤ Get to know the physician a little by noting the framed certificates on the walls showing where he or she studied.

➤ Keep track of your waiting time. If it is longer than 15 minutes, ask the doctor if that is standard and decide whether you want to wait a half hour or longer for each appointment. (You might want to call the doctor's office shortly before you leave home to see whether he or she is running on schedule to save waiting time.)

➤ Ask at which hospital that doctor has admitting privileges. Is it one that is satisfactory to you?

➤ During your visit, note whether the doctor is really listening to you, or if you feel you are being hurried through the appointment.

You will know from your first appointment—whether it is for a specific medical problem, for a physical examination, or for a minor emergency—whether you will want to return to that physician.

Your—and Your Doctor's—Expectations

Besides attending to your immediate health concerns, you will want, over the long term, certain assurances from your physician. Some you will discuss with him or her, and others are unspoken understandings of the doctor-patient relationship.

For example, you will expect your doctor to be honest with you, answering your questions fully, and telling you the truth about all aspects of your condition.

He or she should be expected to check your record before prescribing medication so that you do not always hear, "What are you taking now?"

A doctor should be open enough to concede when he or she is puzzled by some aspect of your case, and

> **Thin Ice**
> Be sure that your doctor knows *all* of the medication you are taking—even over-the-counter products. This is necessary to avoid potentially dangerous drug interactions.

wants to call in a colleague or refer you to a particular specialist. In a similar vein, he or she should not resent your wanting to seek a second opinion in certain circumstances. Some medical plans encourage—even require—a second opinion for surgery. If you want or need one, you can contact your local medical society for a list of surgeons who can provide an objective second opinion.

Finally, you should be able to reach your physician in an emergency situation.

Your doctor expects you to be honest about your medical history and exactly what medications you are taking. He or she also expects you to take the drugs prescribed for you, and for the length of time indicated on the prescription label. You also are expected to report any unusual reactions to those drugs.

A doctor assumes that you trust his or her diagnosis and prescribed treatment (the occasional second opinion notwithstanding).

How To Evaluate a Hospital

It used to be when you went to the hospital, it was simply the one nearest to your home, or the hospital where your doctor held credentials. But in this era of consumerism, the hospital has taken on more importance. You *choose* a hospital. You sometimes choose a doctor by whether he or she is affiliated with the hospital you prefer.

Here are a few points to consider, keeping in mind, of course, that there is no totally flawless institution:

➤ If you belong to an HMO or other managed care plan, you probably will be limited in your choice of hospitals. Still, you can ask which hospitals are in that plan, and whether you can use all the services at each institution. Chapter 23 gives you more information on managed healthcare plans.

➤ Is the hospital you are considering convenient for you?

➤ Hospitals can be categorized as teaching and non-teaching institutions. The former can be particularly good because they often have state-of-the-art equipment, many good physicians, and a 24-hour staff with more than the usual overnight skeleton crew. On the other hand, some studies show there is a tendency for inexperienced doctors at those facilities to order too many tests and unnecessary procedures. You also will be visited frequently by a doctor and a "class" of doctors in training, which you might find disconcerting.

It's Been Said
It may seem a strange principle to enunciate as the very first requirement in a Hospital that it should do the sick no harm.
—Florence Nightingale, *Notes on Hospitals*, 1855

Overall, the best hospital is the one that has had plenty of experience treating your medical condition, whether it's a teaching institution or a local hospital.

➤ A hospital with a large number of doctors on staff who are board certified in their specialty is a good sign that that institution can handle a variety of health problems.

➤ Also good: A sizable proportion of nurses on staff—not "temps" who are there only occasionally.

➤ Many hospitals have a patient handbook. If the hospital you are interested in does, read it over carefully to be sure you agree with its philosophy and principles of patient care. Ask to see their annual report, too, which usually offers more than financial information.

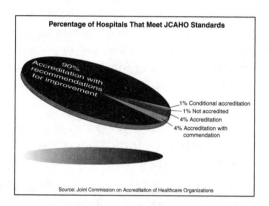

Percentage of Hospitals That Meet JCAHO Standards

90% Accreditation with recommendations for improvement

1% Conditional accreditation
1% Not accredited
4% Accreditation
4% Accreditation with commendation

Source: Joint Commission on Accreditation of Healthcare Organizations

The Joint Commission on Accreditation of Healthcare Organizations (JCAHO), is a not-for-profit group that accredits more than 11,000 hospitals and other healthcare institutions nationwide.

You also can examine various printed materials to evaluate a hospital:

➤ Report cards on specific hospitals (and nursing homes, home healthcare agencies, and mental healthcare facilities) now are being issued by the Joint Commission on Accreditation of Health Care Organizations, a not-for-profit group that accredits more than 11,000 facilities nationwide. Each report costs $30. To see if they have evaluated the hospital that interests you, call (708) 916-5800.

➤ *U.S. News Guide to America's Best Hospitals,* by U.S. News & World Report, expands the popular feature of that magazine into book form, ranking hospitals in 17 specialty areas with listings nationally, in each state, and in 10 key metropolitan areas.

➤ *Helping You Choose a Hospital* is a free brochure from the American Hospital Association, 325 Seventh St. NW, Washington, D.C. 20004, (202) 638-1100.

The Living Will: Carrying Out Your Wishes

You probably have heard and read a good deal about living wills over the last few years, although they certainly have been around considerably longer. As medical science enables hospitals to prolong life, you might want to ask yourself whether you want to live the kind of life they are extending through what may seem to be heroic means. Or, to personalize the issue, if you lapse into an irreversible coma, do you want to be kept alive on a machine?

If you do not have a living will and are unable to communicate your wishes, you could very well be kept alive by whatever means possible, despite your family's insistence that that would not be your wish. The living will is a simple document, usually filled out in part so that all you need to do is add your particular wishes briefly, such as how you feel about artificial feeding and cardiac resuscitation. Some hospitals ask you at admission or just before surgery whether you have a living will, and some will have you fill out a Medical Directives form, which is a statement of your wishes.

Thin Ice
Because states differ in what they recognize in a living will, you might have to have another one prepared if you move out of state. The Department on Aging in your new state can help you with particulars of what is required there.

Give a copy of your living will to your physician for your patient file, another to a trusted family member or friend, and keep one for yourself.

Choice in Dying, an organization that provides information about this and similar issues, offers free living will forms for each state. Call (800) 989-WILL.

Healthcare Power of Attorney: More Important Than a Living Will?

Some physicians and hospitals still are leery about the living will, which seems to them a rather flimsy piece of paper for such important decisions.

You might want to consider an even more solid route to having your wishes carried out: having a healthcare power of attorney or proxy, along with the living will.

The person you name has the authority to make all your healthcare decisions if you are unable to do so. Your next of kin might be able to do that if you can't, but a power of attorney can help settle any family disagreements that could crop up.

You also can get a free healthcare power-of-attorney form from Choice in Dying.

Extra! Extra!

While you are in this thought mode, you might want to request, sign, and carry near your driver's license an organ donor card. Call an area hospital's public affairs department or your local Department of Motor Vehicles to see how you can secure a card, and ask that source whether that card will serve as your wishes or whether your nearest relative also will have a say in donation of your organs.

Hospice Care for the Terminally Ill

A *hospice* is a program for someone who is terminally ill. The aim here is a caring service, with a skilled team of people helping the individual. The team includes a nurse and doctor, of course, and social workers, dietitians, clergy, physical therapists, and the patient's family.

The patient's family is considered and cared for at a hospice, too. This is, of course, a very difficult period in the lives of patient and family. Both are looking for help and support—not just medically, but spiritually and emotionally as well.

That care can be delivered in the patient's home, where members of the hospice team make regular visits and special personnel are on call 24 hours a day, seven days a week. Or, if special attention is needed, the patient can be cared for in a hospital or nursing home, following the hospice concept. The focus of that program is not on cure, but rather on making the most of each day remaining in life by providing comfort, relief from pain, and caring people close at hand.

Another option for the terminally ill, available in more and more communities these days, is moving the patient to a full-time hospice operation. These are special facilities just for the terminally ill, where the emphasis is on a warm, non-hospital-like environment—again, with that support staff.

Hospices can be run by public agencies or private companies. Medicare does pay many hospice costs, but you would be wise to look into the specifics of its allowances. Talk with your physician and contact your state health department. Or, you can call the Medicare hotline at (800) 638-6833.

Finally, for still more information, you might want to contact the National Hospice Organization at 1901 North Moore St., Suite 910, Arlington, VA 22209, (800) 658-8898.

The Least You Need to Know

➤ Medical credentials, of course, are important in choosing a physician but, all things being equal, select the doctor you feel you can trust and with whom you are most comfortable.

➤ If you have a choice according to your healthcare plan, rate and choose the hospital you prefer.

➤ Consider having a living will to be sure your healthcare wishes are carried out if you are unable to convey them yourself.

➤ You might want a healthcare power of attorney along with a living will to make doubly sure your directives are followed.

➤ Hospice care can be a blessing for the terminally ill patient and his or her family.

Paying the Bills

Are we telling you anything new when we say health insurance is expensive? And often limiting in its coverage? Even if you are on Medicare, you will have out-of-pocket expenses for extra policies.

True health insurance security is a mirage. It is unlikely you can protect yourself against the expense of every illness. That can be scary, especially for retirees and those about to be who see Medicare as their salvation, and then learn that program's limitations.

Your best hope is to retire from a company that continues paying your health insurance for the rest of your life and covers your spouse as well.

Oh, you say that isn't you? Well it isn't most of us. What can we do then? Just buy the best coverage we can. And keep our fingers crossed.

Let's see what's out there, and where the holes are.

A Look at Private Healthcare Insurance

If you are still working, you probably are covered by your employer's health insurance plan.

But what if you take early retirement at 56 and opt not to find another job? As we have said, some employers will carry retirees on a company plan, but perhaps there is no such perk where you are. Or what if you are 46 and self employed? Can you find the best coverage possible until Medicare kicks in, way into your future?

Securing health insurance can be a problem at this stage for many people. You might have a few chronic—sometimes serious—health problems. Insurance can come at a steep price, and policies might carry a lifetime exemption for treatment of some of those conditions.

You probably will find that a group plan is more affordable than an individual policy, and it also may offer you coverage in areas where an individual plan might turn you down. So go join a group, right? Actually, yes, if you can. Any organization—local, state, or national—might have... well, not the *perfect* plan, but certainly one you might find very workable indeed, and groups include everything from hobby clubs to professional associations. Some city Chambers of Commerce utilize a program so good that many self-employed residents of those communities join just for the health insurance.

Think about talking with an insurance broker, who has a group of companies from which to choose the best plan for you, rather than an agent who works for just one or two companies.

Extra! Extra!

If you are a military veteran, you can get information about healthcare benefits by contacting your local Veterans Administration office. CHAMPUS (Civilian Health and Medical Program of the Uniformed Services) is a government health plan for former active duty and retired military personnel, their families, some former spouses, and certain other government workers. After age 65, Medicare usually takes over from CHAMPUS. For more information about that program, contact your nearest military health treatment facility.

Managed Care Plans

Managed healthcare seems to be the healthcare buzz phrase for the 21st century, maybe even becoming the *modus operandi* for the venerable Medicare program.

These plans are companies of private healthcare providers that say they can deliver solid services to their beneficiaries at a reasonable premium cost. Each plan is organized somewhat differently, but generally speaking, services might be in one centralized location or among providers in various offices affiliated with that plan. They boast that they cut costs by limiting choices and eliminating extravagant care.

Different kinds of managed healthcare plans are available, such as Health Maintenance Organizations or HMOs (Medicare works with HMOs), Independent Practice Associations (IPAs), and others. With an HMO, for example, you choose a main doctor, called a *primary care physician*, who oversees all your medical treatment. If you need special services that your primary care physician can't provide, he or she refers you to a specialist within the HMO. All of this is covered by your membership fees, but if you stray outside the HMO coverage and choose your own physician(s), you must pay those bills, except in special circumstances. Other programs offer variations on those requirements.

Not everyone is thrilled to be in a managed care plan, of course. While some plans offer high-quality medicine and service, stressing prevention, there are complaints from the public about others and about aspects of all of them. It sometimes takes a long time for the *gatekeeper* (as the primary physician often is called) to refer patients to a specialist, if indeed he or she thinks the patient needs one (a view not always in agreement with what the patient thinks). There can be some concern about the quality of care. The plans may dispense drugs in only the most common dosages, making it necessary for some patients to cut pills. Keep in mind that these plans are laid out to serve the mass of people in the quickest and least costly method for the plan so that the company can be as profitable as possible.

Questions you can ask to decide whether a particular plan is right for you: Is the facility where you will go convenient for you? How much choice will you be allowed in physicians and a hospital? If you need any regular, specialized care, how is that affected by your membership in a managed care plan? Does the plan provide a full range of specialized care? Do you want the option of healthcare outside the plan? If you now have doctors and facilities you are satisfied with, ask them which plans they belong to and you can work from that direction.

Power Words
Managed care plans bring a whole new vocabulary. Doctors are now **providers. Patients** are **enrollees, consumers, clients,** or **members.**

OOOOH...

Not all managed care services are available in every part of the country. Not everyone is eligible to join, either. The best way to get in, if you are not a member now, is through a group plan at work.

Call your state's insurance hotline for more information about what's available where you live.

Managed Care: An AARP Guide is available free from the American Association of Retired Persons. Call (800) 424-3410.

Extra! Extra!

For answers to any senior-related questions, insurance included, you can call the Eldercare Locator at (800) 677-1116, a directory assistance service with access to state and local organizations that serve older Americans. They can help you find local resources. The hotline, open Monday through Friday, from 9 a.m. to 11p.m. eastern time, is a public service funded by the U.S. Administration on Aging. Note, however, that with this number and with other government agencies, the help you are given is likely to get you started, but you probably will still have to investigate on your own locally for the balance of the information you need.

Medicare and How It Works

For many of us, Medicare is like the light at the end of a very long, dark tunnel. If we can just get through our forties, fifties, and early sixties, lugging our imperfect health plans—and our imperfect health—with us, then Medicare will step in when we reach 65. We can breathe a sigh of relief and let Uncle Sam pay our medical bills from then on. Whew—we'll have made it!

It's Been Said

Give me health and a day, and I will make the pomp of emperors ridiculous.
—Ralph Waldo Emerson, 1803-1882

Yes, to some degree, but not totally. This is an imperfect world, and the government insurance program has its flaws too. Medicare will help to a great degree, but we still will have insurance coverage concerns.

Medicare is our nation's health insurance program for Americans over 65, for certain people with disabilities who are under 65, and for those of any age who have permanent kidney failure. It provides a *basic* protection against the cost of healthcare.

If you already are getting Social Security or retirement benefits or railroad retirement checks, the Medicare folks will contact you a few months before you become eligible for the program and give you the information you need to sign up. If you are not getting those checks, you will have to contact the Medicare office three months before your 65th birthday to sign up for the plan. (You can enroll in Medicare even if you do not plan to retire at 65. Indeed, you should because you are eligible then for Part A benefits.)

What Medicare Covers

Generally speaking, there are two parts to Medicare:

➤ **Medicare Part A:** This is hospital insurance that is financed by a portion of your payroll (FICA) tax, which also pays for Social Security. This can help pay for care in a hospital or skilled nursing or rehabilitation service after a hospital stay, for home health visits, and for hospice care. There are qualifications to coverage here, but to list the "limited tos," "participating agencies," and so on would take far too much space in this chapter, and probably run into the next. This is an extremely complicated arena, and a constantly changing one when it comes to benefits allowed and denied.

➤ **Medicare Part B:** This is medical insurance that is financed partly by monthly premiums paid by people who elect to enroll. You automatically are enrolled in Part B when you become entitled to Part A. However, because you must pay a monthly premium for Part B coverage, you have the option of accepting that coverage or turning it down. There are penalties or higher premiums attached to turning it down or enrolling, dropping out, and then re-enrolling in the plan. In l995, the Part B premium cost $46.10 per month. The monthly premiums are adjusted (translation: they rise) every January.

Medicare medical insurance helps pay for doctors' services and many services and supplies that are not covered by the hospital part of Medicare, such as X-rays, outpatient care, and ambulance services.

Filing Claims

When you enroll in Medicare, you will be given a Medicare card containing your claim number. Hold onto that number! No claim will be paid without it. Claims are paid by either an *intermediary* (Part A) or a *carrier* (Part B). Both of those are insurance companies—Blue Cross/Blue Shield, for example—or similar organizations under contract to the government. Hospital charges that Medicare will pay are billed by the hospital to intermediaries. Doctors and medical suppliers of covered services may submit their charges directly to carriers by "taking an assignment." Those doctors and suppliers who take assignment may not charge more than the amount allowed by Medicare.

Even if your doctor does not "take assignment," he or she must send the claim to the Medicare carrier for you. Some charges could be higher than the ones allowed by Medicare, but the doctor cannot charge more than 15 percent above the allowed fee. Your benefit payment will be based on the allowed charge, so your cost will be the amount in excess of the allowed charge.

What Medicare Doesn't Cover (and How To Make Up for That Lack)

You have just read an overview of what Medicare includes. We can be more specific about what the plan does *not* cover:

➤ Most nursing home costs.

➤ Custodial care. This is care at home by a person who is not medically skilled and that is given mainly to help the elder with daily living, such as bathing and dressing. An interesting aside here: Most nursing home patients require only custodial care.

➤ Most prescription drugs.

➤ Dental care and dentures.

➤ Routine checkups and tests directly relating to those checkups (some screening, Pap smears, and mammograms are covered).

➤ Most immunization shots (Part B pays for the full cost of the pneumonia vaccine procedure and helps pay for a few others).

➤ Tests for, and the cost of, eyeglasses or hearing aids.

➤ Routine foot care.

➤ Personal comfort items, such as television sets and telephones in a hospital room.

As just mentioned, there is far more to coverage and exemptions than is within the scope of this book. For your specific questions, you have several sources of information.

You can call the national Medicare hotline at (800) 638-6833 or your state insurance hotline.

The 1995 edition of *Your Medicare Handbook*, a 57-page book published by the Health Care Financing Administration, is available for $4 from Government Printing Office, Order Division, Washington, DC 20402, (410) 786-3000.

Filling in the Gaps

You *can* purchase additional Medigap insurance to protect you from some expenses that Medicare does not cover. In the past, there were a few problems with Medigap policies:

➤ Retirees found themselves inundated with phone calls from insurance salespersons.

➤ More seriously, many Medigap policies being sold contained duplication of coverage with Medicare itself.

Medigap, which is more formally known as *Medicare supplement insurance,* now is regulated by state and federal law. It is a federal offense to sell policies that duplicate a buyer's existing protection (the government has not yet managed to get rid of those phone calls!). Keep in mind as you look into this coverage that you need only ONE Medigap policy, no matter what insurance salespersons try to sell you. Also, be sure what you are buying is identified as Medicare supplement insurance. Other kinds of policies might help with some out-of-pocket expenses, but they do not qualify as Medigap plans.

You can apply for one of the 10 standardized Medigap policies, which offer varying benefits, as soon as you qualify for Medicare. Keep in mind, though, that Medigap is not likely to pay for a nursing home any more than Medicare will. Only about 2 percent of all qualified stays in nursing homes are paid for by Medicare or Medigap.

Here, too, for more information, you can call the Medicare hotline. While you are talking with those folks, ask for a free copy of the *1995 Guide to Health Insurance for People with Medicare* from the National Association of Insurance Commissioners and the Health Care Financing Administration. The guide explains the differences among the 10 Medigap policies and lists the official insurance counseling telephone numbers for each state. Just stay on the line until you are offered the Hold to Talk to an Operator option.

> **Gray Matter Alert**
> Every state—plus Puerto Rico, the Virgin Islands, and Washington, D.C.—offers residents a free health insurance counseling assistance program (HICAP). You can call there with health insurance questions that pertain specifically to where you live. Check under the Department of Insurance Consumer Service division for that hotline number.

Will Medicare Survive into the New Millennium?

First there was Social Security to worry about, now Medicare. It's a nail-biting ride into retirement, isn't it?

The problem here, of course, is that the program is running out of money.

OOOOH...

Power Word
Medicaid is not another word for Medicare. It is an entirely separate program. Medicaid (in California it is called **Medical**) is a state-run plan designed primarily to help those with low incomes and little or no resources. The federal government helps pay for Medicaid, but each state has its own rules about who qualifies and for which benefits. For more information, call your state Medicaid office, listed under the state department of social services or human services.

Founded in 1965 by President Lyndon B. Johnson, Medicare was aimed at the one-third of the elderly in the nation who were living in poverty then, with little or no access to healthcare. Then, like Social Security, the program just grew and grew. Americans have been living longer, for one thing. Technology is responsible for a good deal of that longer life expectancy, and technology is expensive.

How serious is the problem? Medicare Part A, which pays for hospitalization, is expected to be insolvent by 2002. Americans apparently are aware of the problem, and realize changes will have to be made to that sacred system. Suggestions for reform from all quarters include adopting managed care, such as HMOs, instead of the fee-for-service setup of the existing Medicare program. Managed care seems to be the favored solution so far.

If you are in your forties or fifties, you probably will agree that managed healthcare, no matter how imperfect, is better than no Medicare at all. Stay tuned as the tinkering with this program continues.

Some Special Insurance Plans

You read briefly in Chapter 17 how private long-term care insurance (LTCI) can help keep you from total devastation of your assets. Let's look at this policy more closely here, in the context of other health coverage.

This is a relatively new product in the insurance marketplace, with its benefits and exclusions constantly changing. It is also a complex area—aren't they all!—with practically an equal number of pros and cons for purchasing a policy.

One pro, of course, is that LTCI may provide important financial protection against costly nursing home care, among other benefits. On the other side of the ledger, it is expensive, and some people do not have enough assets to protect to justify the sizable premiums the policy carries.

One couple, who had trouble paying their $1,800 annual premium because of a plunge in interest rates with their investments, dropped their policy with relief, also citing its limited coverage.

United Seniors Health Cooperative, a Washington, D.C.–based not-for-profit organization dedicated to helping older consumers, encourages seniors not to consider buying LTCI unless they meet all these criteria:

➤ More than $75,000 in assets, $150,000 per couple (not including home and car)

➤ Annual retirement income of more than $30,000

➤ Ability to make the premium payments comfortably, without having to make lifestyle changes

➤ Ability to afford the policy even if premiums were to increase by 20 to 30 percent in the future

The cooperative, which receives more inquiries about LTCI than any other issue, also cautions against purchasing a policy with combined *triggers*. That means that in order for benefits to kick in you have to have both cognitive impairment, for example, *and* need help with three out of five tasks of daily living. The better policy offers stand-alone triggers—cognitive impairment alone, for example.

For more information about LTCI, you can send for *Private Long-Term Care Insurance: To Buy or Not To Buy* ($2.50) and *Long-Term Care: A Dollar & Sense Guide* ($10), both from United Seniors Health Cooperative, 1331 H Street NW., Suite 500, Washington, D.C. 20005.

The Shoppers Guide to Long-Term Care Insurance is a free publication, available from many state insurance departments.

> **Thin Ice**
> Long-term care insurance frequently is sold over the phone or door to door. Skip those methods and use a local life insurance independent agent or broker.

Insurance for the Terminally Ill

Some companies will buy life insurance policies from the terminally ill, paying them some portion of the death benefit, ranging from 50 to 80 percent. Goulish? It seemed so at first, but now it has become accepted, and indeed new regulations dealing with those companies, issued by the National Association of Insurance Commissioners, have been adopted in some form in nine states so far.

If you are interested in some form of protection along these lines, check with your life insurance company too. More than 200 insurers offer an accelerated benefit that allows those with a life expectancy of less than one year to receive benefits ranging from 25 to 95 percent. If you have cash

> **Power Word**
> Specialty insurers in this field are known as **viatical** companies (taken from the Latin word meaning *provisions for a journey*). You can get their names from the National Viatical Association at (800) 741-9465.

value inside a life insurance policy, you first might want to consider whether a loan would be satisfactory. That way, the difference between the loan amount and the death benefit still would be preserved for your heirs.

Help with Those Claim Forms

If health insurance is confusing, try filling out insurance claim papers after a hospital stay, or even for a major monetary outlay for medical equipment needed at home.

There is help here, however. Many local offices on aging and charitable organizations will guide seniors through the morass of paperwork attached to those forms at no cost.

Some companies have sprung up around the country, too, that will, for a fee, take over the claims process for you. They often can find errors in billing that will save you money. These companies say mistakes are rampant in hospital bills.

You choose. The free service will take on the paperwork, but is not likely to look into whether every charge is legitimate. The companies that charge will check out a bill, but that will cost you. You might pay per project, or you could be charged an annual fee, perhaps around $200, for unlimited assistance that year. For information about those services in your area, contact the National Association of Claims Assistance Professionals, 4724 Florence Ave., Downers Grove, IL 60615, (708) 963-3500.

The Least You Need to Know

➤ If left to your own devices to find health insurance, look into a group plan, check with an insurance broker who represents many insurance companies, and consider managed care options. All are likely to be more affordable, and perhaps easier to secure, than simply picking a company and applying.

➤ Medicare pays a good deal of your healthcare costs after 65, but by no means all of them. You might also want a Medicare supplement insurance policy, known as Medigap.

➤ Medicare is in financial difficulties, but the program, like Social Security, is expected to survive in some form.

➤ Private long-term care insurance (LTCI) can help with nursing home bills, but the policies are costly. You might want to give some thought to this before signing up.

Chapter 24

If Chronic Illness Strikes a Parent or Other Loved One

In This Chapter

➤ How your community can help when you're caring for a relative

➤ Between private home and nursing home: some workable suggestions

➤ Long-distance caregiving

➤ When a nursing home is needed

➤ Concern about you, the caregiver

Whether it's your parent, a spouse, or other relative close to you, a serious long-term sickness in the family will plunge you into a world you did not know existed—that of care for the chronically ill.

If you are new to these concerns, you should know that help is out there—a good deal of it at no cost to you—to assist you and your loved one in coping with the many changes in your once reasonably well-ordered life. In fact, once you start making inquiries in the world of caregiving, you will be amazed at the variety of resources, almost all of them new in the last half dozen years or so. This is a field just being recognized and, because of the increasing elderly population, one that is growing.

Meals on Wheels and Other Community Services

If your relative is at home, but needs some services in addition to what you can provide and he or she can do alone, you first need to be organized in seeking assistance.

On a notepad, jot down exactly what you need, and make a note to ask when you inquire about those services whether there is an age or an income-eligibility restriction.

Meals? Contact your local Meals on Wheels for delivery to your relative of a hot meal each weekday, either free or at a nominal $2 or so charge. There might be other social service agencies in your area that provide food, too, in the form of canned goods and other non-perishables.

Utility bills? Aid with those payments can come from a social service agency such as the Salvation Army (not all of those offices offer identical assistance nationwide). You might also contact your local utility company. They probably have a program directed toward relatives of seniors to ensure that those seniors' services are not discontinued because they did not see the utility bill. They no doubt also have an averaging plan, where customers pay a certain amount toward their bill each month instead of extremely high payments some months of the year and low ones at other times (a plan available to customers of any age).

Transportation? Many local charities, private and religious-affiliated, have a staff of volunteers that will drive seniors on errands and to doctors' appointments. The American Cancer Society will pick up cancer patients of any age, take them to treatment centers, and drive them home.

There is not enough room in these pages to list the wide variety of services available in all but the most remote communities to help the elderly, sick, or homebound. Call your local office on aging or senior citizens agency to see if they can help you with immediate needs.

Whenever you are talking to a government or private social services agency asking for assistance and that office says they cannot help, immediately ask if they know who can. Sometimes those taking calls don't think beyond, "No, we don't do that."

How At-Home Care Can Help

Perhaps your loved one can live at home, but needs some outside assistance. That's when you can turn to home healthcare.

That aid comes in two areas. One is *custodial care*, which includes help with cooking, cleaning, and other chores, and can be just companionship, too. No skills are necessary for those jobs, which average $7 to $10 an hour. (Some local charities and religious organizations offer volunteer "sitters" at no charge.)

The second part of home assistance is *skilled nursing care*, which covers visits from medical professionals. Fees start at around $35 an hour for a registered nurse, $16 for a licensed practical nurse, and $40 for a therapist. A live-in aide charges about $100 a day.

You can hire someone on your own, or you can talk to the several community services for the aging for suggestions on securing this type of aid.

You also might turn to healthcare agencies and nurse registries. Many temp agencies have entered this field in recent years, too—recognizable names like Kelly, Olsten, and INTERIM, among others. They offer assistance on a variety of levels, starting at sitter/companion.

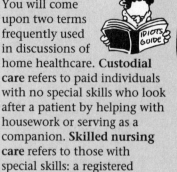

Power Words
You will come upon two terms frequently used in discussions of home healthcare. **Custodial care** refers to paid individuals with no special skills who look after a patient by helping with housework or serving as a companion. **Skilled nursing care** refers to those with special skills: a registered nurse, therapist, licensed practical nurse, or similar medical professional.

When calling for any help, be sure to check credentials and references (agencies usually will have done that screening). Ask about an employee's licensing and bonding. What about liability insurance? Be sure you know, too, exactly what that in-home provider will do for your loved one, in order to avoid misunderstandings.

Some of these services are covered by Medicare, Medicaid, the Older Americans Act, and Veterans Administration benefits. A few private insurance companies pay for home care expenses, too.

Adult Day Care Choices

Is your relative unable to stay at home alone, but needs little or no medical attention? Your solution might be adult day care.

This concept provides the loved one with a stimulating environment and companionship, and offers the caregiver a break of several hours a day with no need to worry about that relative's supervision.

You have two choices here:

➤ You can have someone come in to take care of your loved one. You just read about that option in home health services, where you might be able to utilize a companion/sitter.

➤ You can enter him or her in an adult day care program. There are a wide range of choices here, from local government and religious-affiliated facilities, sometimes in older downtown buildings, to modern new suburban complexes now being built as profit-making ventures. Programs vary from one facility to another, but most focus on keeping the adult occupied with games, songs, light exercise for those who are able, and so on. Some also offer transportation for the relative to and from the day care center, usually at a small charge of $2 or so.

Many day care centers on the local level are free. Fees at others can range from $25 to $50 per day.

At the newer, posh facilities, there are activities rooms, dining areas, garden spots, perhaps a library, coffee shop, and other amenities. They charge an average of $75 per day.

Extra! Extra!

One developer—Baltimore, Maryland-based Deerfield Health Care Corporation—plans to have 73 adult day care centers up by mid-1999, all of them along the East Coast. Some are already in operation.

Day care centers usually run Monday through Friday, although you might find an occasional one open on weekends. Studies show that most who enroll a loved one in a day care program do so just three days a week.

Costs here are absorbed by the older adult or a family member. Medicare and Medigap do not allow those claims, although Medicaid does in some states, among them Florida. Check where you live to see whether Veterans Administration benefits are recognized for adult day care. Sometimes they are.

Day care centers will have the number of medical personnel required by state law, but that could be only a registered nurse. Those who stay here are not, after all, "patients." This is primarily a social, not medical, environment.

In some centers, anyone can enroll, while others focus on those with Alzheimer's or related cognitive illnesses. Naturally, you should check before enrolling your relative to be sure he or she will be comfortable in the facility you have chosen.

Respite Care

Respite care is another outlet to provide a loved one with an opportunity to interact with other adults while you are away on business or recuperating from an illness. Or, you may be on a vacation. You're entitled, you know (more about taking care of the caregiver at the end of this chapter).

Respite care can be having a home health care person to attend to your relative while you are away, but here we will consider taking your loved one to a care facility on a *per diem* basis. He or she will have full medical facilities available there, if needed, plus two or three meals a day. There will be a recreational program, too—whatever the permanent residents of that community enjoy. In most cases, the respite care guest can join in as well. These are assisted living facilities or, sometimes, nursing homes that take in respite care guests to keep rooms filled between long-term residents.

Rates here are also all over the map, but you can expect to pay perhaps $100 to $200 per day. Naturally, you should visit the facility and talk with the staff, even for a short-term visit from your relative.

Extra! Extra!

Throughout this chapter, we offer advice to you as caregiver on the assumption that you are making decisions alone. Naturally, if your chronically ill loved one is able and eager to participate, we assume that you will seek out his or her opinions. These suggestions are not meant to disregard that individual's input.

Looking After a Loved One Across the Miles

Which is worse: Worrying about a close relative you see often, perhaps even live with, as he or she becomes increasingly frail, or worrying about that person when there are hundreds of miles between the two of you?

Well, this isn't a contest. Let's just say both situations can cause many sleepless nights.

If you live some distance from your loved one, and you must, or want to, stay where you are and he or she is in the same situation, there is still much you can do to make that person's life easier—and put some of your fears to rest.

If it is possible, visit your relative to line up the support services you will need to conduct long-distance care. Try to appoint a, shall we say, secondary caregiver there, perhaps a friend or neighbor of your relative's who will call that individual daily, perhaps do some occasional shopping and keep track of any home health aid visits. You can work out a financial arrangement with that individual and give him or her all the phone numbers involved in your relative's care, from local agencies to your own and other family members'.

Still Another Helping Hand

Care manager and *geriatric care manager* (GCM) are words you might hear when caring for a relative. These are professionals who will help assess your loved one's needs and arrange for necessary services. They can be particularly invaluable in long-distance caregiving. For example, you might hire a care manager in your relative's community to oversee selecting individuals to assist him or her there.

Some of these fees are picked up by social service agencies, but other managers are with private companies who will charge perhaps $50 to $60 an hour. A hospital's outpatient planning office or The National Association of Professional Geriatric Care Managers, (602) 881-8008, can help with more information.

Other sources of assistance also are available to you:

➤ Children of Aging Parents (CAPS), publishes a monthly newsletter, several bro-chures, and offers other resources. Membership costs $20 annually. Write CAPS, 2761 Trenton Rd., Levittown, PA 19056, or call (215) 945-6900.

➤ The National Alliance for Caregiving, at (301) 718-8444, is a nationwide resource center that provides information, books, and training.

➤ *Miles Away and Still Caring* is a free pamphlet from the American Association of Retired Persons. Call AARP at (800) 424-3410.

The Next Step: An Assisted Living Facility?

If your relative cannot live alone, but is not ready to enter a nursing home, an assisted living facility may be an excellent solution. Assisted living provides just that—rooms, meals, *and* personal services such as help with dressing and bathing.

Some of these complexes exist by themselves, while others are part of a continuing care retirement community (Chapter 26 tells you more about CCRCs).

You can expect to pay from a low of around $750 as month to $4,000 or more to live in one of these buildings or complexes. They can be less costly than a nursing home, however, in part because they do not provide round-the-clock nursing care.

These services also are paid for by the resident or his or her family.

About Nursing Homes

It is always a difficult, painful decision, but the time may come when your loved one will be best cared for in a nursing home, where he or she will have the full-time attention of medical professionals.

The principal point for you to carry away from these paragraphs—again, space constraints must make this discussion brief—is that, for the most part, when it comes to shopping for a nursing home, you are on your own. It is up to you to check the licensing and accreditation of that facility. It is up to you to visit homes in your area, and to ask for those institutions' inspection reports (and watch the administration try to locate those documents). You will have to walk around with your clipboard, too, noting what you see that is satisfactory and what isn't. Practically no home is going to be without fault somewhere.

Are these facilities as expensive as you have read and heard about over the years? Yes, they are. Nursing homes can cost from $2,000 a month on up—and up. And, this must be paid for out of pocket. If your relative qualifies for Medicaid, look into that assistance. And by all means, read or reread Chapter 17, about protecting assets from nursing home costs.

Extra! Extra!

Consumer Reports, in an August 1995 article on nursing homes (a series continued in its September and October issues), finds the quality of many nursing homes poor, sees little assistance for the patient or family seeking to rate those institutions, and concludes that the best way to find the better ones—besides visiting homes with your own checklist—is calling your state or local government ombudsman, a man or woman who will have received complaints about various institutions and, more important, won't mind telling you the truth about those findings. The National Association of State Units on Aging, at (202) 898-2578, can give you the name of the ombudsman in your state, or the one you're considering, to contact about nursing home information. Geriatric care managers also can offer honest assessments of some specific nursing homes, based on their own experiences.

The *Consumer Reports* article rated 43 chain/religious groups nationwide, calling that "the first objective national ranking of nursing-home chains and religious groups ever published." The results, in brief, showed religious-affiliated homes faring better than other chains, but they were not without problems, either.

A Look at What to Look For

Forget the fanciest building or complex. Look for a nursing home with a caring staff, and your relative will adjust better. That is not to say, of course, that plush facilities can't be concerned about their patients, only that it is important to look beyond decor—or price.

Here are some other points to make this transition easier for both of you:

➤ If Mom has lived in Arizona for the last 15 years and has friends there, do give thought to instinctively electing to move her to a nursing home near your Chicago home. Will you be able to visit her fairly often, with your job and other family obligations? Who else will? Does she have any friends in Chicago? Or will Mom truly be happier in a nursing home in Arizona, where her network of pals there will check in on her frequently?

➤ The visitors angle is important. Nursing homes often are understaffed. Frequently, visitors assist a patient or notice a detail that should be brought to the staff's attention. If that patient rarely has callers, he or she still will be cared for, of course, but that patient might not get the kind of fast attention given those who the staff knows are visited every few days—by folks who might complain about one thing or another.

➤ There is much you will want to look at in any nursing home you are considering. Is the home free of unpleasant odors (not counting the smell of disinfectant which is, at least, a sign of the facility being cleaned regularly)? Are the residents who are able up and dressed at a reasonably early hour of the day? Do there seem to be an unusually high number of patients in restraints? That should be a red light. Are there social activities? What about meals? Are they tasty? Watch the staff to see how they relate to patients. Do they call them by name? Do they seem pleasant, or disinterested or frazzled?

➤ You will want to ask the administrator about licensing and accreditation, of course, and those inspection reports.

It's Been Said

Our society must make it right and possible for old people not to fear the young or be deserted by them, for the best of a civilization is the way that it cares for its helpless members.

—Pearl Buck, *My Several Worlds*, 1954

➤ No doubt, you will want to have a lawyer look over documents you are offered.

➤ Nationally, you can contact the American Association of Homes and Services for the Aging at 901 E St. NW, Washington, DC 20004, (202) 783-2242, for printed material on this subject.

➤ For a free copy of *Nursing Home Life: A Guide for Residents and Families*, contact AARP at 601 E St. NW, Washington, DC 20049, (800) 424-3410.

Caring for the Caregiver—You!

This is a tough business, looking after a chronically ill loved one, perhaps in addition to a job and still having children at home. Even if you are retired and do not have that extra burden of earning a living, there will be fatigue, tension, and some rough days.

You are doing a wonderful job—perhaps one that others couldn't or wouldn't undertake. But while you are tending to your loved one, you need to be taking care of yourself, too:

➤ **Take a break from your responsibilities.** Say yes to offers of help, even if you know those folks won't do the job exactly the way you would. Or, hire a sitter when you can and go out. Take advantage of day care centers and respite care for longer breaks. Even if you do little but rest during those hours, take them. You need and deserve time off.

➤ **Watch your diet.** While you are making sure the nutritional needs of your loved one are met, you could be neglecting your own.

➤ **Your relative may sometimes be cranky, argumentative, or abusive.** You may feel resentment and often experience burnout. Your feelings are natural. Try to detach yourself from your loved one's behavior and focus on other things, one of which might be happy memories of past years.

➤ **Join a support group.** Some groups are for caregivers in general, while others focus on a specialty area, such as families of Alzheimer's patients. Just talking with others going through what you are can help enormously, allowing you to return to your duties refreshed.

Do you have a computer? Many of the major online services offer assistance for the caregiver, whether in the form of tips or with a social arena for chatting with others in your position. Specifics about these services can be found in Chapter 29, "Are We Having Fun Yet?" You might want to call a few services to see what they offer in this area and then compare programs.

➤ **It is important to realize and accept when the time has come, as it sometimes does, for your relative to move to a nursing home.** You have done the very best that you can for him or her, but now it is better for a full-time facility to take over aspects of care that you cannot provide.

➤ AARP offers the video *Survival Tips for New Caregivers* for $12. Call (800) 424-3410.

The Least You Need to Know

➤ While elder care can be expensive, there are some community agencies that can help with a wide variety of programs, from meals to "sitting" to home repair. It will take some phone calls around the community to locate those services, but many of them are free or at a nominal cost. It will be worth the effort to find them.

➤ Day care, respite care, or having a sitter/companion come to your loved one's home all offer him or her an opportunity for interaction with new people, and you some hours of free time. Take advantage of them as frequently as possible. Some services charge a fee, but some are free.

➤ It will take some time setting up your resources, but caregiving *can* take place across a long distance. Perhaps a geriatric care manager can help in coordinating the support you and your loved one will need.

➤ The major criterion in evaluating a nursing home is that it should have an attentive, caring staff. Also, when investigating nursing homes, know that you will have to do much of the evaluating yourself.

➤ Very important: Take good care of the caregiver!

Part 6
Retirement Countdown

Well, time certainly does fly, doesn't it? Here you are, about ready to attend another retirement party and... it's your own!

Perhaps you have planned well, and absolutely cannot wait to leave the workplace. But maybe you are 61 or 64, and now you must plunge into this new life you can't quite believe has arrived. You? Retired?

What will it be like? Retirement could be nearly one-third of your life. Those days can be filled with enriching, enjoyable experiences that also bring new pleasures from relations with family and friends, and from enjoyment of your home. There is travel, perhaps another paying job, school if you like, volunteering and... well, read on. This is a long part of the book because there is so much for you to do. Good luck! Enjoy!

Chapter 25

3-2-1 Blastoff

In This Chapter

➤ Some personal points to mull over

➤ The importance of talking about this major change in your life with immediate family and close friends

➤ A final look at any budget surprises

So you are planning to retire in a year or two or three. You find that your financial portfolio is pretty much in order, but there are other issues that might still be unresolved. The rest of your life, for one, and what you will be doing with those days when you walk out the office door for the last time. Let's take a look at a little more work you can do to be certain you enter retirement as well prepared as you can possibly be in areas of your life that it might not have occurred to you will be affected by that retirement date.

Are You Ready? A Seven-Question Quiz

Here is a test to help you see how ready you really are to depart the salt mines, or how much work you still need to do to retire gracefully and productively. Just jot *yes* or *no* after the queries. Interpretation of your responses follows the quiz. Answer these questions:

1. You are chairing a project at work that will be completed six months after you retire. Can you imagine the team functioning well in your absence?

2. If you have accepted an early retirement offer, have you come to terms with that decision?

3. If you are at the regular retirement age at your company, do you want to continue working there so badly that you have thought about asking management if you can stay on longer?

4. Have you at least begun to think about what might interest you after retirement? A part-time job? The kids and grandchildren? Volunteer work? Spending time with friends?

5. You are at a party shortly after you have retired. Someone asks you, as they customarily have at these things over the years, "And what do you do?" How do you reply?

6. An important consideration these days: Are you and your spouse in agreement about your retirement, and whether he or she will continue working or will also retire or resign?

7. Are you and your spouse in agreement about where you will live after you retire?

How did you respond? Let's see:

1. If you cannot, it might not have sunk in yet that you will be retiring, or you might be fighting that very real upcoming date. Naturally, you must do your job, even if it means planning a product, service, or conference to be realized six months after your departure. But do keep in the back of your mind that you *will* be somewhere else then. That new mindset is important for an easy transition from work to retirement.

2. It can take a good deal of work on your part to come to terms with a forced early retirement—even if you were not that thrilled with the job anyway. A handsome financial package can ease the shock somewhat, and your knuckling down to find another job will help, because this retirement might have come before you were ready, age-wise or in any other way. Look back a little, which is understandable, but look forward a good deal!

3. If you are in good health, doing good work, and sense that management might want to keep you on a while longer, it probably won't hurt to ask. Keep it light, though, and be prepared for a "No, but thanks for asking" response.

   If you want to stay on because you sense that you will be desperate without that work and retirement seems an abyss, you should give some careful thought to preparation (or lack of it) for those non-working days.

4. You have to make some plans, even if they change frequently. They can be vague ("Maybe I'll take up golf. I'd like to get involved in some sport or other.") or they can be more specific ("Now I'll have time to serve on the board of the condominium association/Boys Club/Friends of the Museum."). That thinking will at least get you to make the leap in your mind from a daily job to retirement activities, and plant the "I really have to think about all this" seed. Eventually, you will firm up your plans.

5. Any answer is fine, as long as you are comfortable with it. You can say "I'm retired," or "I'm retiring next year," or "I just retired as a math teacher at Elm Street High," or "I'm retired, but I've been doing a lot of work lately with the League of Women Voters." It *will* startle you, though, the first time you answer that question at or just after retirement. After all, you might have been giving the same answer for decades!

6. It helps if there is harmony between you and your spouse about those very important issues. Often, if the man is retiring, the woman, who might be a few years younger, might want to continue working or start her own career.

   If there are serious conflicts between the two of you on this important subject, perhaps counseling will offer a solution. As stated several times in this book, retirement is a major life change, and you might need some outside help getting on track for the years ahead.

7. This can be another toughie, but caring couples usually work out the issue, even if it results in a kind of choppy compromise. The man who looks forward to heading for Florida to golf and

Gray Matter Alert
A consultancy, if that is possible in your field, could be a segue from working full time at your company to retiring full time. Also, some corporations hire retired workers as temps, as the need arises, because those former employees know the workings of the company. If you'd like to stay on where you are, you might look into both possibilities.

It's Been Said
Archie doesn't know how to worry without getting upset.
—Edith Bunker

fish immediately after retirement, and the woman who wants to stay home to be near the kids and grandchildren, will obviously be pulling in different directions. Sometimes a compromise is two homes—one owned in the hometown and the other rented in the vacation locale. Sometimes it is importing family and friends to the new permanent home miles away for frequent visits, and hopping back home, often by the spouse who misses it the most.

If no progress is made through compromise without one party feeling put out and angry, the answer to question 6 might apply here too: Seek professional counseling.

Is Your Spouse Ready? A Five-Question Quiz

The heading here is addressed to the retiree, but the section that follows is, of course, for your spouse, significant other, companion, or whoever it may be who shares your home and life in such an important fashion. For ease in reading, we'll continue to use *spouse*. So hand these questions to him or her, and no kibitzing, now:

1. Are you in agreement that this is the time for your spouse to retire, or do you want him or her to continue working?

2. Are you prepared for the changes in your day-to-day life with this retirement? Have you talked them over with the retiree?

3. Do you realize that retirement, eagerly anticipated or not, can affect your spouse dramatically—that he or she may need your support then more than at many other times in life? This is particularly true if your spouse is being forced into early retirement.

4. Do you have a support system of your own for dealing with your spouse's retirement?

5. This is the same as the retiree's question 7. Are you in agreement about where to live after retirement?

About your responses:

1. If age makes it mandatory that your spouse retire, then there is no room for discussion. But if you want your spouse to work longer, perhaps to earn more money, or maybe because you're working longer, have you discussed the matter with him or her, or does the prospective retiree just have a sense that you are not supportive of this move? Talk this over honestly. Retiring is a big enough change for both of you without hiding important feelings about the very deed itself—its timing, necessity, and so on.

2. If you do not hold an outside job, you might feel the retirement change almost as much as your spouse that leaves the workplace. It will affect your daily life that much.

   In any event, or in any other scenario, think about how the household will work now. Will you cook together? Clean together? Do everything as a couple? For many spouses, the answers will be doing some things together, but having some separate social activities, making for a continually fresh exchange of news and ideas. Household duties may well change from who did what in previous years, but do discuss freely what you'd like (having her come along with you on errands, maybe stopping for lunch along the way) to what you'd absolutely abhor (having him accompany you grocery shopping all the time).

3. While some whoop for joy at retirement, others can suffer a mild depression once there is no more familiar workplace. Those who are being ushered out of their job against their will can be particularly susceptible to depression. Your spouse will need your encouragement, your suggestions, and your pointing to the positive life ahead (although it is up to the retiree, of course, to chart his or her own course for the future). If depression runs too long, or is all-encompassing, you will probably want to seek medical help.

4. You need friends or family members, aside from your spouse, with whom to discuss the changes in your lives these days, and the ups and downs as you move into a new routine. Many women do this easily. Some men might have to make more of an effort, perhaps talking with one of the children or a good buddy for insight and advice. It will be worth it, and will bring a fresh prospective to the issue or problem concerning you.

It's Been Said
Extremists think "communicating" means agreeing with them.
—Leo Rosten, *A Trumpet for Reason*, 1970

It's Been Said
Happiness? That's nothing more than health and a poor memory.
—Albert Schweitzer

5. The answer here is the same as the retiree's answer number 7. Fortunately, most couples are in agreement on moving or staying put, and have looked forward for several years to enjoying the decisions they have made.

When both of you have finished the quizzes, exchange answers. That can bring some surprises, but will certainly offer both of you a chance to discuss large or small points of the upcoming retirement that have either gone unspoken or have been taken for granted by one spouse, but certainly not the other. This is a good opportunity for dialogue!

The Retirement Budget Dry Run

Tick-tock, tick-tock. You are now two or three years from retirement. Here is a good way to be sure you can live, and reasonably well, on what you have been calculating in the earlier parts of this book.

Select two months—any two ordinary, consecutive months with no year-end holidays or vacations during that time—and see if you can get by on what you expect to have coming in during your first few retirement years. Add everything in, at the amounts of money you expect, and have a test run. If you don't already know, you can contact Social Security for an estimate of your benefits, and get pension and 401(k) totals from your employer.

You can conduct this test for just two months, but do *think* about an entire retirement year during that time. If you budget your retirement income from pension, Social Security, and savings at $22,000 per year, for example, and you now are earning $34,000, you might have $12,000 left over if you don't increase your spending after retirement. Or consider this: Estimate your retirement expenses at 70 to 75 percent of your gross salary at the time of retirement. How does that figure compare with your retirement sources of income?

Just for fun, and to get a broad idea of where your money will be going during the transition to retirement (the heavy preparation, of course, took place in Parts 1 and 3 of this book), answer the questions in the Expenses quiz to the best of your ability. Then, note the difference in certain expenses now versus later, and the cause for that spending. Do the two totals almost cancel each other out? If the After Retirement expenses are higher than the While Employed ones (not likely), you'll have to take into account the need for a retirement income that will pay for that increase.

Expenses Quiz

List 5 expenses you will have while employed that you will NOT have after retirement.	Annual Cost	List 5 expenses you will have after retirement you do not have now.	Annual Cost
1. _____	_____	1. _____	_____
2. _____	_____	2. _____	_____
3. _____	_____	3. _____	_____
4. _____	_____	4. _____	_____
5. _____	_____	5. _____	_____
Total	_____	Total	_____

How will your expenses in retirement compare to what you are spending now? Here's a quiz to help you find out.

What If... It Isn't Enough?

Engage in this test run once or twice a year. If you find too great a disparity between your expenses and expected income during these tests, you will have time to go back to the drawing board and work the numbers again, so that the ledger is in better shape by your actual retirement. If you are continually running short, ask yourself why. Will your needs be greater than you had budgeted? Perhaps you plan a part-time job after retirement that will bring in some money to add to what is lacking now. You also will learn during this experiment where your interests lie and where you have a hard time cutting back. Is it lavish gifts for the grandchildren? Travel? Do you like to dine out often, with an emphasis on "dine?" You'll learn where the weakness is in your retirement planning and see that you truly have to cut back—or earn more money.

This will not be a totally scientific study, of course, because you are still working and have job-related expenses like commuting, lunches, and so on. Your housing may change when you retire, with different figures for rent or mortgage payments, and auxiliary costs. But if you try this dry run, even in its imperfect state, you will have a good idea of what it's like to live on a shrunken income while there is still time to do some fine-tuning before actually having to live on those retirement moneys with no safety net.

The Least You Need to Know

➤ Retirement is a major change, even when it is joyously welcomed. It's natural to feel a little shaky at the outset.

➤ While a spouse can help you with plans for your new life, it is truly up to you to make this new "passage" as successful as it can be.

➤ Last chance! Try living on your retirement income for a few months each year during the last two or three years you are working. If you can't, go back to your budget for some adjustments.

Chapter 26

Another Look at Housing

In This Chapter

➤ Choices for last-minute planners

➤ Life changes, home changes

➤ Housing options you may not have known existed

Now that you're inching closer toward retirement, your earlier decision about where to live after The Big Day may be in the process of changing. You might have discovered (and if you haven't, you will in the next few pages) that there are options you would not have known about or considered a few years ago—manufactured homes or communal housing, for example. Or perhaps, after reading about it, a life care community looks good to you about now.

What follows is a mini-smorgasbord of still more housing suggestions. See what we mean when we said earlier that you will have so many options in this area that your retirement home is likely to be two or more addresses over the years?

To Mortgage or Not To Mortgage

This would not have been a question with your first, or no doubt, any other, home you have owned. Pay cash—Hah! But now it is a consideration. Perhaps now you have cash from the equity buildup in previous homes to pay for the one you buy now without financing it. Should you?

Alas, there is no clear answer here. This is a personal decision, based on your current financial situation and needs for the future.

If you pay cash for your home, will you still have money for emergencies in an accessible fund? Remember that you can't sell a home quickly for instant cash. Do you have a savings plan for the next 10 or 20 years that will keep up with rising costs of living? Or will paying cash for a home strip you of all those needed moneys?

You might want to go with cash if your investments are in low-return CDs, for example. Why pay 8 or 9 percent interest on a mortgage loan while CDs are earning 5 or 6 percent?

Another reason for paying cash is purely emotional. If you are going to be nervous carrying a mortgage into retirement, then go with owning your home free and clear. Don't let that debt spoil otherwise good days ahead.

Yes, you will be giving up the mortgage interest tax deduction if you pay cash. Many retirees do not claim a lot of deductions, and the amount of interest on a low mortgage (maybe $50,000 or so), might not exceed the standard deduction allowed. If you itemize deductions, it might pay to consider that tax break in the cash versus mortgage decision.

Gray Matter Alert
When you sell your home, you have two years to buy another before the profits from that home are subject to taxation.

Some retirees choose to divide the money they realize from a home sale, making a large down payment on their next house, and investing the balance to help their nest egg grow. The down payment helps keep mortgage payments low. That's a good way to go, too, depending on whether you will have enough in savings for the coming years.

Redesigned Homes for Retirement Living

The retirement home you planned in your forties might be different from one you now want or need in your sixties, seventies, or even eighties, in a way you did not expect. Now you will be looking for some design features to make life a little easier for you, your spouse, and guests to your home, either presently or in the future.

Although 70 percent of the population—regardless of age—suffers from a disability at least once during their lifetime, most people do not equip their houses to handle mobility or vision problems.

If you will be house hunting soon, here are some good features to look for. A bonus for you: Real estate agents say homes that include some of these design elements make a property more marketable (when selling, you can offer to put things back to their original state if that's what a particular buyer wants):

Thin Ice
Studies show that many older people resist thinking about and implementing alterations in their homes as their needs change. They simply stop using something that gives them trouble, narrowing what they can do even further.

➤ Take a good look at the exterior of the house that interests you. Will the facade require constant upkeep? Maybe you won't have to do that work, but you will have to pay for someone to handle the constant painting, for example. That goes for landscaping, too.

➤ Can you construct a ramp to the front door, if it is needed?

➤ Be careful of too many—or any—steps or stairs. Make sure that stairwells are well lit and prepare to install a handrail if there is none.

➤ Doorways 36 inches wide can accommodate a wheelchair. If you cannot find any of that size, be sure the house you choose is adaptable if the need arises.

➤ Thick carpeting might be too difficult for a wheelchair to cross. Carpeting not so plush is better, but bare wood floors are better yet. Be sure a house you look at with wall-to-wall carpeting has more than subflooring, in the event you choose one day to take up the carpet.

➤ Do you plan on having a workshop in your retirement home for all the projects you've been saving until you have more time? If you will have a basement, your space will be heated, but you might want to consider heat in the garage of your home if that's where the workshop will be. You'll be more comfortable and able to work there any time of the day or night, or any time of the year. You can have central heat extended into the garage, or opt for electrical units installed along the baseboard in that space. Both jobs should be done by a professional.

➤ At least one bathroom should be large enough for a wheelchair to turn around. It would be wise, too, to have at least one shower stall, instead of only bathtubs. You can install safety bars in the bath(s) near the toilet and tub areas.

Here is an interesting statistic to help you look seriously at any home you are considering these days. By one estimate, 20 to 40 percent of those in nursing homes are there because they do not have services and housing that would enable them to live at home independently.

Adapting a home for easier living is, like the aging population itself, a growing field, with much literature for the retiree. For helpful suggestions in and around your home, you can write for *The Doable Renewable Home: Making Your Home Fit Your Needs* and *The Perfect Fit: Creative Ideas for a Safe and Livable Home.* Both are available from The American Association of Retired Persons, 601 E St. NW, Washington, DC 20049. Or, you can call (800) 424-3410.

Shared Housing, or Co-Housing, or...

Semantics, it'll kill us. What we are talking about here, with slight shadings in meanings, is co-housing, communal housing, mutual housing, shared housing, and extended family housing. All these terms describe unrelated people living together in some new lifestyle, or at least officially new.

This is a fascinating arena, in which professionals are conducting experiments in housing styles that allow for independence among residents, yet foster a sense of community and, for the elderly in particular, take away some of the burden of living alone.

There are several hundred of these communities across the country. Some are new housing developments for buyers of all ages, who own their homes and then share common areas, such as dining facilities, daycare, and laundry. Others are houses, built by private developers especially for sharing, with each residence having a bedroom/bath suite, and then two or three residents sharing the living/dining area and the kitchen. Still another segment of this market is existing houses that have been purchased and remodeled by government agencies for use as "group homes," where four or more retired residents of that community share the dwelling.

Thin Ice
A zoning alert: Some communities have statutes against unrelated persons sharing a home, although your having one housemate is not exactly a group home. If you do have more than one sharer, check with your local office on aging or senior services department for clarification of this issue.

You could be many miles from some of these newcomers on the housing scene, although as the huge number of baby boomers reaches retirement age, no doubt those facilities will become more numerous.

For more information, you can contact the National Shared Housing Resource Center, 321 E. 25 St., Baltimore, MD 21218, (410) 235-4454.

Here is another source. You can send for the booklets *Making Home Sharing Work for You: A Planning Guide* and *Shared Living Residences: The Most Asked Questions*. Both are part of the *Housing Options for Seniors Today* series published by Cornell Cooperative Extension. Send $1.20 for each booklet to Media Services Resource Center "Topics," Cornell University, 7 Cornell Business and Technology Park, Ithaca, NY 14850.

The Most Popular Sharing Style

This is one that can help with your living situation right now. If you have a too-large house, you might take in a sharer—someone who is not a boarder, but who has full run of the house, using all of its facilities.

If you don't have someone in mind, you can contact your local council on aging or senior services department, which often can help with finding a house sharer, either someone your own age or—another growing option—a younger person, perhaps a single mother and her child, or someone who might be willing to do some chores around the house in exchange for a lower rent. A student attending a local college might fill the latter bill.

Make sure all rules with these co-sharers, whether friend or stranger, are spelled out before anyone moves in. You might see a lawyer to have a simple lease drawn up, or perhaps your local office on aging can help.

The flip side of all of this is that if you are seeking someone with a house to share, you, too, can contact those local offices, looking to make a match with an individual they have on their books with a home to share. You also might be in a community with group homes.

Continuing-Care Retirement Communities

Continuing-care communities are words you will hear over and over again as you shop for a home when you retire. Sometimes also known as *life-care communities*, the concept is growing as the aging population increases.

Continuing-care retirement communities, more familiarly known by the initials CCRC, are sprawling complexes where buyers generally move through in phases:

1. Independent living, where you purchase a home in any style the community offers, such as a ranch or patio home, condominium or cottage; or you might rent an apartment.

2. Assisted living, where there is some help with meals and other services.

3. The health center or nursing home, which provides skilled nursing care.

OOOOH...

Power Word
Skilled nursing facility is a term you will see frequently when reading about long-term care. The federal government, which administers Medicare and, with each state, the Medicaid program, defines a skilled nursing facility as one in which there is 24-hour nursing care under the direction of a physician. Other healthcare insurers and providers may have a looser definition of the term.

Every community is different—not only in its look, but also in rules and regulations, healthcare coverage and, of course, fees charged.

Yes, continuing care is expensive. On the other hand, you know that once you are in that community, if you become ill, according to the terms of your contract, you will be cared for as long as you need to be. That concept is what is making those complexes so popular. (A reassuring note: Most CCRCs have a policy that residents will not be forced to leave if they outlive their assets.)

Most CCRCs charge an up-front fee that covers the living unit and part or all of future healthcare costs. How much can that up-front fee be? Anywhere from $10,000 to more than $500,000. Some communities refund a portion after a specific period of time if requested, or allow refunds on a sliding scale. Besides the fee, there is a monthly cost to residents that can range from several hundred dollars to $3,000 or more. Care varies according to those fees charged, and can run from extensive (life care) to pay-as-you-need-it services, which is what residents who pay the lower entry fees often choose.

Extra! Extra!

As you begin looking into retirement homes, you might want to refer to *Retirement Living Communities*, compiled by Deborah Freundlich (Macmillan, $24.95). The book is a national directory of more than 400 full-service housing communities. Various styles are included, including developments adjacent to and affiliated with colleges or universities. Retirement communities had to follow specific criteria to qualify for a listing; they had to offer healthcare, 24-hour security, and certain other specified services.

Some Suggestions When Looking Around

How can you tell which are the well-run (translation: financially sound) CCRC communities? How can you tell what you can afford when plowing through pages of figures in a community's documents offered to prospective buyers?

Here are some tips:

➤ Look at the communities carefully, of course, and talk to residents. Don't move in too soon—when you are too young—or you may not find friends with compatible interests. The mid seventies seems to be the most popular entry age in CCRCs.

➤ Keep in mind that you are not buying profit-making real estate here. This is a totally different concept.

➤ If money is a serious concern, you might choose renting an apartment over any home purchase. In many complexes, you do not have to pay an entry fee when you rent. That rent, which might be $1,000 a month, for example, might cover such services as meals, although you probably will pay for healthcare as you use those facilities.

➤ Have a lawyer, perhaps an elder law attorney (these attorneys are discussed in Chapter 20), read every document you are handed for admission carefully. Be sure that you understand what you are purchasing and some of the finer points of CCRCs. For example, when residents are transferred into the assisted-living or the nursing-care facilities, who is it who makes those decisions? You? Staff healthcare professionals? Your family?

➤ You can read more about nursing homes in Chapter 23, "Paying the Bills."

For more information about CCRCs, contact the Continuing Care Accreditation Commission (CCAC), which is run by the American Association of Homes and Services for the Aging. CCAC looks closely at the quality of those residences, including their financial stability. You can ask them about accreditation, too, of course. Call (202) 783-7286.

The American Association of Homes and Services for the Aging publishes printed material that also can help in the decision-making process. Call (202) 783-2242.

Moving in with the Kids, or Vice Versa

Here is a housing style that will either make you smile and bring on warm feelings... or have you rolling your eyes. If it's the eyes, you had better move on to the next topic. This will never work for you.

But, you smilers, let's give this some thought. Two households can live as cheaply as one in many ways. If you all get along just fine, why not share? It can work for economy, and for the companionship.

A few points about joining generations to keep in mind: Never give the kids all your money if you're moving into their home, or if they are moving into yours, for that matter. You never know about your future wants or needs. Also, having no money puts you in a no-power position in that relationship. If the kids need a hand and you can afford to help, by all means offer, if you like. But make sure they get some help, not all your assets. Keep these points in mind:

281

Gray Matter Alert
These paragraphs discuss your moving in with your child, or your child making a home with you, but there is another option, of course, and that is your moving in with a parent or having him or her live with you. With Americans living longer, it is not unusual these days to see households consisting of an 88-year-old parent and a 65-year-old son or daughter.

Thin Ice
If either you or your child is planning to add a room and bath and perhaps a separate entrance to your home to accommodate a relative, first check your local government agency to see what you are allowed to do from a zoning standpoint. Once you have that permission, you can go ahead with the building plans (subject, of course, to a building permit and town inspection).

➤ You had better have some house rules. Perhaps your kids' children are grown and gone, but if there are some of them still at home, decide now whether you can be called on for baby-sitting or day care, and whether you will charge for that assistance. Speaking of your grandchildren, will you be able to discipline them freely? That's an important point to discuss, too.

➤ While you are in the dialogue mode, it would be wise for all of you to talk about housekeeping, too. Will you be expected to pitch in? Are there some chores you would prefer over others? Are there some it is assumed you will undertake (which might come as news to you!)? What about home repairs? Better discuss it all and apportion work fairly. The more you straighten out beforehand, the less chance for misunderstandings and hurt feelings later.

Actually, those decisions and compromises might be easier to make these days when everyone is involved in outside work, taking care of the home, volunteering, attending school, baby-sitting, playing marathon bridge games, or participating in other activities that keep them on the move. A house full of busy people often doesn't sweat the small stuff.

➤ Both sides should pay something toward the running of the house, even if the amount is prorated according to how much money that individual can comfortably manage. It will boost the self-esteem of the one who pays less, and will register with the one paying more that the other is not a guest, but a paying, contributing member of the household.

Mobiles? Manufactured Homes? Which Are They These Days?

You might have been seeing the term *manufactured homes* a good deal recently. What exactly are they?

These are "houses" produced in sections in a factory—parts that can even include carpeting—and then shipped to the building site where the sections are assembled to form a house. They can be very attractive indeed. In fact, in some communities, you cannot distinguish them from traditional homes built on the site from the ground up.

Manufactured houses are less costly for developers, and for you too. New homes come in a variety of styles, from luxurious to quite simple. An average three-bedroom, two-bath, multi-section manufactured home, loaded with amenities, such as a fireplace, will cost around $40,000 (including installation, but not including land). Larger homes can carry $100,000-plus price tags. Carports and garages are extra.

Resale manufactured homes range in price from less than $20,000 for small units to well into what you would pay for a new house, if it is in good condition and in a solid, well-maintained manufactured home community.

These homes must adhere to standards complying with a 1976 federal code set by the U.S. Department of Housing and Urban Development. Yes, they were once called *mobile homes*, but now, because the newer ones never leave their original site, that term is no longer in general use. You may see it in some of the older *mobile home parks*, however, and some salespeople and others in the business use the term because it is familiar to many buyers. Table 26.1 shows that manufactured homes have come a very long way from their very humble beginnings.

Table 26.1 From Trailers to Manufactured Homes

Year	Development
1930s–40s	Aluminum trailer is eight feet wide, and can be hauled on a highway behind a car.
1950s	The first 10-foot-wide models are introduced. Manufacturers put two together for *double-wides*.
1960s	The 10-foot-wide models grow to 12 and 14 feet wide. Each state has its own standards for construction and transportation. Now known as *mobile homes* and placed in *mobile home parks*.
1976	The federal government begins to regulate construction of mobile homes.
1980	The federal government changes the term *mobile* to *manufactured* home in all its laws and publications, to reflect the changing nature of the product.
1995	One out of every three new single-family homes in the country is a manufactured home. Shipments in May are the highest since August 1974. In July, industry estimates are that 325,000 to 350,000 manufactured homes will be sold in 1995.

Source: Manufactured Housing Institute

A Look at Communities

If there are manufactured homes on land the buyer owns, and if they are not going to be moved (they likely are not), they are considered real estate and can qualify for financing with a mortgage.

There also may be manufactured homes on leased land. They are considered personal property, and are financed with a loan from the manufactured home retailer or from a bank.

Thin Ice

Are manufactured homes safe? The federal government keeps tightening regulations, as news circulates of some homes being flattened in major storms. However, those are usually the older, smaller mobile homes. Owners of all manufactured houses buy the best home owners insurance protection they can, and then just hope a Big Blow doesn't hit *them*.

If you are interested in a home on rented land, be sure to ask the park owner the questions a renter would ask about any property: Does the community have covenants to which one must adhere? How long is a lease? To what does that entitle a resident? Who handles maintenance? And here's one for you to learn the answer to: What happens if the park owner decides to sell his land? Where does that leave you and your home?

If you want to have a manufactured home erected on land you own outside a manufactured home community, be certain your municipality allows that housing. Some do not, although restrictions against them are easing as the factory-built homes become more attractive and government regulations tighten. What will you pay for a lot? Whatever land costs in the area that interests you—and that can be anywhere from a few hundred dollars or less per acre to more than $50,000. Location is everything in real estate, remember?

When Renting an Apartment Is the Best Option

With all this talk about houses, you might find yourself stirring with impatience. "I've had enough of houses," you say. "When I retire I want to chuck home maintenance, and even home ownership. Is it so terrible to want to rent an apartment?"

These days it is not, and indeed there are many retirees who feel the same way you do. They sell their homes, invest the profit, and rent an apartment. Interest from that investment helps with the rent, or perhaps the rent is low enough to be such a difference from the mortgage payments of previous years that no help from investments is needed.

Actually, with houses appreciating slowly in the 1990s—in some parts of the country, not at all—you do not stand to make the killing that some sellers did in the 1980s. And the money you would have spent on the down payment for a home—money that would be tied up as long as you owned the place, with no interest accruing—could well earn a tidy profit for you elsewhere.

Generally speaking, over the long haul it is wiser to own than to rent. But you are not just starting out with home owning, raising a family, and needing the space of a house, so why buy one if you don't want to? These are your years, remember?

It's Been Said
The fellow that owns his own home is always just coming out of a hardware store.
—Frank McKinney Hubbard

With Some Help from the Government

If you will be on a very limited retirement budget, you might want to look into U.S., state, or regional government-assisted rental housing for seniors. These are complexes—high rise or garden style—where the government charges below-market rents for tenants who qualify for financial assistance.

Sometimes Uncle Sam owns the complexes; sometimes they are in the hands of private developers who are subsidized so that they are able to realize a market rent for their units.

Many of these communities are very attractive, well run, and desirable, and have long waiting lists for admission. When we say long, we mean if you are interested in moving into one in two or three years, you had better look into getting your name on the waiting list immediately!

For more information, you can call your local housing office or housing authority.

The Least You Need to Know

➤ Even if you will be tightly budgeted, you will still have housing choices in retirement, such as sharing your home, renting an apartment, or perhaps living in government-assisted apartment complexes.

➤ Some retirees prefer to be with others their own age, but you might opt for an age mix. That can work with a younger house sharer, or by living with your kids.

➤ Whether you share your home with a friend, stranger, or your kids, it is important that you discuss all aspects of the arrangement so that everyone understands rights and responsibilities and there are no unpleasant surprises a short time into that arrangement.

➤ Continuing Care Retirement Communities (CCRCs) can offer a lifetime of care, for a price. Be sure to closely investigate any community you are considering, and note services provided, including the extent of healthcare coverage.

Chapter 27

Family Matters and Other Relationships

In This Chapter

➤ Adaptability wins, rigidity loses in retirement lifestyles

➤ Remarriage, and some changes it can bring

➤ The importance of friends—just like family, for some

Family comes to the fore as work days recede. Perhaps family was always more important to you than the job, but let's say there is more time now for relationships. Shifts can occur in family groupings, and with friends, too, in retirement years.

You might marry—or remarry. Children might marry or remarry. Perhaps there will be more grandkids. Grandnieces and nephews, too. And it's quite possible for a 66-year-old parent's 47-year-old child's 21-year-old daughter to make that retiree a great-grandparent! Eeek! Or wow! You may make many new friends, too, if you move to another community or another part of the country. You can make new friends even dipping into new activities where you are now. Here are a few words on what to do about change, so that both those important networks—family and friends—will be strong, to be enjoyed to the fullest.

If It's Just the Two of You—Some Adjustments To Be Sure

That first full day of retirement is apt to be an eye opener. It will likely be without structure, and will pass quickly, perhaps from your—and your spouse's—wanting to fill the hours to make it special. Eventually, though, and perhaps as soon as Day 2, you will want some structure to your days, if not to replicate working life, then at least to have a pattern you will quickly grow to recognize. Here are some ideas—more follow in Chapter 29—to get you started thinking and talking about new ways to spend your time, actually getting out and doing these things, and staying socially connected:

➤ **Look for another job!** Some will, you know, especially those faced with an unexpected retirement at an earlier age than they expected.

➤ **Sightsee in your town.** You know how it is said that New Yorkers never visit the Statue of Liberty and other tourist sights in their city? Maybe you've overlooked what *your* town has to offer. Take some day trips and explore.

➤ **Look into what you've never done that might be just the spark you and your spouse need right now to perk up this start to the rest of your life.** Head for stables and go horseback riding, if that is something you've always wanted to do. Plant a tree. Begin growing your own tomatoes. Hiking to a nearby destination, swimming where you've never been before—all offer new experiences (and, you'll notice, are good exercise and get you out of the house).

➤ **If you are a 1970s, or '60s, or '50s couple, maybe it's time to update yourselves.** Toss out the rules(?) that say the husband does this around the house and the wife that. Take your cue from today's young marrieds, who share household chores along non-gender-related lines. For example, if you've always been ho-hum about cooking and he loves it, let him do more, or most, of it. If you suspect that she'd be better at managing the budget and paying the bills, and she's game, let her do it.

➤ **Do some visiting together, calls you have been meaning to make and somehow never got around to with the busyness of a daily job.** Invite yourself to your child's apartment for dinner, and call on an ailing relative. Arrange to meet friends and have lunch at an elegant spot to celebrate the retirement and perhaps renew a friendship that had been back burnered over the years. Remember the saying, "Make new friends but keep the old, one is silver the other gold."

It's Been Said
Grow old along with me! The best is yet to be, The last of life for Which the first was made.
—Robert Browning

➤ Pick up with as many old friends as you can, friends you might have lost contact with, or been reduced to holiday greeting cards as communication over the years. You might be delighted at the ease with which you pick up chatting with them again after so many years. Friends, especially those who know you from way back, become important in retirement years, now that child-raising and the daily nine-to-five grind do not take up such a large chunk of your time.

If you get the impression by now that you are being asked to test some new waters, you're right. It's easy to slip into comfortable pre-retirement routines (TV, walking the dog, cleaning house, grocery shopping, and so on), but with the huge gap of empty time in the middle of the day now, you have to be creative. Making an effort in these early days means you will find your style together sooner rather than later, and your days will fall into a new pattern, as busy as you want them to be, but always open, of course, to delightful surprises.

Yours, Mine, Ours (When Two Families Are Combined)

Remarriage a few years before or into retirement can bring new pleasures, one of which can be your new spouse's family. The "children" are probably grown by now, and you can consider them new friends.

That is how most of those situations work out, but your new family might need some work on the togetherness front. Most kids are happy for their parent to have found a companion with whom to move through retirement. Those who are not could be concerned with inheritance issues. That aspect of remarriage is considered in Chapter 17, "Protection for Your Possessions." Here we will say, that with an effort on both sides (if one is needed), you and your mate can succeed in blending this new, grown-up family.

Compromise, of course, is the name of the game, just as it is in marriage at any stage of life. Yes, your stepchildren are probably grown and away, but your spouse has spent 25, 30, or however many years with that child—years you know nothing about—and has forged a relationship that could come as news to you.

Maybe Helen is on the phone with her daughter, Paula, 3,000 miles away, every two or three days. "Why does she have to talk to a grown woman that often?" you ask. "And the phone bill!" Perhaps you can't understand why Stan keeps running over to help his son, Dave, with Dave's new business at every phone call from the younger man. Can't Stan let that adult run his own career?

In both instances, it pays to be tolerant of those long-standing relationships and the dynamics behind them, which you might not yet understand. For example, Dave could

It's Been Said
She saw every personal relationship as a pair of intersecting circles... Probably perfection is reached when the area of the two outer crescents, added together, is exactly equal to that of the leaf-shaped piece in the middle. On paper there must be some neat mathematical formula for arriving at this; in life, none.
—Jan Struther in *Mrs. Miniver* (1940)

have had an earlier business go under, or he is not that great with numbers, so Stan is helping with the books. Or there is some other factor at work that could help you understand what you see as excessive "helping" on Stan's part.

Talk over what you do not understand, not in an accusing tone, but just making conversation. A lot will come out in casual chit-chat that can illuminate situations that are puzzling to you, helping not only the stepparent/stepchild relationship, but also the bonding process of a new, united stepfamily.

Although you might like your spouse's family perfectly well, you also might not want to spend that much time with them when they visit, but rather continue your own pursuits. Perhaps you and your partner can work out a schedule in which you are away fishing for a few days the way you'd like, when Cindy, Bob, and the kids visit for a week, for example. But you will come back two days before the gang leaves to spend some time with them, including dinner out for the whole "family."

You will probably be expected to show up at certain functions held by your new family: weddings, christenings, funerals, family reunions, and the like, whether you like those people or not. You will not be able to wriggle your way out of many events, but this is part of the package in marriage or remarriage, and you will no doubt plant a smile on your face, be pleasant, and try to enjoy yourself as much as you can.

All of this compromising, you know deep down, will be worth the effort. It will be reflected in your spouse's happiness, and in overall family harmony—both families that might, somewhere down the road, become one beautifully blended clan.

Lending Money to the Kids

This section can apply to your children, or those of a new spouse.

Parents are sometimes asked for a loan or a monetary gift. Sometimes it's $20 until payday, but on other occasions, it can be several thousand dollars for the down payment on a home. How should you handle these requests?

It's easier if you're both the parents of that child. In a stepfamily, one concern is likely to be, "Does it come out of *your* money or *our* money?" Another might be one partner's annoyance at his or her spouse's child asking for money ("You make it too easy for him" or "She's always testing how you feel about her by asking for money"). Both of those responses call for honest talk between partners. After all, this is a family that is here to stay, and you want things to work well.

Here are some good rules to follow when lending money to the children, to help both you and them—and your bank account, too.

➤ If you are worried about your financial future and feel you simply cannot offer that child a loan in the amount he or she needs, by all means reject that request, explaining your position if you feel comfortable getting into your finances with the kids. Some parents do not.

➤ To avoid misunderstandings later, be sure everyone involved knows whether this is a gift or a loan that you expect to have repaid. If it is the latter, will you charge interest?

➤ Any loan for more than $5,000 should be treated like a business arrangement, with the terms for repayment in writing. If your child has a history of not paying back money borrowed, either on time or at all, and if having that money returned is very important to you, you might want to lower that figure to $1,000, or perhaps even less. You can have a lawyer draw up a payment schedule, or you can purchase a standard form at an office supply store. You can change terms and payment dates as often as you choose, but the schedule, official looking as it is, should impress your child with the seriousness of this agreement.

➤ Consult an accountant for the best way to give or lend money with the fewest repercussions to your bank account and tax situation.

➤ You and your spouse, and the child, should feel free to discuss all aspects of the money to be borrowed—what it is to be used for, how everyone feels about this debt, and, of course, all of the other points listed here.

> **Thin Ice**
> If you have been asked to co-sign your child's mortgage, keep in mind that that obligation is taken into account by lenders should you want to borrow money someday for starting a business, buying a second home, or some other major expenditure. It is considered *your* debt, even if your child has made every mortgage payment on time.

Grandparents' Legal Rights When Divorce Separates a Family

"If I'd known grandchildren were so much fun, I'd have had them first." You may have seen mugs, T-shirts and other paraphernalia printed with that slogan. Grandkids are likely to be a special delight of retirees' lives.

But not all grandparents are able to enjoy those experiences. With the high divorce rate these days, sometimes one half of a divorcing couple—the half with custody of the kids—can move right out of the older generation's lives. That has been making for a lot of bereft grandparents in recent years. Sometimes the tie is broken through distance, but on other occasions that parent does not want to be reminded of the marriage that failed, and that includes the reminder of in-laws. Remarriage of the custodial parent puts the grandparents at an even farther remove. It would be too confusing for the kids, the remarried parent now asserts.

Thin Ice
You might want to be careful about going too public with your desire to see your grandkids, or being too bitter about their custodial parent. Judges making these decisions might turn down your request if they think you're going to create more conflict in that child's life.

Finally, there are some instances where it is the death of a spouse that has seen the remaining parent cut off any relationship with that spouse's family.

While some children say rifts are the result of problems with their parents over the years, more grandparental losses stem from the reasons just mentioned.

Whatever the explanation, the effect is the same: The grandparents have no contact with the kids at all. But just as children deserve caring parents, they also need, if it is at all possible, the attention of doting grandparents, with their unconditional love. It's part of their birthright, too, to be able to trace their family history through the presence and stories of the older generation.

What You Can Do

Does this sound sadly familiar to you? Grandparents in your situation have fought for and won laws in recent years giving them the right to seek visitation with their grandkids when contact has been cut off after family breakups. Grandparents in every state have the legal right to demand visitation. You can engage a lawyer to fight for that right. You can lobby for continual reform of those laws, and you might also want to join a support group, several of which are springing up around the country. If you contact the National Self-Help Clearing House, 25 West 43 St., Room 620, New York, NY 10036, (212) 354-8525, they will put you in touch with the regional clearinghouse nearest you, so that you can see if there is a grandparents' support group in your area.

Living Together without Marriage

There are all manner of households today that do not constitute the traditional nuclear family. There are same-sex house sharers and opposite sex ones. There are those sharers engaged in a romantic relationship and those for whom *platonic* is the operative word.

If you are new to home sharing, you will no doubt want to make sure there is space in the house or apartment that is yours alone. If there isn't an entire room for each of you to have separately, then a nook will do, or even, in close quarters, a desk and chair that is "hands off" to anyone but you.

It's good to get the legalities of the partnership out of the way quickly, such as whose name is on the lease or mortgage, drawing up a will, or creating any other legal document, depending on the depth and length of the relationship. Several of those are considered in Part 5, "Law and Medicine—What You Absolutely Need to Know."

When it comes to *home*, some people who are living together—friends or family members who are not spouses—opt to buy a house together. The ownership style they choose is *tenants in common*, which means they can leave their share of the house to whomever they choose in their will. That's different from married couples, who usually buy as *joint tenants with rights of survivorship*, meaning that after their death, ownership of their half of the property reverts to the partner.

The best protection is a written agreement spelling out all possible scenarios in your relationship and resolutions to them, drawn up by an attorney. That way, if any problems arise, from one party wanting to sell and move on, to how paying of house-related bills will be handled, the sharers involved can consult that document. Some house sharers say they have run frequently to that paper during the first several months of the living-together arrangement, but then it was filed away and not referred to again.

Some Special Strategies for Living Alone

Many in this country, of whatever age, prefer to live alone in a household they set up just to suit themselves. Others would rather not, but still they do live by themselves.

A number of singles are doing just that these days, especially those in retirement years. There are some 7.4 million Americans age 65 and over living alone in this country, according to a 1993 U.S. Census Bureau study. That's from a total population of 18 million over the age of 65.

Just as there are strategies for every other aspect of retirement, there are some tips for doing this the best way possible for maximum enjoyment:

➤ Most single folks do know how to get out and do things, but without the socializing of a workplace (which might include bowling or softball with the company team, frequent lunches with coworkers, and so on), you might find yourself having to jump start your social life in the early days of retirement. That workplace socializing will be either entirely, or for the most part, missing in your new life.

➤ Sally Stayhome would like to travel, but being single, and with friends she can't usually coax to go along with her, she stays home. She thinks any trip she would take alone would be more a trial than a good time. Tina Traveler, on the other hand, is also single, and also can't always depend on friends for traveling companions. She goes everywhere her budget allows, however.

Traveling alone these days does not have to mean totally alone, if you do not want to be. Tina, for example, takes many Elderhostel vacations (there's more about them in Chapter 28, "Travel Time"), where there is a group of "students" her age just waiting to be friendly. She can share a room, too, if she doesn't want to stay by herself. Most travel agencies these days will help singles hook up with others of similar interests if they do not want to travel alone, for trips virtually anywhere in the world. If Sally sounds like you, all you have to do is ask, and you can travel with new friends or meet them there, expanding your horizons about a thousandfold.

➤ Can a single retiree be happy in a retirement community seemingly populated exclusively by couples? Yes, of course, unless he or she can't bear the thought of being age segregated, in which case it's certainly wise to skip that kind of housing.

One problem with some seniors is isolation and loneliness, and both can be overcome in a community of people who do have age and a variety of social activities in common. The majority of single retirees are women (and we are talking about never married, widowed, separated, and divorced "singles"), who often find themselves socializing with other women or with married couples in those communities.

It's Been Said

Let this be your motto—
Rely on yourself!
For whether the prize be a ribbon or throne,
The victor is he who can go it alone!
—John Godfrey Saxe, *The Game of Life*

Single men of retirement age are not as numerous, and while some are more outgoing than others, they, too, can find in a seniors-only community just as much socializing as they would like (maybe more than they would like from some female residents!).

The tip repeated so often in these pages when it comes to scouting specific housing styles applies here too: Talk to residents of any community you are considering. In fact, ask at the administration office if you can talk with a single resident, to be especially sure your questions and concerns are addressed. Perhaps you can arrange with the administration to be invited to some social events at the development. That goes for communities of any size. You will want to know what awaits you in famed Sun City, Arizona, with its population of 60,000-plus, for example, as well as in the many smaller developments with just a few hundred residents.

The Least You Need to Know

➤ You will have to keep busy working at relationships—with your spouse, kids, stepkids, grandchildren, friends—all your days. Situations shift, and new needs arise, but as you grow older, you will appreciate all of those contacts, perhaps as you never have before.

➤ A new marriage can bring a new stepfamily. That can mean many new joys, and a few compromises, too.

➤ Lending money to the children calls for straight talk—between you as a couple and with the child receiving the loan.

➤ Living together, unmarried and perhaps just as friends, can be a positive, enjoyable step for retirees, not to mention a way of keeping expenses down.

➤ If you're single you're probably already used to making your own social life, but you might find in retirement the need to push just a little harder. The absence of workplace socializing will create a void that will need to be filled.

Chapter 28

Travel Time

In This Chapter

➤ Seeking travel bargains, some especially for retirees

➤ What's new on the 60-plus tourism scene

➤ Special holidays where you'll meet kindred souls

Ask prospective retirees how they intend to spend much of their time when they have stopped punching the time clock, and many will reply "travel."

Packing one's bags and leaving town can mean different things to different retirees. Many will visit their network of family and friends nationwide frequently in retirement. Others look forward to exploring new locales, too, but for short hops, such as a few long weekends away each year. Still others are looking for adventure and the longer trip, thousands of miles from home sweet home and light years from the familiarity of that life.

Many retirees want to learn a thing or two while they are on holiday, and choose their vacations by that criterion. No matter where *you* plan to head post-retirement, you are, of course, looking for fun, too, and memories to store.

Well, the time is here, so let's go.

Travel Agents Versus Doing It Yourself

If you are planning your third trip to England, you may want to do it yourself, foregoing the services of a travel agent. But if you want to visit Brazil for the first time, you probably will make a beeline for a travel agent's office.

A travel agent can book a trip for you, from airfare to cruise reservations to hotels to car rental and any extras you need for a good holiday, such as travel within a country. He or she is more than a booking agent, having been trained to draw from you exactly what you expect from a trip, the style of accommodations you like, your price ranges, and so on.

A travel agent also will know about specials—a London theater package that you are not likely to have heard about, for example.

You pay nothing for that personalized service. The agent is paid a commission by the airline, hotel, and so on.

Yes, you can use an agent if you want to just have a hotel booked, but it makes sense to let that professional handle the airline ticket and other purchases necessary for your trip while you are at it. Do agents know everything? No, naturally not. A few may push spots that are familiar to them over those that they know little about, and places and services that pay them the higher commissions. But for the most part, you will find their help invaluable.

Thin Ice
Some airlines have been making efforts to put caps on commissions they pay to travel agents. To make up for that loss, some travel agents will pass a small fee of $5 to $10 or more on to their customers for a ticket purchased. Not all fares are involved and not every travel agent is doing this. You might want to check to see how your agent is handling this.

An agent usually can help if there is a problem with your trip, too, such as getting a refund for unsatisfactory service or no service at all.

This is not always possible with tour packages, however. You hear from time to time about tour operators going bust and leaving vacationers with no place to go after they have paid a few thousand dollars for their holiday. Those travelers can't always find the operators—and neither, often, can the travel agencies. Or, at least, neither group can get those operators to come up with a refund.

Packaged tours are certainly popular vacation styles, especially with retirees. How can you avoid finding yourself in that dreadful position? You might pay with a credit card, which gives you some leverage if problems develop. Perhaps you can put your money into a bank escrow account instead of making out a check to the tour operator. Travel insurance is another option.

Finding an Agent

How do you find a good travel agent? As with most other products and services, the best route is to ask for a recommendation from friends who have had experiences, good and bad, with local agents.

The American Society of Travel Agents (ASTA) offers several booklets: *How To Find a Good Travel Agent*, *How To Avoid Travel Problems*, *Car Rental Tips*, *Tips on Tipping*, and *Traveling Abroad*. Send a self-addressed stamped envelope with first-class postage for each booklet (eight booklets will fit into a #10 business envelope). ASTA is at 1101 King St., Suite 200, Alexandria, VA 22314. The phone number is (703) 739-2782.

Some Other Travel Savings

It's a big world out there, with enough travel choices to make your head spin—far too many, of course, even to give you an overview in these pages. Here are a few specially tailored ideas, though, that you might find of interest as your thoughts increasingly turn to getting away in retirement:

➤ Senior citizen discounts are available for what seems like everything these days. Make it a rule to ask, no matter what you are purchasing and whether or not you have a specific credit card or membership. You'll be surprised how often you can get at least 10 percent knocked off a quoted price. A driver's license is usually sufficient identification.

➤ Ten percent? You might be able to do better. Regardless of what you are buying in travel-related services, ask "Is this your lowest rate?" Sometimes the one originally quoted to you, even with certain discount cards, isn't the best, and you can improve on that figure.

➤ Traveling by train around America can be pleasant, leisurely, and very cost effective. Ask Amtrak about discounts for seniors that can run as much as 25 percent.

➤ The hottest place to get travel discounts these days might be online. Several travel-related businesses offer price breaks to anyone who books through a computer system.

If you have a computer with a modem (and you might want to spring for one to enjoy in retirement; more about that in Chapter 29),

OOOOH...

Power Word
The word **seniors** is open to interpretation in the world of sales these days. It used to mean age 65 and above, but now it is often lowered to include youngsters of 50. So begin asking about discounts once you turn 50.

you can access a world of travel information and magnificent looks at travel destinations, as well as practical, money-saving advice and bargain offers.

Join one of the online services, which you can do with a phone call and a credit card. Costs are low—usually around $10 a month, with extra charges for extra use. Here is a selection of services and their 800 numbers where you can start your travel searches. Each has a different repertoire of programs, and each has its own style.

America Online: (800) 827-6364
CompuServe: (800):848-8198
Delphi: (800) 696-4005
GEnie: (800) 638-9636

➤ Check your library or bookstore for travel-related books especially for seniors. You can find excellent price-saving tips, as well as information on other aspects of travel over 65 (or 55 or 50 or whatever age they are considering *senior* these days). Also, if you are not already in the habit of reading one or two of the travel magazines, pick up a few. You can enjoy armchair traveling while planning your own first few trips.

The Popular Elderhostel

This is an enormously successful learning vacation program that used to be available to those over 60, but then in 1994 the minimum age of eligibility was lowered to 55. Spouses of any age are welcome, or you may bring a companion who is at least 50. Today, some 250,000-plus "students" attend Elderhostel sites annually, at 1,800 participating not-for-profit institutions.

It's Been Said
I grow old learning something new every day.
—Solon, 638?-559BC

Programs are held on college campuses, at learning centers, state parks, ranches, and in unusual spots, too—a monastery for one. The college scene is a common one for Elderhostel vacationers. They live in dormitories—some plain, some new and plush—and eat in the dining hall with students. The food is institutional fare, but hearty, although special diets cannot be accommodated.

You learn about a wide variety of topics (they are taught on an adult level, but do not require previous formal education). Typically, you will take three non-credit courses, taught by professionals in those fields, during your five or six days. The three areas of study are varied—one subject might be on a political theme, another might be on some aspect of computers or music or a look at Southern writers or psychology, or a few hundred other themes. The third course could be a tour of historic sites in the city where the Elderhostel group is meeting.

Classes run about an hour and a half for each course, leaving you plenty of time for extracurricular activities, which can be planned by Elderhostel or at your discretion.

Programs are held in the United States and 47 other countries. Abroad, that five or six days is usually a two- to four-week holiday.

An Elderhostel U.S. vacation will cost around $300, which includes absolutely everything except your transportation to the college campus, state park, or other locations. That's pretty inexpensive for an all-inclusive vacation these days. Elderhostel holidays abroad are not inexpensive, but they are reasonable. One 20-day trip to Eastern Europe, for example, cost a little over $3,000, round trip from New York, which works out to a daily rate of $150. Part of the appeal of these vacations is the folks you meet—your "class-mates." These are people with a variety of interests and a love for the academic setting. They find Elderhostel programs enriching, broadening, and just plain fun. Many lasting friendships are formed among Elderhostel groups. Some involve getting together when the individuals are back at home, while others consist of friendly "students" just reuniting at a succession of Elderhostel holidays.

Extra! Extra!

A social activist and a university administrator began Elderhostel in 1974, basing the program on Scandinavian folk schools, where adult workers who could not attend college were taught various subjects. You might want to read *The Story of Elderhostel* by Eugene S. Mills.

For more information about national and international learning vacations, contact Elderhostel at 75 Federal St., Boston, MA 02110 (617) 426-7788.

Yours for Mine—House Swaps

You might have read articles over the years about folks who have traded their home for someone else's, to experience a different kind of vacation in a foreign country. Some have swapped their place for an area that is new to them in these 50 states. Overall, this is a vacation style for those who are more interested in new travel experiences than they are worried about someone they don't know staying in their home.

The beauty here is that you can not only visit another country, but you also can live like the residents there. Instead of an expensive hotel, you are staying at no cost at all in a house or apartment belonging to your corresponding swapper.

> ### Extra! Extra!
>
> Trading homes, as the business we know today, began in the late 1960s when a New York schoolteacher formed the first organization, Vacation Exchange Club. He and fellow educators were looking for a low-cost way to travel abroad. Today, there are more than half a dozen swap clubs nationwide.

Can there be problems with all of these strangers staying in one another's homes? Just a few have developed over the years. The occasional snags seem to be

➤ Prospective swappers who cancel their vacation plans at the last minute, leaving the family they're trading with high and dry

➤ A difference in housekeeping standards between swappers (a concern that can be worked out in the exchange of letters between the two prior to the vacation)

I'm Sold—What Do I Do?

You join one of the home swap agencies, so that you can find a family with whom to trade. You can, of course, trade your place on your own, advertising in the local paper for the community where you'd like to vacation, but these organizations can be easier. You'll get someone who is on your wavelength and knows what to expect from the process.

All the swap organizations publish a book annually, sometimes with periodic supplements, of listings from members who talk about their home and where they'd like to visit. You read that book and write to those individuals living where you'd like to holiday, telling them about your place. After an exchange of letters, and sometimes pictures and phone calls, the two of you make a match.

You pay only for your listing in the swap directory.

Give yourself plenty of time to find a home to visit. Swaps can take about a year to conclude, between waiting for your listing to appear, and then contacting potential homeowners or tenants. Be flexible, too. If you can't get exactly the city or country you want—hey, it's a big world. Have two or three alternate choices, and get busy trying to nail down one of those homes to trade.

Here are two home-swap organizations in this country that can help:

➤ Vacation Exchange Club
P. O. Box 650
Key West, FL 33041
(800) 638-3841

Cost: $70 for an annual directory (including a listing of your home), plus monthly updates for homes of 16,000 members worldwide.

➤ Intervac U.S.
P. O. Box 590504
San Francisco, CA 94159
(800) 756-HOME
Cost: $65 a year ($60 for seniors 62 and over). The directory is published in four installments, with 10,000 listings in 30 countries.

Buying Timeshare Vacations

Want to buy just a bit of a vacation home? Here's how this works. You purchase a portion of a year at a resort. Your week or two buys you a fully furnished apartment, perhaps for as long as the resort is in operation or maybe for a specific time, such as 30 years (each resort has its own purchasing style that might vary slightly from one to the next). You also have the use of the recreational amenities that go along with that resort. Usually, 50 weeks are offered for sale with each unit, with the resort holding two weeks open each year for cleaning and repairs.

You can pay anywhere from $2,000 to $20,000-plus for a week of time, depending on where in the world you buy and whether you are interested in high season there or the downtime. The size of the unit and the degree of lavishness of the complex enters into the equation, too, of course.

Extra! Extra!

Timesharing is now a well-regulated and popular enterprise, after a rocky spell several years back. The entrance into the field of Marriott, Hilton, and other respected names in the hospitality industry, especially the magical name of Disney, has contributed to its new legitimacy. A stronger industry association has helped too.

The most popular timeshare locale in this country: Orlando, Florida. A town undergoing a good deal of construction activity these days, and one that appeals to a number of retirees, is Branson, Missouri, with its many entertainment facilities, especially country music theaters. Several new timeshare complexes are open or scheduled to open there, including one by the Welk Resort Group, headed by Larry Welk, son of the late bandleader.

You might like to spend a week at Orlando or Branson or some other spot by yourselves. Or maybe not. The beauty of buying a week or two also means you might have the family visit. Apartments can sleep four, six, or more. Of course, you could prefer to head for the hills and let the kids and grandkids have the place to themselves.

There's something even better about timesharing: You can use the time you have bought to trade for a week or two in some other resort anywhere in the world. Some timesharers have never returned to the resort where they originally purchased an apartment. One stay was enough. Now they're seeing the world on trades.

Once you own a timeshare unit, you can register with organizations that arrange those bookings.

Cautions: Don't consider your apartment a real estate investment. It isn't. You are buying vacation time—that's all. Don't expect a profit from your purchase either. Timeshares can be difficult to sell, with competition from newer, fancier resorts opening all the time. You may find, though, that with trading, you can always use your timeshare in one form or another, and so you will not be interested in selling.

The American Resort Development Association (ARDA), the trade association for the industry, offers free printed material about timesharing for consumers. They are at 1220 L St. NW, Washington, DC 20005, (202) 371-6700.

You Can Rent, Too

You can also rent a timeshare unit, which is a good idea prior to purchasing one. The national average rate for one-bedroom apartments is around $650 a week. That will probably sleep four, since there is usually a sofa bed in the living room (larger units with two bedrooms will cost more). You can very likely do better than that rate in the off season where you want to go, and by contacting the unit owner directly instead of dealing with the resort's rental office. Look for timeshare rentals in the classified columns of the newspapers where the resorts that interest you are located. If you want really top-flight rentals, such as in London or Hawaii, you might advertise in such national papers as the *New York Times* or *USA Today*. Dealing directly with timeshare owners also might get you a better price when you want to buy.

Rental RVs for the Road

Recreation vehicles (RVs) are an economical way to travel, and one with thousands of enthusiastic devotees.

The beauty of the RV, of course, is that you are spared hotel and restaurant bills (unless you choose to eat out or choose a motor home with no eating facilities), and car rental fees by having a small house on wheels right there with you in your travels.

When you want to rent an RV, you will have a variety of styles from which to choose—some modest, some large and lavishly appointed. You can rent one that sleeps four, has a kitchenette, and perhaps a bathroom for $400 to $500 a week. If you want to step down a little to a model that provides only sleeping accommodations, the charge is likely to be $200 to $400, depending on the luxury level of that selection.

Thin Ice
If you take a grandchild or your pet with you on an RV holiday, be sure the campground where you want to stay allows kids and pets. Some do not.

Price-wise, a good deal depends on which type of RV you select, of course; whether it has microwaves, VCRs, and other conveniences; and, to a great extent, on which season you choose for your travels.

Parking, Prices, and Addresses

After a day's touring, you will come to rest in one of the nation's more than 16,000 public and private campgrounds, where you can pay anywhere from around $10 to $20 per night for just a parking spot, to $30 to $50 for a site that has water, electric, and sewage hookups.

You also might factor in getting around eight miles per gallon for your home on wheels—not exactly a bargain if you are traveling a long distance.

You can save money on these trips, though (aside from the obvious hotel, car rental, and the like). You might join an RV club; there are about a dozen around the country. Many of them offer members special discounts, which reduce fees at campgrounds. For a complete list of RV clubs, write the Recreation Vehicle Industry Association, P. O. Box 2999, Reston, VA 22090. Or, call (703) 620-6003. The association also publishes a free catalog of publications about RV camping.

For information on renting an RV, you can contact the Recreation Vehicle Rental Association, 3930 University Drive, Fairfax, Virginia 22030, or call (800) 336-0355. They publish *Who's Who, RV Rentals* for $5 and *Rental Ventures*, a book of tips for those vacationers. That book sells for $3, or $2.50 if you also purchase the $5 publication. You also can call one of the largest RV rental dealers in the country, Cruise America, located in Miami, Florida at (800) 327-7778.

The Go Camping America hotline offers material on where to camp. Call (800) 47-SUNNY.

Finally, if you enjoy this vacation style so much that you'd like to buy your own RV, look up "On the Road, RV Style " in Chapter 7.

The Least You Need to Know

➤ Using a travel agent can take away some—or a lot—of the worry about the logistics of major trips.

➤ Now that you will have the time, try some vacations that call for a more leisurely approach to travel, like RVing along the nation's highways or swapping for a home abroad.

➤ Always inquire about discounts. To qualify for some of them, you will need specific credit cards or memberships, but others will come to you just for being 55 or 62 or whatever the minimum age is for that product or service.

Chapter 29

Are We Having Fun Yet?

In This Chapter

➤ Checking out new leisure opportunities

➤ There's a paying or volunteer outlet for every talent

➤ The bottom line: Stay active

Much of what follows is nothing new really. Doing volunteer work, going to the library, working out—you might have dabbled in some of those activities over the years, or you might have been quite serious in your participation.

But there had always been work before. And never enough time left over after job and family considerations to make those interests more than peripheral to your life. Now they can play a more important part in your days, which is indeed good news because all of this can be fun. It also can be good for you.

They say in order to have a good life in retirement, you need exercise, the right diet, an overall feeling of usefulness, and a network of family and friends. Sounds like a good recipe for life at any age. In fact, many retirement seminars are called *life planning* seminars.

How To Meet People, at New Hangouts and Old

"Come for dinner... Would you like to join... We're having a meeting... Some of us want to go..."

You might hear those opening lines often in your early retirement days, and unless the offering is so totally unappealing that you really would rather stay home and wash the dog (or even the cat, which says a lot), then go out and do it. Go for dinner. Join the crowd. Attend the meeting, and maybe even speak up if you feel particularly strongly about something.

By going almost everywhere initially, you get out, meet new people, and learn something new. You stay connected, in touch, and in tune with the times. You also discover what truly interests you, which activities you'd like to pursue further, and which new friends you'd like to get to know better. It's a process of elimination, narrowing down your opportunities to the choice few you want to hold on to, but if you don't make a major effort, you won't have enough of a pool from which to make a selection.

It's Been Said
All happiness depends on a leisurely breakfast.
—John Gunther

If you haven't given much thought to what you'd like to be doing, write out some goals (a handy worksheet is included here). These goals will at least get you started during the first few months or first year of retirement.

Jot down your specific retirement goals, whether lofty or ordinary ones.

Personal Goals for the First Few Months to One Year After Retirement

Aim	1st Step	Any Obstacles Anticipated?	Made It! Check When Goal Reached
1. _____	_____	_____	_____
2. _____	_____	_____	_____
3. _____	_____	_____	_____
4. _____	_____	_____	_____
5. _____	_____	_____	_____

Good Morning, Sunshine

Here is an interesting phenomenon you already might be enjoying: retirees gathering for breakfast at a neighborhood coffee shop or diner. Sometimes it's in a hometown where the participants have known one another for years, and sometimes in a retirement haven where they are all new friends. Often, it's a daily ritual, but it can be a once-a-week event. They sit around a table for four or six or more, cluttered with dishes and coffee cups, and talk and talk and talk.

Sometimes these are groups of men and women, but other times it's men only. Perhaps that's because women often get together at lunchtime. Maybe you've been invited to come on over to one of those groups, or perhaps you'd like to start your own. Go for it. It's a great way to begin the day, particularly if it follows a brisk morning walk. In any event, sitting around gabbing with friends over a meal, with no need to look at one's watch, is bliss at any age.

Back to School, To Study or Teach

Quick now, which subjects would you like to learn more about? American History? Spanish? Astronomy? Computers? English Literature? Maybe there are several areas of interest you'd like to poke around in, learning as much as you can about those subjects.

Now you can. And you will have plenty of company. A 1993 survey by the U.S. Census Bureau showed there were 81,000 Americans age 60 and older enrolled in college.

There are thousands more *auditing* (sitting in but not participating and not taking exams) college classes, and an even more sizable throng attending noncredit adult education schools to learn subjects from mathematics to Oriental cooking to script writing.

Whether you have always wanted to return to school for a degree, to attend college for the first time and continue until you are handed your sheepskin, or you just want to spend a few evenings a week learning something new, you have hundreds of courses to choose from almost anywhere you live.

Gray Matter Alert

Ask about *Learning in Retirement* programs at any college you contact. There are almost 200 of these study groups offered nationwide, usually under the auspices of a college or university. The programs vary from one school to another, and cover every subject imaginable. There has even been one on building a light plane from a kit! How can anyone say school is boring?

Many colleges will allow adults over a certain age to audit for-credit courses free or at a nominal fee of $10 or $15. Most adult education programs are quite inexpensive—some charging as little as $10 for a noncredit course. If you want to go to school and seriously pursue a degree, ask at a few colleges near you and you may be surprised to learn about the financial assistance, especially lower tuition fees available for seniors and academic programs designed specifically for the 60-plus set.

Do we hear "Oh, but if I start school now, I'll be 71 by the time I get my degree." Well, one day you'll be that age anyway. Wouldn't you rather be 71 and a college graduate?

Age certainly did not deter Helene Rosenblatt, who received some national publicity (articles in the *New York Times* and the *Chronicle of Higher Education*) when she graduated from Cornell University in 1994 at the age of 70. Ms. Rosenblatt had started college in the 1940s, but then dropped out because of the war. With her diploma in hand from Cornell's College of Human Ecology, the graduate said she planned to seek a position working with seniors.

"Now, Class..."

Here's another idea: Why not teach? If you have a master's degree in your specialty, you might inquire about college teaching, perhaps one course a day or two a week. On the adult education level, no formal education is necessary, as long as you know your subject well. Or you might consider teaching a course from your home, perhaps just for a handful of students. Zoning regulations should not be a problem if you are meeting just once a week for a semester or two, and your students do not park in your neighbors' parking spots.

Wonderful Work: Volunteer Opportunities

Volunteer work is a worthy—even important—retirement activity that you may have been engaged in for years during your work life. Now you have more hours to devote to your special interest. Or, if you never had the time before, this is an excellent opportunity to find your niche and contribute.

More than one-third of all Americans—89 million people—do some type of volunteer work, according to a survey conducted by the Gallup Organization. One of the fastest growing groups of volunteers? Those age 75 and older. Table 29.1 shows how the volunteer crowd breaks down by age group.

Table 29.1 Americans Volunteer! Here's a Breakdown by Age.

Age Group	Percentage Volunteering
18-24	45%
25-34	46%
35-44	55%
45-55	54%
55-64	47%

Age Group	Percentage Volunteering
65-74	43%
75+	36%

Source: Giving and Volunteering, 1994, Volume I, Page 41, Independent Sector

If you are not plugged into a volunteer slot of your own, first give some thought to what area interests you. Helping with Meals on Wheels, painting scenery for the little theater, working with AIDS or Alzheimer's patients, reading books for the blind, helping out at a shelter for the homeless—while the good news is that you have hundreds of volunteer choices wherever you live, the not-so-great report from the trenches is that so much help is needed in so many areas.

If you live in a large metropolitan area, there is likely to be an office of volunteers connected with the city government, acting as a clearinghouse for those who want to help. If there is no such department in your town, you can go directly to places that interest you—hospitals, schools, nursing homes, cultural institutions, and so on.

It's Been Said
Each morning sees some task begun, Each evening sees it close; Something attempted, something done, Has earned a night's repose.
—Henry Wadsworth Longfellow

Eek—a Mouse! You and Your Computer

Maybe you're one of those folks over 40 who cannot bear to think about computers, let alone actually use one. Or you might be 67 and so computer literate that everyone comes to you for advice. For the most part, these next few paragraphs are for the former—the timid. But you who are proficient, stay around. You might learn something new.

But What Will I Do with It?

If you become at least minimally proficient with a computer, you will expand your world in many new directions:

➤ You can look for a part-time job, if you like. So many positions these days require knowledge of that big, gray box.

➤ You also can communicate with your children and grandkids, which can be enormously satisfying if your family is spread across the country. You can "chat" with each member personally via computer and save big bucks on your telephone bill.

➤ You can start a diary or journal or family history. It's much easier to erase and begin again with a computer than it is writing by hand or even typing.

➤ You can purchase software programs on virtually any area of interest to you these days, including home repair, help with your taxes, travel destinations, retirement investments, and so on.

➤ You can transfer many of your written files into the computer, and update them more easily than you could on paper.

➤ You can make new friends, and maybe even find Mr. or Ms. Right online. You will find services directed at retirees, such as SeniorNet, a San Francisco-based online network for people over 55. It now has 13,000 members, and is available through America Online at (800) 827-6364. Its purpose? It just gives members an opportunity to "talk" and make friends.

➤ You can purchase programs that will enable you to play all sorts of games, solve puzzles, figure out mysteries, and enjoy hours of fun at any time of the day or night that you feel like switching on your machine.

Okay, I'm Sold. Where Do I Learn?

To pick up this skill as economically as possible, you can sign up for an introductory course at an adult evening school; be sure it's something like "Introduction to Computers" and not an introduction to a specific program. Rates here can be all over the place, depending on where you live in the country, but dig around for the school offering the lowest rates. Some cities and towns offer special courses for seniors at low $25 or so costs. Maybe there will be a city-sponsored training school where you live, teaching a number of skills, including computers, for $25 to $50 for a one-day workshop.

You might do better with a tutor, having someone sit with you at home teaching only you. You can ask around for a tutor at colleges with computer courses, or check with your friends and neighbors for someone to help. You might be able to hire your 10-year-old grandchild to teach you, but you may not want to take that route to learning. One survey of a few retirees showed they would be embarrassed to have kids teaching them about computers. You may feel that way too.

Do I Need a Brand-New Computer?

You don't have to buy a brand-new computer. As you talk with computer whizzes in your circle of friends, you will learn that some used, older machines can be just fine for what you want to accomplish, and can save you several hundred dollars over the purchase price of a new system.

Just be certain to tell your computer guru what your plans are so he or she can be sure you will buy a machine capable of doing that work. Ask, too, if what you are considering purchasing can be upgraded one day. Technology is moving so quickly that, although you want to save money, you don't want to buy a used machine that will be no good to you a year or two later.

Exercise for Fun and Fitness

Well, for fitness anyway. It might not be that much fun for the half of the population that says "Oh, just leave me alone here on the sofa. But before you go, would you move that bag of chips over this way?" Up and at 'em! As mentioned earlier in this chapter, exercise is one important component of an enjoyable retirement. We are not talking about participating in a triathalon here, just enough movement three times a week to keep as fit as cardiologists would like us to be.

That can be raking and weeding in the yard, taking a 20- to 30-minute walk a few days a week, or perhaps swimming.

You might be able to join your local mall walkers. Many shopping malls around the country open at 8 a.m. or 9 a.m. to allow anyone who wants to walk through those seemingly endless passages. Sometimes the mall sponsors the walks, and sometimes an area hospital sponsors them. That sort of organized exercise appeals to seniors, and can turn into quite a social event too. Of course, one should not follow up the walk with a jelly doughnut bought at the food court. That's a tsk-tsk.

Another almost painless way to get and keep moving is through some of the wide array of exercise videos on the market these days, targeted to seemingly every physical condition (or lack of condition). Start with one for the most out of shape, and you can work your way up the fitness scale to those sufficiently challenging. Exercise machines, either yours at home or the ones you use at the health club, can offer a good workout, too. Some health clubs have special programs for seniors. Be sure that you have your doctor's okay before investing in machines or club memberships and before engaging in workouts from the more lively exercise videos. Another option: Some communities offer exercise programs for seniors as part of their adult education curriculum, and some hospitals have those classes, too. Both charge well under $100 for the course. You might pick up enough to keep you going with a regular routine on your own after the course ends.

Creative Juices

If you have an artistic bent—and talent—you can find much to do, certainly on a volunteer, or perhaps on a paying, basis.

You might check out salaried positions with theaters, orchestras, and the like, if that has been your dream in pre-retirement days. But you are likely to find, not surprisingly, 1) the competition is so fierce you almost have no chance or 2) there is no money involved in many of those jobs you thought paid at least something.

So you adapt. If you really wanted to play with the local symphony, you might still be happy with a smaller chamber group or teaching from your home. Or maybe it's the symphony itself that's more important than the playing. You might be able to land a paying part-time job at the office there, or perhaps one as a volunteer with the local Friends of the Symphony group. Ushering at a day's event might be a paying job or strictly volunteer, but in either event you will get to see the symphony at no charge. All of this applies to local theater, too.

Gray Matter Alert
When checking out communities where you might like to retire, visit the town's public library. The free printed material on the counters will give you a good idea of the resources in that town. Check the bulletin board, too, for notices of activities. If that library carries the Elderhostel newspaper, that's a good sign there is a significant retiree segment in that community.

Creative people usually know where the paying opportunities are, few as they may be, and will be persistent. Writers will try out as contributors to the local paper. (Does it have a regular "Seniors" column? Perhaps you can start one.) Artists will give lessons, either private or at the adult education level, while still going on with their own painting or sketching that is so important to them. Here, too, of course, volunteer opportunities are far more numerous.

Look around you, and by all means keep trying to find a slot that's perfect for you. It can be rewarding for you, of course, and for the rest of us—well, we can all use more beauty in our lives in the form of art, music, dance, and literature.

The Library Is More Than Books These Days

If you used to dash into your local library every week or two while you were working to pick up a few bestsellers and then hurry out again, you're in for a surprise.

If you take your time to look around now—you'll see displays of books on audiocassettes, both current bestsellers and literary classics. These can be particularly valuable for company when you take those walks, or for use in your car, either for long trips or daily errands. Videocassettes have come to many libraries, too, offering current movies at no charge. Can't get out of the house? Many libraries will send you books, videos, and so on. If you are visually impaired or have difficulty holding a book, some will send you an audiocassette player along with the tapes you request.

The library means even more these days. There are lectures held there on a variety of topics, and there often are book discussion groups, pegged to current bestsellers, the Great Books series, or some other theme a member has proposed. If your library does not have one of these groups, you might suggest one. Many libraries also have small rooms where civic or other community groups can meet, which you might want to keep in mind for any organization to which you belong. Finally, every library has a busy children's department with many programs for the kid set. Taking your grandchild to the library to pick up books and staying for a special presentation there for youngsters is a great way for both of you to spend time together.

Helping Out

If you want to get involved with the library's workings, you might be able to serve on the board of trustees. Sometimes those are politically appointed positions, but in other communities, volunteers are welcome. Many libraries also have a Friends of the Library volunteer group which, through book sales and other activities, raises money to buy extras for the library that a municipal budget often cannot afford.

Also, because of budget cuts at many libraries, volunteer positions in the library itself have become available—stacking books, answering inquiries, or whatever else can be done at the volunteer level. You do need a Master of Science degree in Library Science to be a librarian, but there are few if any educational requirements for volunteering there.

Leisure without Guilt

You have seen in the earlier parts of this chapter that it is not a difficult thing at all to become busy after retirement—sometimes with activities that are of service to the community, and sometimes with those that are just fun.

As long as you feel you are contributing in some way—in volunteering, in helping out family and friends, or whatever the criteria is you have set for yourself—do enjoy all the social opportunities that come your way in retirement. And don't bother with the ones you just don't want to do. You don't feel like weeding right now, even though your neighbor is working furiously in his yard? Then don't do it, and don't feel guilty about staying right there on the porch with your book. You don't really want to campaign for a local political candidate, even though you plan to vote for her? Say no. You have earned that right. These are *your* days, and they can be so sweet when the pressure of battling the workplace is over. You paid your dues with that job, and now come the benefits filtering down from those years. Accept and enjoy them, with no apologies.

The Least You Need to Know

➤ Meet new people and try new activities in several areas. That's how you'll decide which pursuits you'd like to continue through retirement and which acquaintances you'd like to see become friends.

➤ If you cannot secure a paying job, part- or full-time, in the field you love, you almost certainly can find a volunteer slot in that arena.

➤ Stay fit—you'll have fun with whatever pastimes you choose that much more.

➤ Enjoy these retirement days, doing as much as is possible, and exactly what you want.

OOOOH...

IDIOTS GUIDE

Words for the Wise

Adult day care A community-based group program designed to meet the needs of functionally impaired adults through an individual plan of care. It is a structured, comprehensive program that provides a variety of health, social, and other related support services in a protective setting during any part of a day, but less than 24-hour care.

Amortization The gradual reduction and finally elimination of a debt (usually a mortgage loan) by making periodic payments over the term of the loan.

Assets Anything having your own commercial or exchange value.

Assisted housing In the context here, government-sponsored buildings or garden complexes for seniors who qualify for rent reductions. Not to be confused with assisted living.

Assisted-living facility A building or complex offering some help to residents with tasks like bathing and dressing, and providing meals, but not full-time nursing care.

Boarder An individual provided with regular meals and lodging, usually in another's house.

Care manager Also called a *geriatric care manager*, an individual affiliated with a healthcare facility or a private company who helps assess an elderly person's healthcare needs, and then arranges for them.

Caregiver Generally, an individual looking after the health and other needs of an incapacitated spouse or other close relative.

Common stock Units of ownership in a public corporation. Although the claims of secured and unsecured creditors and owners of bonds and preferred stock take precedence over the claims of common stockholders, common stock usually has more potential for appreciation.

Compound interest Interest paid on accumulated interest, as well as on the principal.

CMA (competitive market analysis) An estimate of fair market value in real estate based on a comparison with similar properties currently for sale or sold recently.

CPI (Consumer Price Index) The measure of change in consumer prices as determined by a monthly survey conducted by the U.S. Bureau of Labor Statistics. Also sometimes called the *cost-of-living index*.

CCRCs (continuing care retirement communities) Housing style where retirees buy into, and move into, in sequence, three separate stages: (1) independent living, (2) assisted living, and (3) nursing home care—all of which are part of the same community.

COLA (cost-of-living adjustment) A periodic increase in pension payments usually tied to a rising consumer price index.

Condominium A housing style where a buyer owns his or her apartment unit outright, plus an undivided share in the complex's common areas.

Cooperative A housing style where a buyer purchases shares in the corporation that owns the cooperative building. This is personal property, not a real estate purchase.

CC&Rs (covenants, conditions, and restrictions) Limitations imposed on a piece of property by a seller of real estate and incorporated into the deed. CC&Rs survive change of ownership.

Custodial care In a home healthcare context, helping an elderly or disabled person with cooking, cleaning, companionship, or similar aid requiring no special skills.

Disability For purposes of Social Security, a physical or mental impairment that is expected to keep a person from doing any "substantial" work for at least one year. Generally, monthly earnings of $500 or more are considered substantial. Or one must have a condition that is expected to result in death.

Entitlement (1) A right to benefits specified by law or contract; (2) A government program providing benefits to members of a specified group.

Equity (1) In real estate, the market value of property minus the amount of existing liens; (2) In investments, the ownership interest possessed by shareholders in a corporation—stocks, not bonds.

Executor or Executrix Named in a will, an individual charged with dispersing the deceased's estate, paying bills, distributing inheritance to heirs, and so on.

Healthcare power of attorney A legal instrument through which an individual names another person to make healthcare decisions for him or her in the event that individual is not physically able to convey those wishes.

Homeowner associations Community of residents (in single-family homes, condominiums, or any other housing style) bound by specific written covenants of dos and don'ts that must be adhered to by all residents.

Hospice A program for the terminally ill, emphasizing support for patient and family. Can also be a building devoted to that care.

Intestate Dying without a will, as opposed to "testate"—having a valid will.

Keogh A tax-deferred retirement plan for self-employed individuals.

Lien A charge or encumbrance against property for money. A lien can be voluntary, such as a mortgage, or it can be involuntary, such as a tax lien or a mechanic's lien. To pass clear title to a property, all liens must be removed.

Liquidity The ability to convert assets into cash or cash equivalents quickly without significant loss.

Living will A document spelling out one's wishes for medical care to hospitals and physicians if it becomes impossible to communicate those wishes personally.

Managed healthcare Companies of private healthcare insurers claiming they can deliver care at a reasonable price to policy holders by limiting choice of physicians and enforcing other restrictions.

Manufactured homes Houses made in a factory, with parts shipped to the building lot, where they are assembled and the house is erected.

Medicaid A state-run healthcare plan, with federal government contributions, to help lower-income residents.

Medicare The nation's health insurance program for Americans over the age of 65, those eligible for Social Security disability, and those with chronic kidney disease.

Mutual fund A pooling of money into a fund operated by an investment company and invested to make a profit. The money is raised by selling shares and is invested in a professionally managed portfolio of stocks, bonds, options, commodities, real estate, mortgages, and other securities.

Net worth Your assets minus your liabilities.

Nursing home A facility offering residents rooms, meals, and round-the-clock medical care if needed.

Portfolio The combined holding of more than one stock, bond, commodity, real estate investment, cash equivalent, or other assets by an individual or institutional investor. The purpose of a portfolio is to reduce risk by diversification.

Power of attorney Also known as "durable power of attorney," a legal instrument through which an individual appoints another to handle his or her business and personal affairs in the event of an incapacitating illness.

Preferred stock A class of stock that pays dividends at a specified rate and that has preference over common stock in the payment of dividends and the liquidation of assets. Preferred stock does not usually carry voting rights.

Principal In this book: (1) The face amount of a mortgage or loan; (2) The balance of a debt obligation, separate from the interest owed; (3) In investments, the basic amount invested, exclusive of earnings.

Principal residence For those who own two or more properties, their voting address and the place they have chosen based on tax benefits and other criteria, with their other home(s) considered secondary.

Provider A term for a physician in managed healthcare plans.

Quit claim deed A deed that operates as a release, giving up any claim on the property.

Respite care Having a healthcare aide come in to stay with an elderly or ill individual or, if that person is able, having him or her stay at an assisted living facility or nursing home for a specified period of time, usually just a few days.

Roomer One who occupies a rented room in another's house.

Skilled nursing facility According to the federal government's definition, a facility in which there is 24-hour nursing care under the direction of a physician.

Tenancy (1) In real estate, ownership or holding of property; (2) Temporary possession or occupancy of a property that belongs to another, as in renting an apartment.

Timeshare A vacation style in which buyers purchase a week or two in a resort, entitling them to a furnished apartment and recreational amenities at that complex for that time each year for as long as a contract states, which can be for the life of the resort.

Townhomes Usually an architectural style—two-story attached buildings operating under the condominium form of ownership.

Trust Used instead of, or along with, a will. A style of leaving assets that takes advantage of tax breaks and other elements of estate planning that might be more favorable to an individual and his or her heirs than a will.

Vesting An employee's right, acquired by length of service, to share in employer-contributed benefits in a pension fund.

Viatical Used in the context of terminally ill insurance, where policyholders with a life expectancy of less than one year can receive a portion of death benefits while they are still alive.

Yield The ratio of income from an investment to the total cost of the investment over a given period of time; in other words, what an investment has paid.

Index

G

H

I

M

S

u

V

W

X-Y-Z